In The Safety Of His Wings

A Test Pilot's Adventures

D1525161

Jack Schweibold

Pictures are from personal albums, Allison historical photos (compliments of Rolls-Royce), National Aeronautic Association (used by permission) and public domain.

All Scripture taken from the *Holy Bible, New International Version*®. NIV®. Copyright©1973, 1978, 1984 by International Bible Society. Used by permission of Zondervan. All rights reserved.

Art Work is Copyright © 1995-2002 Nova Development Corporation and its licensors, used by permission.

ISBN: 0-9769186-1-7

Published by:
Holy Fire Publishing
531 Constitution Blvd. Martinsburg, WV 25401
www.ChristianPublish.com

Printed in the United States of America and the United Kingdom

Special Thanks

To my family and friends who have encouraged me in writing this book.

Dedication

Dear Grandchildren,

This book, although an autobiography of grandpa, is a gift to you from your grandfather and grandmother as it has taken the two of us, with God, to start our family and see it grow to a point we can pass on our memories. These are thoughts (mostly grandpas), hopes and prayers about the past and for the future. Temper a lot of the crazy stories and outlook with the fact that our generation was born into families that did not know much about Him. Our life story is effectively about how we came to know Jesus Christ intimately over these years.

The legacy we pass on is the precious gift of faith, a heritage of love for God and family. You may be disappointed not to find a lot of stories directly about you, as we have intentionally left those for you to personally write to your own grandchildren. We are very pleased and proud of your parents for the fine job they have accomplished in raising you and thank God every day for each of you. We trust that this book will be a remembrance of how special you are to us and how very much you are loved. Thank you for enriching our lives.

Love and joy,
Grandpa Jack & Grandma Sharon

"For whatever is born of God overcomes the world. And this is the victory that has overcome the world – our faith."
1 Jn 3:4

"For the Mighty One has done great things for me--holy is his name. His mercy extends to those who fear him, from generation to generation."
Lu 1:49-50

TRIBAL LEGAND

Our Great Great (maybe an extra Great) Grandfather Schweibold is believed to be one of two brothers, ages 17 and 19, who left Germany alone in 1849. They arrived in New York City aboard a clipper ship during a wave of emigrants from Europe. Almost a third of these were German, escaping severe economic depression, unemployment, and political unrest. With the coupling of steam power to tall mast clipper ships in 1840, Atlantic passage became reasonably priced … making freedom and adventure feasible.

Once on ground in New York, pipelines were established to move the overwhelming number of young people crowding the docks westward … to provide cheap labor for farmers and emerging industry. By 1849 the Erie Canal, running from Albany, N.Y. on the Hudson River to Buffalo on Lake Erie, had been extended to Toledo, Ohio. From there, newly established railroads continued to the far West. With barge passengers only paying 1½ cents per mile or crewmen riding free, it can be envisioned that the brothers easily made it to Ohio where they were eventually split between Toledo and Columbus.

The two were probably raised tradesman, whose skills and hard-working natures eventually earned them a living during the industrial revolution, my grandfather, Elmer Schweibold, was a pressman in a Toledo printing shop. Though two ensuing world wars involved their mother country, the Schweibold clan stayed rooted in Ohio rather than return to Germany. This allegiance showed they must have cherished their new freedom and opportunity in America. Our family was given birth from the Northern Branch of the Buckeye tree, in Toledo … and was eventually grafted into the Ray E. Crouse and Helen Elizabeth Cheetham families.

This set of relations was of English and French descent that most likely followed the same immigration path, settling in the Southern Michigan and Toledo areas. Most all were of academically sound background: teachers, chemists, engineers and one an owner of an early Henry Ford Dealership. Through those period wars, the German, English and French probably never would have joined forces until … Mom Schweibold knew her son, Jack (that's me) needed help. She advertised for a woman in the local paper and your Grandma Sharon, a princess of only 14, answered the call. Everyone thought it was a good match and these feuding countries were united through marriage in the heartland of America.

"A good name is more desirable than great riches; to be esteemed is better than silver or gold"

INDEX

1

World Record Attempt

"Army 213, Army 213, this is SPORT, do you read?" I faintly hear the controller call. "You just cut inside that last pylon, enter an immediate left turn 270 degrees . . . or you will blow the mission!" I hesitate to respond, hadn't slept for over two days. I'm exhausted. Reluctantly, I slowly roll the ship into a lazy left bank. The forces on the cyclic control stick at these altitudes are so heavy that I wrapped an elastic bungee cord around it; fastening ends of the cord between doorframes, to help relieve the flight control steering pressures. This reduced some of the left lateral force but I hadn't taken another wrap on the cord since passing 20,000 feet over an hour ago. Fatigue is setting in.

Juggling the cord to take up another winding, I slump slightly forward and Howard Hughes' experimental helicopter slips higher in speed; it only takes another two knots to enter high-speed rotor stall. The violent shaking rattles me back to a minor threshold of alertness. I neutralize the controls and allow the speed and angle of bank to drop back within a safe flight envelope. Terminal rotor stall will flip the craft inverted . . . and at this altitude with little, if any, expectation of recovery. Once upside down, bailout through the rotors is not an option; the only hope is to be thrown clear if the aircraft explosively separates.

"Continue the turn!" yells SPORT, forgetting the formality of radio call signs . . . they know I am hurting. "You've got thirty-five degrees to go yet."

"SPORT" is the Spatial Positioning and Orbital Radar Tracking facility at Edwards Air Force Base in California. I apply a shallow bank to the left. "We'll call your rollout assuming you hold a constant rate of turn . . . good we see you turning. Get ready to roll level on the count . . . three, two, one rollout!"

I struggle through the next three laps of the sixty kilometer speed course, in the Army's attempt to capture the Unlimited Class World Helicopter Distance Record for the United States.

"Mr. Schweibold! Listen up!" the flight surgeon calls curtly to get my attention. I know his voice. He had called several times before, but now I can sense his growing concern. "Check your oxygen supply again."

"It's still half full and turned to Emergency, 100% safety flow," I respond. I'd been flying fighters and bombers for years, pressurized and un-pressurized, trained in altitude tanks, the works . . . physiological altitude equations were nothing new, but I still can't analyze what is going wrong.

"How are your nails?" he replies on queue.

I pull my left glove off and stare through a fogging visor to inspect my finger tips, "Rosy red!" I say softly, hoping for some other reassuring direction. Silence, he is still looking for some sign of hypoxia that might be contributing to my exhaustion. "How about taking a couple of those No-doze capsules I gave you?" he finally adds.

"Took several over the past few hours," I admit, to turn off his interrogation. Don't want to tell him I had already choked down the whole box of twenty-four tablets hours ago, lack of caffeine is not the problem.

"Can you hold on for two more laps?" the Engineering Project Manager asks comely, "It might be best to bring you in now. You've already set the Light Weight Class Record." However, I understand nobody really wants an early termination. Months and years of effort have gone into designing and building this ship . . . but half-a-pie might be better than none at all.

Air is leaking from my mask; I reach up and pull the mask straps tighter with my still naked but now cold hand . . . leakage stops as the mask seals in raw crevices of cheek. Two more laps feel marginal and fuel is already bumping on empty. Softly I rely, "We're, we're . . . going for it". I can only listen now, no vocal resource left. I can't understand, four miles high but I'm drowning. . . .

My whole body is shutting down. If a person's life is supposed to flash before a drowning man, the first I can remember is . . . it was a pitch-black night. Grandpa Elmer walked me out to the center of the Railway Bridge spanning the Maumee River in Toledo, Ohio. There was only open grating beneath the tracks, with the glassy river reflecting occasional stray lights. Every step, like now, my every breath on this flight . . . brought impending death. When we got to the center of the trestle, silence was broken by a horn down river, then a louder horn BLASTED from the bridge control house . . . I jumped . . . and jumped again as the whole trestle started turning.

12

I can remember holding tightly to grandpa's leg. When it stopped at ninety degrees, we were left in the middle of the river . . . separated by two chasms of water, one to be filled by a giant coal freighter passing almost silently just ten to fifteen feet away. At that very moment grandpa told me . . . my dad died a few hours earlier. The night became very black to this five-year-old boy as the steamer's lights faded in the distance.

2

Called to Fly

First School Day, Mine Stunk!

Long gone, years before urban renewal, my first grade school building was on busy Monroe Street, down and across one block from the Toledo Art Museum. Back then, there was no kindergarten, you started school once you reached six that calendar year. Since my birthday was in November, I started out as a young five-year old, without the manly nurturing of a father. Within the first week, I encountered my first "Fear of Man". Recess was on a stone corner lot in front of the building. A tall chain link fence kept the dodge ball played by girls from going into the street. The boys commanded the swings and monkey bars. Sport for the first day was for several of the boys to hold my arms and legs across the bars while the bigger guys used me as a punching bag. Mrs. Ruler, my teacher, wasn't too compassionate as she washed my nose but said I could join the girls in dodge ball the next day. To the little kid in me, it sounded like a comforting option; however, there were too many other dark corners, like the cloakroom and restrooms to consider . . . they became as violent as the playground. The better solution was just not to return to school.

For the next two and one half months, I became Junior Caretaker at the local mortuary. After crossing Monroe Street at the museum light, the left turn toward school took me past the local mortuary. I remember hiding under my father's casket and not wanting to leave it the day he was buried. The area seemed quite comforting. Adjacent to the sidewalk, was a sunken driveway fronted by a brick wall. This drive sloped down to a covered hearse port for the storage of two vehicles, here a double door led into the lower basement and viewing room. I never entered this area but had visions of bodies stacked in the caskets lined up for display.

I continued to sit in and around the hearses through Thanksgiving when the weather became too cold . . . so, I just returned to school. Mrs. Ruler was quite surprised and asked where I'd been, "Out of town, we had to live with my grandma for a while". It wasn't a total lie; I did stay with

15

my Grandma Nanny, sometimes. She lived in a small trailer two lots from a railway switchyard. I always dreamed of being an engineer.

"Good to have you back, take the same desk," Mrs. Ruler greeted. Some of the kids knew where I had been hiding out and had envied my freedom. Mom remarried later that year and we moved to Cleveland Heights, Ohio. Dick Cordrey was a Mechanical Engineer and even though he was registered 4-F with the draft board for a crooked little finger, the military still assigned him defense positions. I only finished 3a in the third grade; one needed to pass 3b to make it to the 4th grade. We moved back to Toledo the beginning of my fourth year and since they didn't know what to do with a 3b, they promoted me to the 4th grade! I made up for it though; I tried to attend school as LITTLE as possible.

Mom and Dad both worked and this gave me a lot of unmerited freedom; actually, I think I was just ignored. By now, I had become street savvy and found I could travel around Toledo by trolley and bus, with transfers all day for a penny. In those days once inside a movie theater a person had unlimited stay. There were double features with no limit on repeats.

Some theaters were only a nickel, and I soon learned to hit the higher priced ones as the main attraction let out. By backing in as the crowd exited, I would call to "Mommy" at the candy stand or restroom. It never failed. My ten cents a day for lunch would let me load up at Woolworth's 5 and 10-cent store, take one of several bus lines sight seeing and spend the rest of the afternoon in the movies. My favorite was the Granada Monster House, always a double-decker Frankenstein /Wolf man combo topped with one of 60 chapters of Superman or Flash Gordon.

Later I hit the real jackpot when Grandma Cordrey worked as cashier in the Princess Theater. This didn't help during school days but she could get a buddy and me into the costly first run flicks free . . . without sneaking around! This was a real outreach for her. I hadn't been able to talk with her very well since the first day I stayed with her when I was six or seven. Her house was beautiful, all fresh and white inside and out. On that visit, I encountered an interesting phenomenon. If you draw a line with a lead pencil, starting on the door of the screened in front porch, run it around the porch, continue around the living room wall, dining room, bedrooms, doors, etc., you finally return to the original starting point. I was so excited to tell Grandma Barbara . . . but not as excited as she was! Don't know how she lived to 106, maybe it was because she didn't see me much after that. Now, I wish I had some of her genes.

A Boy's First Love

Grandpa Jack Cordrey always had a sparkle in his eye. I think he was disappointed in me for all the pencil mess but later he treated me like a man. Maybe I got to Grandma where he couldn't. At 14 he checked me out solo in his outboard boat docked on Sandusky Bay in Lake Erie. By High School I shed the truancy dilemma. An association with DeMolay, a junior Masonic group introduced me to a bunch of good friends and a "one true and living God". Together, they got me headed in a positive direction. On weekends I could drive to the bay. Those visits would bring long days of good fishing. I don't think I caught many fish, but the quart of olives I'd eat each trip filled the empty space.

My first car was a 1942 Studebaker, secured several months before my 16th birthday in 1951. It was destined to become a non-classic. The absence of domestic automotive production from 1942-1945 left a void of eight to ten year old cars that would normally fit the pocket book of a under-employed high school student. So, commanding even a '42 wimpy Stude was a real privilege. Actually, Dad Cordrey was quite wise in helping select this gem. Low horsepower prevented me from becoming the local drag champion and at $0.13/gal for gasoline . . . it was economical. A side advantage from the folks' side may also have been that I never saw it draw a girl to the running board on its own merit! Also, it served well as a training ground for basic mechanics, and Dad was ever helpful in teaching about things like plugs, points and condensers. I don't think I ever would have made it in a mechanical environment without that tutoring. The Stude's main and terminal downfall was being a rust bucket. On the way to school one day while making a swift left turn at the end of the first block, my bowling ball leaped off the rear seat and made a perfect strike through the right doorpost. The ball was retrieved from the gutter, structure bent back in place and the car soon retired to the junk yard.

The replacement auto WAS a classic, Charles Lindberg's 1938 Olds Club Coupe! Purchased from his cook's wife, it was a straight eight, side flip-down seats in the rear with front and back radios. We couldn't see a movie at the drive-in over the long hood, so we would back in and watch out the rear window . . . but who watched the movie? I should have kept it; today it would be worth big bucks . . . it could have retired ME!

Uncle Sam Wants You!

That's what he said, "I want you!"

At nineteen, while meandering down the street in downtown Toledo, Ohio heading for the Princess Theater, I was faced with a poster sign at the curb. It was a red, white and blue Uncle Sam in beard and top hat, pointing a finger at ME. Old Sam was saying, "I want you . . . as a Navigator!"

As I look back on the situation, I don't know if it was the warmth of finding someone who wanted me or the excitement of the four jets flying in formation over his shoulder. Anyway, my eyes finally ended at the plaque below that said, "Come in and see if you qualify." The sign's arrow pointed to the Post Office next door where a hungry recruiting sergeant waited in his office with teeth that gleamed like a barracuda's.

"Well," I thought, "Nothing to lose."

My Uncle Dick, after flying me at 16, convinced me I didn't have the coordination to become a pilot! But then, maybe I didn't need to be coordinated . . . just to be a navigator. After all, I had already been in the Naval Reserves as an enlisted man for a year and a half. "They couldn't get me" . . . so I thought.

I sat down and took a test. WHAMO, I passed the simple 30 questions with "flying colors" and qualified for an all expense paid, *no obligation* trip by overnight Pullman train to Chanute Air Force Base in Illinois. For a guy that had just quit the wholesale hardware business that morning as a stock chaser, it was at least something to do . . . and paid for! And as for being in another branch of service, seems there was a special discharge available for anyone who qualified for an Officer's Candidate School in another branch of service. The qualification process was to pass the tests in Chanute. I could depart any convenient Sunday in the next 30 days. I left two days later.

Trains were not new to me. At eight my parents and grandma, Nanny, would board me at terminals in Cleveland and Toledo to travel between the cities alone. This couldn't be a reasonable situation with kids today.

By nine, Nanny had taken me by train to Pensacola, FL and at eleven to Norfolk, VA. Both times were to see Uncle Dick who was a Naval Aviator; to see him get his wings and then the Distinguished Flying Cross for sinking the first German U-boat. Obviously this was where I got my interest in aviation and was almost fatally discouraged when he flew me and told me, "You do not have the coordination skills to be a pilot!" However, he did let me wash and wax his plane to pay for the evaluation ride. Fortunately, he never saw my algebra grades or he would have convinced me navigation was out of reach, too. I never would have boarded that Pullman. It is interesting to see that in years to come I would sometimes suffer the same shortsightedness in viewing my own children . . . as they would occasionally misread their offspring.

The overnight sleeper was an experience. Previously I had only traveled coach, which meant sitting and sleeping on suitcases stacked in the isle. WWII trains had been full to the brim with solders and sailors on leave and traveling between assignments. Now during the Korean Conflict I was getting the comfort of a private sleep car, this potential officer billet was starting to look pretty cush!

After checking out all of the miniature conveniences secreted throughout the cabin, I realized that I was being programmed to comfortably shave, shower and potty the rest of my life in a Boeing 747 sized restroom. It would have even been tighter if there were an occupant in the lower bunk! Being aviation minded at the time, I decided on the topside berth for the night. I can't remember ever having trouble sleeping on those suitcases as a kid, but this softer bunk didn't lead to easy slumber. Rattling westward across Indiana, we effectively paralleled the new Indiana Toll Road but at a jerky and much slower pace. At night, clanging bells would announce an approaching intersection, where headlights would spotlight the bedroom window before the bells faded off into the distance. Not much rest for someone hopeful of arriving bright eyed and bushy tailed for a week of exams. However, Champaign, IL, was a sleepy college town and my letter of authorization gave easy entry to an even more relaxed WWI/II vintage military base.

This first day was uneventful and allowed some thirty potential inductees to check out a bed roll, wander around the little town by foot and then grab some early shuteye. In the quiet of the barracks it seemed I could hear faint voices calling from the rafters, "Come fly with us, Jack. Come fly. . . ."

3

Double Vision

Flight Physical

The next morning found us beginning three days of testing. By Thursday afternoon, only ten of us remained to take the flight physical on Friday morning. Celebration was in order; unfortunately, I went along with the peer pressure and headed to the Cadet Club for a couple pitchers of beer with the survivors. Not accustomed to imbibing, I was lucky to navigate back to the barracks.

The physical was a breeze, one of the doctors said I would have to get my weight UP six pounds to one hundred thirty eight pounds by the time I reported for class. We marched back to the office where three of us were told we washed out on the physical . . . I had DOUBLE VISION! This explained a lot of things. I never enjoyed reading, had trouble concentrating on school stuff and dropped out of Ohio State and Toledo Universities. Today I would have instantly qualified for drugs as an Attention Deficit Syndrome candidate. The train ride home was less than uplifting, no cheering friends or relatives; I guess my uncle was right.

The next two months were spent licking wounds and seeing several eye doctors to address my vision problem. I had to see several because none could find a defect with my eyes! I had apparently heard one of my buddies at the original physical talk about seeing two lights while looking at the night eye chart. So, as I entered the darkened room, a red lens was put over one eye and the doctor shone a penlight on a wall grid. He asked how many lights I saw. Initially I saw a red one and a white one . . . and then the eyes focused NORMALLY to see one pink light. But, thinking I needed to see two, I FORCEFULLY focused them apart and could see two! The doctor seemed quite attentive to my ability to keep them apart so long and checked my chart as having double vision. I imagine my ½ pitcher of beer relaxed those eye muscles a little, too, an early lesson about the negative effects of alcohol.

With a fistful of "No Double Vision" letters stuffed into an envelope, I sent a Letter of Appeal to retake my physical. I received my fastest response from any government agency . . . "NO!" In fact they included a copy of a multi-service regulation stating, "A candidate rejected for any officer training program may not reapply for the same program within 12 months." My fate was sealed.

Need a Job? - Persist!

It's funny, when we fail to get something on our own merit; it only makes us want it more. I had my tongue hanging out for that Navigator School assignment . . . and got it cut off! I took the only path I had left, go for the job anyway, the same advice I give employment seekers today. I headed for Chanute AFB the very next morning. I needed a job and my eyes were no longer looking to the future riding a Navy mop in my reserve squadron. My eyes were toward the skies, with the Air Force!

Westbound in Charles Lindberg's Olds on the Ohio Turnpike, I was now dejectedly paralleling the railway tracks I had so recently traveled. What could I accomplish? Well, I did know they started a new test class each week and I had nothing to lose!

I arrived at Chanute around 8 pm, parked on a side street outside the base gate and strode confidently to the guard post. "Lost my pass, I'm in the cadet barracks," I murmured like a dumb, sheepish civilian. This was Thursday night and they had given us a one night pass until 10 pm after passing our written tests. It had been printed on a slip of 3x5 paper and could have been easily lost . . . it worked.

"You officer types are all the same, you're cleared to Tiger Barracks, Bucko," the guard sarcastically replied and waived me through.

"Whew, the first wall scaled", I thought, as I lay down on the bare bunk mattress when the lights went out. Even being cold, I didn't have any trouble sleeping that night . . . I had made it inside the fortress!

The next morning I fell into formation and just like the previous trip, the group was paired down to just 10 (now 11) men. Breakfast was exceptionally good this morning and just what I needed as my stomach was getting quite queasy. As before, we continued down to the dispensary for the flight physical. Once in the waiting room, the orderly collected each applicant's forms. This was the moment of terror. "Where is yours?" they asked.

"Oh, they ran out up at Headquarters and said you'd have some blank sets," I replied without hesitation.

"Lazy SO_'s", an orderly snapped back. "Here, fill these out. You can catch up at the end of the hall." I knew right where they would be!

If the last exam was a breeze, this one was a whirlwind, and I only saw ONE PINK light! At the end of the day I was handed my forms . . . stamped, "PASSED A-OK!" The march of eight men back to headquarters was agonizing, I had come to the end of my rope; maybe the military could court-martial me through the Naval Air Reserves! Many similar thoughts were racing through my mind as we entered the assembly room. The same Captain that dismissed me three months ago . . . addressed us as, "New Aviation Cadets", and welcomed us to the corps. He called each man forward and diligently went down their tests scores, starting with the highest, assigned their starting class dates and dismissed them individually.

I remained the lone man, except for the Captain. "I don't have any more papers. I wonder where they are?" he questioned dumbfounded.

"Oh, you put them in that bottom file cabinet drawer three months ago," I replied with all the confidence I could muster.

"What!" he screamed back shrilly. I tried to explain. He said, "You can't do THAT. No one has ever done THAT!" In disbelief, he opened the "REJECTED" drawer, pulled out my file and just stared at it. Then he slowly moved to a door marked "Commander's Office", opened it and said, "Major, come see what this idiot has done!" They talked and rifled through my file, then the Major approached, sizing me up from head to toe . . . I felt pretty small.

"Mister, you must really want to fly?" the Major questioned.

"Yes, sir!" I boldly replied. My limited military experience had already let me know that with an address of "Mister", things were going to get very official.

"Your letter of appeal has already been answered stating you can't retest for another nine months. What don't you understand?" Before I could even attempt to answer the question for which I had no answer, the Captain came to my rescue. "Did you see these scores?" he asked the Major, "It would be a waste to turn him down."

I didn't know silence could last so long. "Why do you have checked that you want to be a Navigator? Your grades qualify you for Pilot Training," the Major probed.

"Didn't think I'd pass the test, sir," I sputtered back.

"You've got the highest score this week, CADET Schweibold," continued the Major, "Why sit in the back seat staring at a scope when you can be flying the plane? It's your choice. There is a 9 month wait for a Navigator class and 12 months for a Pilot class. Which will it be?"

I was almost tongue-tied but seeing the pilot wings on his chest, I said proudly, "I want to be a pilot like you, Sir. Besides, an extra three months with my girl would not be shabby."

"Cut his orders for Flight School", the major directed as he left the room. I think all three of us felt justice had been served.

4

Soloed!

Better than Sex?

After qualification for cadets, there was a twelve-month waiting period before my class assignment. I had only considered navigator training. Now suddenly, I faced the prospect of being a pilot. A  friend of my uncle agreed to take me as a student and give me lessons in his Talorcraft BC12D for the astounding sum of three dollars per hour for the plane plus three dollars per hour for his instruction.

I believe every young man's prayer is, "Lord, don't let me die before sex." If he says otherwise he's a liar . . . or hasn't prayed yet. A good thing about flying early in life, it redirects some of those troublesome drives, at least temporarily . . . as our vision turns toward the skies. After eight hours, I soloed from the instructor's farm field, made three "touch-and-goes" at a local airport and was released for restricted solo flight.

My FIRST unsupervised departure found me dropping into my uncle's airfield, a small grass strip between cornrows at full height in August. I had arranged to pick up my unauthorized friend, Jan Berry. Jan, probably the largest of my acquaintances, for the first time showed his girth as he stuffed his near three-hundred pound bulk in place. On lift-off, we noticed a summer thunderstorm moving in from the west, so we decided to go just once around the field. I'd never observed the seriousness of shear force, 45 to 55 mile per hour frontal winds.

By the time we turned downwind, I had already cranked in a compensating crab angle of thirty-five degrees; never dealt with wind like this. On final approach, the wind was directly ACROSS, not down this narrow grass runway. With landing speeds of forty miles per hour, my crab-angle increased to 35 degrees. I was looking at the runway out the

SIDE window. On the high flare to land, gusts zigzagged us out over the corn, fifty feet on BOTH sides. We wouldn't make it; we'd have to return to the city airport with a favorable runway direction . . . and be caught with my illegal passenger. Attempting a go-around, I applied full throttle to the 60-hp engine, pulled the nose up and . . . inadvertently stalled-out due to turbulence, high angle-of-attack and the unaccustomed weight of my passenger. By accident, the plane made a BEAUTIFUL 3-point landing ON the runway.

As we taxied in, Jan said, "Great job Jack, I guess I didn't need to be so worried, you are a super pilot!" Little did he know, we should have plowed up an acre of corn and popped it with the ensuing fire! I took off, hotfooted ahead of the storm, landed, and tied the plane down while welcomed rains drenched my shirt to camouflage the dripping sweat. If flying was going to substitute for premarital sex, I just learned that illicit flight might get you in just as much trouble!

Never Be Late!

When I shipped off to flight school, the military sent me specific instructions about when and where to report and even included a coupon for a government airline ticket. It seemed pretty simple to show up on time with all this detailed help. Toledo to San Antonio in the mid-50's required a stop in Dallas for plane change. Dallas' new terminal was impressive. The echoing sound announcing my flight departure brought added dramatic impact, "American Flight to San Antonio will be delayed for . . . Tornadoes!"

This wait, now extending to four hours, was certainly going to impact my due time of 1600 hours (5 p.m.); however, I figured a wait for severe frontal activity would be an acceptable excuse, and besides, each hour we waited meant the cyclones were probably slipping off our course. I was soon to learn it would be neither; this was one of my bumpiest rides ever and NO one was happy about my 1900 hours (7 p.m.), LATE arrival!

Arriving after the 5 PM curfew placed me directly in the hands of the upperclassmen, a fate worse than landing in a swimming pool of piranha. These guys were a ragtag band of disheveled, bloodstained gladiators, clothed only in a torn T-shirts, dirty shorts and muddy tennis shoes. As they shot grimacing smirks, they informed me they'd just returned from physical training hour and would be waiting on the field for me on Tuesday . . . to see what I was made of! They didn't need to wait; they already knew I was mush!

26

Once in the barracks, I got the one remaining rack. It was right next to the head, the john . . . or whatever else you want to call the stall, bedside twelve naked stools flushing throughout the night. I had already been sworn into the Air Force, so this meant I was officially AWOL! As I attempted to squeeze my tornado excuse into the interrogation process, they informed me I had been due a day earlier on Sunday, not Monday! In an attempt to hang with my girlfriend an extra few hours before leaving Toledo, I misread the calendar by 24 hours. Harassment continued well beyond the 2200 hour (10 PM) lights out. I wasn't permitted sleep until after 3AM, when these bloody jocks could go to bed knowing they had singled out their first candidate for . . . WASHOUT!

The 0430-hour revelry was a b-l-u-r and once rolled-out in the Texas cold summer morning, clad only in T-shirt and pants . . . a frigid, shivering **burr-r-r-r** set in! Roll call lasted forever, when they got to "Schwerverboard, Shiverbald" and other intentionally spastic mutilations of the family crest, time stood still. Back inside, only a few minutes were allowed to shave and dress for breakfast. I was the only man who showed up in civvies; the balance of thirty double-time marching cadets had been issued a set of green fatigues. Was I a target . . . or was I a target? You bet, every passing upperclassman shot a verbal salvo that day and they were marksmen! While we stood at attention in the mess line, every departing senior assaulted us . . . and they didn't miss me!

The tables were set with an upperclassman at both ends, with four to five underclassmen lining both sides. Permission had to be requested and received for every action taken by an underclassman. Whenever six empty glass-sized milk bottles hit the table, each underclassman had to answer up at attention, "SIR, request permission to ask a question, SIR". The last man to respond would be addressed, "Cadet ask question asked!" The late underclassman would reply, "SIR, request permission to depart for a refueling mission, SIR," to which he was granted permission to march across to the milk line and refuel. All the while, the two end table upperclassmen would be throwing questions to, "The 37th cadet on my left, listen up!" If that man missed or the wrong man responded, they would get the next refueling run. This table combat was supposed to develop your peripheral vision and thinking under stress. The one thing quickly learned was to drink lots of milk in one gulp, as food was too difficult to masticate when being called to response at attention . . . with mouth empty; otherwise, "bombing recon" requests had to be solicited to retrieve ejected food.

While everyone else headed for their first day of academics, I was shuttled over to headquarters for a disciplinary hearing, "Cadet Schweibold, AWOL", was the announcement. I expected to be drummed out of the corps this very first day; instead, I was fortunately taught what AWOL meant in Cadets. "Away With Out Leave" equaled . . . "Always Walking Off Laps on the Tour Ramp." I received a "24 Gun Salute", twenty-four demerits and twelve hours on the tour ramp. Since an hour on the ramp was also assigned for every weekly demerit over twelve, I came into Cadets with twenty-four tour hours ahead of my closest wingman! My codename was, Ramp Master!

Broken!

Leaving Headquarters, I traded even for a pair of green fatigues, I got the fatigues . . . they got my hair! Well, at least I didn't stand out as severely from my other one hundred and forty-eight classmates. By noon, I was able to catch up with them at physical training, one hour of calisthenics ending with a two-mile run. No, it wasn't the bloody event I expected . . . the trauma witnessed the night before was just the aftermath of good-natured sports activity when the graduating cadets matriculated from pre-flight school. However, the two-mile run was worse. I had been the slowest boy in high school, always finishing the 100-yard dash last out of four hundred kids. I never ran a mile before in my life, yet alone two!

No, I didn't finish last but limped across second to last, with a wonderful prize . . . the last five won another mile! As we struggled around the course again, mostly in an agonizing walk/run/walk, we saw the formation departing to the barracks . . . we could only savor being late for remaining classes and becoming "dead meat" for upper-class predators.

This process of no sleep, harassment, and double time physical activity continued day and night for three weeks in the

Upperclassmen took turns holding hourly barracks inspection throughout the night

28

same unwashed pair of fatigues. They stood alone in their salt shell at night, but I couldn't. The only positive thing was that as a stinking, rotting group of underclassmen during daytime fatigue wear, the upper-class would only belittle from a distance . . . and then from upwind! They saved close encounters for after shower time at night, when they could deprive us from our most precious commodity . . . sleep. I was being broken!

They had done their job well, singled out a runt; not drowned in a bucket like a deformed animal, but just humiliated to be washed out of the corps. SIE, Self Initiated Elimination . . . quitting, was not an option. I had already dropped out of two colleges, I couldn't handle returning home as a total failure, again. Then a way appeared. On Saturday, the bulletin board announced that whitewashing the barracks would replace Monday's drill time. Eureka, I figured that a position on the roof, coupled with a straight-leg-freefall from two and a half stories, would score at least a broken leg. After all, rats caught in a trap are known to chew off their own legs. Conceivably, a medical discharge from cadets would transfer me to a two-year hitch as an enlisted Airman and an honorable return home. I was trapped and . . . about to be broken!

Happy Hour

The Sunday morning bugle blew at 6 AM, an hour and a half longer in the pad. Sunday meant some free time . . . at least for those without tours to march. The ol' Ramp Master would be marching four hours in the morning and four after lunch, with no end in sight; not much incentive to get up. Waiting in formation for morning muster, the barracks roof appeared to grow higher as it sat blocking the rising sun. Resolve for the jump was confirmed. After roll call, the Flight Captain informed us we could attend Happy Hour. I figured this was a time we would all "hang-around-the-barracks" (doing chin-ups from exposed water pipes) while forced to listen to upper-classmen's stale jokes. I volunteered, thought it might delay the Tour Ramp. So, after morning chow, our formation split with half of us begrudgingly singing double-time cadence enroute to Happy Hour.

Surprise! We pulled up in front of the Base Chapel. Happy Hour was Church. One hour of absolute total PEACE! Once in the chair, I collapsed immediately and wonderfully asleep . . . for one whole, uninterrupted hour! No upper-class torment, running, marching or square meals at attention . . . just total, unconscious rest. Several buddies eventually shook me. I can still remember trying to stay in Never, Never Land. "Don't miss formation," they kept yelling. After returning for change to "Class A" (full dress) uniform, white gloves and brogan boots . . . I hadn't missed the Tour Ramp, I asked permission to ask a question. "Ask question asked," responded the Leader.

"Sir, request to know if we get Happy Hour privileges next Sunday, Sir?" I snapped.

"Yes, we can't keep you bumbling pussycats from Sunday Happy Hour," replied a sarcastic upper-classman, who had obviously drawn the short straw to blow an hour of his Sunday free time. Suddenly I saw light at the end of the tunnel! If I could hold out until next Sunday morning, I could get another hour of wonderful, priceless sleep. The next day's barracks whitewash didn't find me vying for a topside position. Instead, I claimed a new chemical formula, HFH^2 ... Holdout for Happy Hour!

During the next three months, I slept wonderfully through every 60-minute service. The seniors eventually marched off to actual flight school and we moved to an upper-class-position. Revenge, oh, yes! I did my share to torment the new kids on the block, but I was first to volunteer marching the "pussycats" to Happy Hour. After all, I was still marching weekends on the Tour Ramp and didn't have anything else to do for amusement. I continued to sleep through a couple services; I had a lot of z-z-z's to catch up while my sharp classmates visited San Antonio on weekend passes. I was never to get a pass at this base. Actually, this twist of torment turned to my good. As the months of August and September moved above 100 degrees, we sat out tour hours in study hall. This set me straight with academics, a form of one-ups-men-ship on those without demerits!

In a month or so, I started staying awake during Chapel. On one Sunday a real fire-and-brimstone, Hell snort'n Southern Baptist Chaplin got my full, undivided attention. The Holy Spirit convicted me of my sin, His righteousness and a future judgment to come. What I heard was HEAVY on the judgment side. I knew well I was a sinner, didn't understand righteousness . . . and sure wanted forgiveness from that judgment stuff. After the sermon, the Chaplin invited those that would like to talk with him to go forward. Fortunately, there was another classmate to return the troops. Without hesitation, I went with the Chaplin into the next room. I can't say I'd ever seen people "go forward" before. I just needed to talk about MY judgment!

It sounds so simple to say I accepted Jesus Christ on the strength of one verse, John 3:16, *"For God so loved the world that He gave His only begotten Son, that whoever believes in Him shall not perish but have everlasting life.*" The Chaplin probably read the next couple of verses, too, but I did know that Christ took my judgment on Himself and I was free of sin AND guilt. As I was moved quickly out the door because of others waiting for counsel, I asked over my shoulder, "Sir, if God loves me so and I love Him . . . why am I here learning to be a combat pilot or a crowd killer (our affectionate name for a bomber pilot)?"

"Typical question, son," he replied. "Come back next week and we'll discuss it. Until then read John in that Testament and pray . . . for the answer." Back at the barracks and under the covers by flashlight, I read John in the Gideon's New Testament he had handed me, and I prayed. Weeks passed, but like most chaplains, he never returned. I kept this to myself . . . and my prayer was eventually answered years later, but God had started a wonderful work in me that day. In weeks past, Chapel had saved me from a broken leg, now He was saving me from a broken life . . . thanks, Lord!

Happy Hour brought hope to this harassed cadet one Sunday in 1955. Maybe he'd get to fly a T-Bird Jet Trainer like this one parked aside the barracks.

5

Flight School

Singled Out ... Again

Life is a continuous learning process. In Primary Flight Training, I came up against a formidable foe . . . the docile looking T-34. My first flight in this modern Beechcraft military variant of their civilian Bonanza was to be a relaxing "freebee". It recently replaced the Air Force's old ground-looping T-6 Trainer. The flight should be a snap. It was really meant to determine student aptitude to divide us so one instructor wouldn't be overburdened with four slow students ... real Dumbo's. Yes, well even Dumbo learned to fly.

We sat in an old WW II Squadron Flight Operations Building on the aircraft ramp. About seventy-two of us flew in the morning and seventy-two in the afternoon. It looked more like a training shack for WWI Jenny's than the eventual Air Force Academy. Eighteen instructors sat in three ranks of tables with four students each, except for me! They singled me out to sit alone at a table; I didn't even have an instructor. The Squadron Flight Commander took the podium, I must have so blown the flight that I would be first to get pink slipped. After all, my uncle said when examining my flight aptitude, "There is no way. You are too uncoordinated to ever be a pilot!" I should have listened.

The Commander stepped down and headed right for my table, isolated in front of his podium . . . everyone held their breath, I was fish bait! I stood, snapped to attention and saluted his arrival. "At ease. Sit down, Cadet," he replied. "How do you pronounce that nametag, Mister?"

I stuttered out, "Sch-w-ei-bold, Sir," I stammered.

"Aren't you sure, Mister?"

"Well . . . I guess so, Sir" I sheepishly replied. We took our first flight.

On returning to the briefing table, he let me have it, "Schweibold, you lied on your application!" Silence . . . you tried to hide it, a lot of you guys do . . . but you've flown before. How much time do you have?"

"Just soloed, sir." as I lied again, hiding my big forty-four hours."

"Well," he said, "I don't care how much time you have, you're mine and I want you CERTAIN about everything here! I have to run this Squadron, I only have time for one student, and my student WILL be the BEST. You will solo FIRST, your grades will be TOP; flying, academically, physically . . . ." as he surveyed my anemic frame. Well, maybe not physically but militarily, flight wise and academically. You got me, Mister!"

"Yes, Sir." Better than the being the first washout, I thought.

"Your problem is, these first couple weeks in the air will be spontaneous to you. Everyone else will struggle and get in the learning mode. Soon they'll zip right past and whip your butt!" he challenged. "You falter . . . and make me look bad in front of MY troops, and you are past tense around here!"

I didn't need to reply.

"Recovery from Inverted Flight"

He not only became my most terrifying and demanding instructor but my most life-saving; however, he first proceeded to prove himself right. Everything went well through solo and the first flying phase. I was his Prima Donna and made him look GREAT. On the first morning of Phase II, we experienced an obvious cut. Several tables were missing one or more students. By the time we got back to the barracks that night, those men and all of their belongings were gone, leaving only . . . bare mattresses. Rolled up on their naked springs, they looked more like cold headstones on fresh graves. Buddies were gone and their names were never spoken again. One could have been mine.

The next morning we moved into advanced maneuvers and aerobatics. Right on schedule, our plane with the Squadron Commander was the first one with "gear up." He had just briefed me on "Loops and Recovery from Inverted Flight". We climbed straight up to 10,000 feet, made our two level clearing turns, and then he took the controls to demonstrate the loop. I was next, I dropped the nose on the Texas north/south fencerows, holding it on the section line with rudder and pulled the nose up to enter the maneuver. As the airspeed dropped off passing vertical, the throttle was advanced and the aft stick relaxed to pull through the top where the throttle was reduced and back pressure on the stick applied to pull out at the bottom . . . all the time keeping the nose on the section lines with the rudder and wings level with the ailerons. "Repeat that and see if it was a fluke", he commanded. I did two more that seemed to get worse, not better . . . it had been a fluke.

34

Then he rolled the ship over on our back, which left me hanging by the shoulder straps. "Follow me through on the controls!" he shouted. Nothing felt right . . . now we were just there, hanging upside down. My feet fell off the rudders. "Forward control pressure, add right stick, and feed in left rudder," he added.

What did he mean, LEFT rudder? That's cross-controlling!

"Let the aft pressure relax as you roll out and return to level flight, see how simple that was?" I didn't answer. He continued, "The goal is to lose as little altitude as possible, no more than a couple hundred feet. This maneuver trains a quick roll recovery if you inadvertently get upside down on turn to final approach or in an unusual condition . . . your turn," he concluded.

I climbed back to 10,000 feet, added the two clearing turns when he abruptly rolled the T34 on its back; again hanging me in my straps looking through the canopy, transfixed by the Texas turf two miles below. Then I did what many a greenhorn did . . . I barfed all over the canopy. Do you know that vomiting upside down fills your nostrils and makes it worse? Sitting behind me, he saw my distress and rolled the ship level, where the slop and crud dripped slowly from the roof. The flight ended. Once on the ground I was given a couple of buckets of water and the job of cleaning up the mess. I wanted to keep throwing up. Silently my instructor stomped off to his office. I knew if this sequence was repeated, MY mattress would be bare tomorrow. I began praying for bad weather. God answered, the next two days found us grounded with 500-foot ceilings. Those nights I made like Batman and practiced hanging upside down from the upper bunk.

"Checkitus"

Three days later we were inverted again. "Now roll out," he shouted. I slowly started the right roll, was late getting the left rudder in and immediately panicked and pulled the stick aft. This resulted in a classic split "S", maximum diving descent. "Get the throttle off!" he screamed . . . I was frozen on the controls. I felt him pull the throttle and start the stick back to pull out. "Lost 6,000', more than a mile," he chided. "At low level, you'd been buried . . . deep!"

I knew, I knew.

"Get back up there and try again, this time hold the nose forward longer and roll through faster!" Three more split "S's" followed; he was getting mad and tired of blacking out on the recoveries. He was in the back seat pulling more "G's" and being older, he blacked out first. Finally,

35

I got one . . . half-right. I was shaking all over . . . I knew everything was over. It was time to go back.

He flew back to base, taxied in at high speed, swerved into the parking space . . . jamming on the brakes to a stop, leaving the aircraft sitting, bouncing on the nose strut! It was over. "Meet me in my office immediately, cadet!" he loudly snapped. I could see empathy in the surrounding crews. They knew what that meant.

I caught up with him as he was turning to sit at his desk. When he saw me enter, he grabbed the desk, whirled it around and slammed it against the door, baring my departure. It was a small office at the rear of the building immediately outside the Squadron Briefing Room. I had already passed the lowered eyes of my classmates being debriefed by their instructors. He sat down in his chair, staring at me with two burning eyes. Trembling inside, I spewed, "Sir, Cadet Schweibold reporting as ordered, Sir."

"Mister, that's the WORST lesson I've lived through since I've had this command. Wipe off that window!"

I stood dumbfounded.

"At ease, Schweibold!" he kept on, while throwing a shop towel at my feet. "Well, pick it up, stupid," he continued to shout . . . so everyone outside could hear. "Pick it up and wipe off that window."

I slowly bent over and picked it up, still staring blankly.

"Unzip your flight suit".

I did.

"NO ... Drop it to the crotch!"

I "bottomed" it.

"Now, wipe off that window," he screamed, "right there, where your belly button is!" pointing to my stomach. "So you can see out of it when you've got your head up your as _ and LOCKED! Now get out of here. I never want to see you again!" he ground into my raw ears.

As I turned to leave he added, "Wait! Get your butt back out in that airplane, go practice that recovery for one hour. If you come back alive, I'll have a check instructor waiting for your exit flight!"

I was scared. I left, staggering out of the room with everyone watching . . . opened mouthed. As I pulled the door closed slowly behind me, the knob ripped out of my hand. "HERE, use my back cushion and then leave it in the ship for my next flight!" as he slammed the door. I headed for the flight line . . . but not before stopping in the head. At least now, I wouldn't get sick while up solo.

This flight spent more time in unusual attitudes then level! I got to where I would lose less that 100' in the recovery. Why couldn't I do this with the boss aboard? Survival instinct, I guess. As I taxied the T-34 slowly back to its berth, I knew this next flight could be my last. There was the check instructor, we had seen him take out four or five of our buddies the past week . . . he had a vibrant copy of my Pink Slip on the top of his clipboard. "Are you ready, cadet?" he asked as the prop came to rest.

"As ready as I can be," I wearily replied. I knew how a blindfolded prisoner of war felt on his walk to be shot. The only difference was that I looked through a salt-stained visor while taxiing to my execution. But I made it! A climb, two clearing turns and two perfect recoveries, I just used my only permitted pink slip.

Likewise, the Squadron Commander just sacrificed his very best shot at getting his point across. In his displayed anger, he gambled his reputation before the entire squadron . . . while loving his student enough to give him one final chance to fly. He had played his last wild card.

The next morning I reported to another briefing table where I received a new instructor to become my father image the balance of time at Hondo AFB. While I have no problem remembering the Commander, the one and only gift I recall receiving from this second instructor was his wisdom: "Soon, the Korean War will be over, pilots again will be worth only a nickel a dozen ... but remember: there will always be a job for the best!" Thanks to these two mentors, I have never been a day without a job and have done my utmost to extend their "Be the Best" challenge to my family, employees, students and counselees. Positive motivation works, too.

2 Timothy 4:2 Preach the Word; be prepared in season and out of season; correct, rebuke and encourage--with great patience and careful instruction.

Fighter Pilots

Finally finishing the T-34, we moved into the T-28. This bigger engined ship served as a trainer and stepping-stone for both fighter and bomber transition. Its big 800 hp Wright radial engine started and operated like the recips on transports and bombers we would soon be flying. Once in flight, the "28" paralleled the performance and handling characteristics of the T-Bird Jet Trainer. Civilian landing patterns typically involve a wide, left-hand pattern or straight-in approach to landing. We utilized the military overhead pitch-out pattern in landing. This permitted us to enter down the runway, 1,000-feet over the touchdown point, reduce the throttle and circle down to the runway. The advantage of this close-in circling approach is that the pilot is able to make the runway if the engine quits, by increasing or decreasing angle of bank. Little did I know how often I would employ this technique when engines say, "Goodbye!"

The T-28 could also be fitted with armament racks for bombs, guns and rockets, making it the ideal option for counter insurgency combat. All of the basic flying skills learned in the T-34 were quickly adapted in the T-28, even recovery from inverted flight. With more power, aerobatics were a snap. Switching seats to the rear, a full hood pulled over the canopy, exposed us to our first taste of flying on instruments. The secret was to develop a consistent revolving crosscheck, rather than become fixated on a few or one gage; however, in a pinch, the old cadet motto slipped into play . . . one peek is worth more than a dozen crosschecks! The problem with that motto was those who depended on the "peek", probably never developed the required proficiency and became our washout statistics for the instrument phase. We were destined to loose 75% of our starting class before receiving wings.

The author climbs aboard his T28 for an aerobatic flight.

One night at this base, the outbound upperclassmen celebrated their Saturday at the Cadet Club, our class still faced an earlier curfew. Squires, my roommate, and I "racked out" by 10 pm. We were softly playing an unauthorized record player to cover the noise of revelers returning at midnight. We had commandeered the front room, next to the outside door where we had fewer steps to formations; however, it didn't work well this night. Suddenly, the main entrance door slammed open. Someone yelled, "Who's got the music on?"

Waking from a light sleep and thinking it was a drunken, harassing upperclassman . . . I hollered back, "What do you think this is, a purge or something?"

Then, our door swung open and two of our base Tactical Officers blasted in. One of them grimaced and continued in high pitched voice, "Mister, you don't know what a purge is . . . YET!" On Monday I learned what a "purge" was; it was to be me. They summoned me to a Cadet Evaluation Board hearing for "Insubordination". Little did I know that the officer I'd answered was Jewish. I'm certain his families had recently lived out a real purge, Hitler's extermination of ten million countrymen. Fortunately, his fellow officers must have recognized his sensitivity to the issue. The Board dropped the insubordination rap and I rightfully ate a "6 & 12", six hours on the tour ramp and twelve demerits for playing music after hours. While the frustrated "Tac" Officer couldn't very well get at me, he did nail poor Squires with a 72-Gun Salute, thirty-six hours on the ramp and seventy-two demerits . . . for having unauthorized food in his dresser drawer, an opened package of peanut butter crackers. My buddy Squires hadn't left me wounded in battle. He testified for me at that board hearing . . . nearly killing him!

It wasn't that I was prejudiced; my parents had raised me to be tolerant of all. In reality, until half our barracks (those not walking tours) went to a Texas beach on Padre Island with one of my closest cadet friends, our own corps-elected Cadet Commander . . . would I became aware that his being black was significant. We were playing touch football on the beach, when several cars of Texans pulled up around us. We battled our way out of a race war . . . all over one black man they didn't want on THEIR surf, the TOP man in our squadron. Similarly, we didn't leave him wounded on the beach. I don't think the Texans realized they were taking on a formation of "fighter pilots!"

Pr 18:24b " . . . But there is a friend who sticks closer than a brother."

Bombers are Beautiful

Halfway through the T-28 was a milestone. Tour ramp duty was completed and this "Ramp Master" finally saw a couple weekends of liberty in San Antonio. Don't know how the class was split after graduation from Hondo, but half of our remaining seventy students or so were assigned to Mississippi for singles and I was assigned with the balance to multi-engines, the "Big Ones". The venerable B-25, medium bomber, would become my home for the next year.

Climbing aboard through the bottom escape-hatch ladder the first day sent shivers up the spine. We flew with an instructor and two to four students. While one student was worked over in the left pilot's seat, a second watched from behind in the navigator's bench. It would be his turn to fly next and he would have the advantage of seeing the maneuvers in advance. The third cadet was stationed downstairs in the bombardier's position, the nose greenhouse, to watch for oncoming aircraft. This was the resting spot reserved for the man rotating from direct instruction; he could strip to the waist and let the sun dry his sweat-drenched body. Any additional observer would crawl through the bomb bay catwalk and strap into one of the side or tail gun turrets to look for traffic from the rear.

Relaxing in any of these positions, it was easy to let your mind drift to the valiant heritage of your ship. It was named for General Billy Mitchell, who, for defending his far-reaching vision of the strategic use of bombers in the mid-20's, was court-martialed by the Army and drummed out of the service. Years later, a squadron of Mitchell's took-off from Admiral Halsey's carrier, the Hornet, on a mission so secret the pilots didn't know

40

their destination . . . until AFTER being launched. They were our first weapons to strike the heartland of Japan at the beginning of WWII. After dropping their bombs, most were lost at sea or crashed on the China mainland but this mission let the enemy know they were vulnerable. It vindicated General Mitchell and boosted the morale of our still shocked nation. As the Marines flew the Corsair in frontline combat, the Army Air Force flew the B-25 in close air/ground support to retake the Pacific Islands. It's a good thing we didn't carry live guns or we students may have gotten caught up in nostalgia and shot each other down.

Preparing for the B-25, we were all doing one-hand pushups, chin-ups and leg squats. Once the instructor pulled a throttle to simulate an engine-out condition, we had to roll in full aileron and hold opposite rudder to maintain track. Without modern day boost systems, we held barn door-sized control surfaces against 150 mph gale force wind . . . with mere muscle. By the time I wrestled the beast around the pattern for a landing, I'd be standing on the rudder with locked leg, muscles shaking! I'd be well ready for the greenhouse rest position; the difficulty was staying awake while soaking up the sun.

My most testing encounter with this forgiving brute was returning from our solo night cross-country mission. A buddy and I teamed to fly two hours west into New Mexico, land at a staging field, switch seats and return to base. He landed in NM on a small, narrow-width strip; I returned to Reese and landed on our wider runway. After flying all night at higher than normal altitudes, I setup for the sight picture I had seen in New Mexico. The wider runway now "appeared" close. I rounded out 50-100 feet too high . . . and stalled, dropping "Beast" from a substantial height. We hit so-o HARD it knocked off our headsets and hats, drove chins into chests, dropped most switches that were up or neutral to DOWN positions. This turned lights, blowers, wipers, etc. "on" or "off" from their normal positions. My copilot slumped into the right corner, lifted his mike to his lips and sputtered, "Schweibold, that was the hardest landing I've ever seen." Unfortunately, his mike switch also toggled down . . . from intercom to transmit. As we turned off the end of the runway in total darkness, because all exterior lights were turned off, the tower came back, "Invisible aircraft, let us know when you're off the runway . . . and then write that ship up for a hard landing!" It was a long wait during the inspection. If damage was found, my bunk would be empty . . . with only two weeks to graduation.

During the year at Reese Air Force Base, Lubbock, Texas, we witnessed several weather systems. One was a dust storm that appeared as a solid, vertical wall of black cloud turning day into near night. Once it hit we couldn't see the next barracks, consequently we sat for two days and watched sand drift in miniature dunes INSIDE our rooms. It was easy to see how endless days like these during the 30's formed The Dust Bowl. The most devastating front brought a tornado and baseball sized hailstones through the main gate, shredding our roofs, B-25's and adjacent cattle. When the tally was taken, we lost the fabric control surfaces and Plexiglas windows on all but three of our hundred aircraft and dozens of cattle lay dead along the fences. My 51' Volkswagen Bug rolled into a flooded drainage ditch and floated four blocks through the base streets before washing aground. We worked night and day to refurbish the control surfaces and install new Plexiglas in our bombers. It was a week before I could salvage the car. I found the engine still underwater and its body pulverized by hail. But who cared about the car, my B25 showed its strength . . . and passed its Hard Landing Check!

Graduation

When starting multi-engine training, our small surviving band of cadets merged with Naval Academy and West Point four-year graduates desiring to switch to the Air Force. I guess that was a reasonable option for them since I originally changed from the Navy; however, that placed a burden on us cadets. Since they were now flying as fully commissioned officers, they outranked us, were probably academically more astute and didn't have to put up with military training, demerits and the tour ramp. Likewise, they came with some baggage we didn't carry. Most of them had recently married (or activated secret marriages) bringing some of their own extra responsibilities. Grades were important and mutual competition became evident as we positioned for first pick of available graduation assignments.

Actually, the tour ramp became a non-event. Physical training even ended for a time. Our Annapolis/West Point Squadron was hit a hard blow; two men were stricken with polio, one died. Our own cadet ranks continued to thin when one of our men was caught cheating on exams. He had marked multiple answers on score sheets. Then, one week they changed from punched-out opaque score sheets to clear plastic overlays . . . where they could SEE his multiple marks. At that time I was second-in-command of our Cadet Squadron, I was also President of the Cadet Honor Counsel. All military cadets police their own honesty. Here, the kid who had the stickiest fingers on the block faced the decision to shoot down one of our own. Our board's finding was that he had lowered all of our grades, especially since a diligent friend just washed out on academics. It came down to, "If he cheated in Flight School, he might cheat on a mission." His fellow cadets emptied his bunk and maintained the integrity of the Corps.

Yes, I made graduation. Class 57-Tango received our wings and commissions in late summer. My girl back home had saved her money all summer and flew in with Mom for a few days. Commencement was in the base auditorium, housing a class of more than a hundred graduates. We cadets walked across the stage, received our gold Second Lieutenant bars and joined the Annapolis and West Point officers to receive our wings. Then, by class rank, we continued across the stage to select our assignments from the board. I remember getting fifth choice; significant because the first four went to Military Transport duty in Hawaii and California, leaving the fifth and sixth to squadrons in Europe. As I reached for the French slot, I saw Sharon over the edge of the platform . . . I knew if I hit the Continent, I'd never see her again. Instead, I selected one off the bottom of the board, an extended training billet to Helicopter School. I'd never seen a helicopter up close, didn't know anything about them . . . but some day I might want to fly commercially and I believed vertical lift might have a future. Most of the other assignments were to the Strategic Air Command flying B-47's and 52's in the Arctic. The bottom students filled the remaining 24 Helicopter School slots . . . no one else must have thought much about helicopters. I pinned my wings on Mom; she deserved them. I hugged and squeezed Sharon, a long time.

After Mom and Sharon left and the pressure of school was off, we had three months to casually sit around the base waiting for our assignments to start after Thanksgiving. The Volkswagen took a lot of attention; it looked like the Jolly Green Giant had taken a hammer to the metal. After the insurance company fixed the many dents and paint, it looked pretty good but after a few weeks of driving, the engine blew. It had apparently soaked too long underwater. The closest Volkswagen Dealer was 90 miles north in Amarillo. Squires lent me his car to tow it but I needed another driver, as Squires couldn't make the trip . . . he was still marching tours. A chap volunteered, he was the squadron "ladies man".

Even though school was over, I was still learning. All the way north he talked about chasing down some chicks. Surprise! As soon as we hit the hotel, he ORDERED one from the bellman, along with a bottle of whiskey. Not my picture of a date. Once in the rooms I could hear the girl-of-the-night arrive . . . and through the walls, HIS pleas of, "Please tell me you love me." That was enough. If he was the envy of the troops, would I end up like him? I already had a girl that I was pretty sure loved me. I KNEW I loved her, despite the fact that those words had never been spoken. I called Sharon the next day in the midst of a telephone strike; we connected . . . for life!

PR 18:22 He who finds a wife finds what is good and receives favor from the LORD.

6

Honeymoon Time

You give a woman enough rope and she can ring a wedding bell, Sharon blessed me by ringing ours at a Presbyterian Church in Toledo, Ohio, December 27th, 1957. She had everything under control; all I needed to do was show up with a ring. I had already purchased the set at Zale's in San Antonio, Texas; even paid it off. I was bringing into marriage two costly children she'd financially adopt, a four-hundred dollar bill for my uniforms and a twenty-seven-hundred dollar loan on a new 1957 convertible. Things were tight but we had possession of three important items: clothes to keep a job, transportation to get back to base and a ring to prove she was mine.

The church was dressed in a special setting, freshly decorated from the Christmas candlelight service. It was dark except for the soft glow radiating from the window and altar candles. Sharon lit the whole church with her radiance as she entered . . . with her dad frantically trying to stay

in step. Dad Crouse came out of the big band era, Glenn Miller, Ray Anthony, Benny Goodman, etc. - - but the wedding march was a step that he just couldn't swing to! As he got closer, I saw he was probably slipping in his tears as he was letting go of his baby girl.

Other than kissing her, I don't remember anything until we were southbound out of Toledo for San Antonio. I had only two days to get back to base. Here she took the reigns of the Chevrolet and said "Whoa, Big Fella! We're stopping for a honeymoon." Stumbling into the motel in Findley, Ohio, I sheepishly signed

45

the register as Jack Schweibold and Sharon Crouse; can't remember if I ever changed it, but the proprietor could probably tell we were okay by the rice falling from my hair onto a shiny new ring. This at least started us with a humorous moment every marriage needs. It was worth saving real loving for the honeymoon!!!

Humility

If we are going to be used by God, He will keep us humble. While at Oxnard AFB, we had dozens of successful rescues, each one memorable on its own merit. If it seemed exciting and challenging to us, it must have been a much more awesome event to those we were attempting to serve . . . they were already in a traumatic situation. While we were used to our four-ton monsters, their elation when first sighting us would sometimes slip to trepidation, fear and trembling. They were suddenly face-to-face with a screaming beast advancing and brandishing whirling blades, a roaring engine and a surprise downwash . . . the latter capable of tumbling even the hardy. If conscious, the distressed person must make an immediate decision whether we were friend or foe!

Others would normally be involved to help make the decision. These good Samaritans would vote for us as the most expeditious transport from remote or restricted areas. They didn't want the person(s) to die in THEIR arms. Once we had the distraught aboard, the immediate helpers could go on their way or assist with further recovery efforts.

My very first rescue attempt was just that, an attempt! I had only been on base a couple of weeks and I was eager to hit the sky. Lt. Ken and I were the duty pilots assigned to rendezvous with a Navy Destroyer outbound from Long Beach NAS for the Orient. A seaman aboard was suffering from appendicitis. The captain didn't want to return to base and the doctor didn't want to care for a sick man the whole trip. We were the convenient enroute transport option. The ship continued at half speed while we set a course to intercept at sea. As we approached from their 4 o'clock position, radio contact was established and the captain responded to Lt. Ken's request by turning the cruiser into the wind.

46

Upon reaching the ship, we flew alongside to view the position of the man to be transported. He was located on a mesh stretcher, about two-thirds the way aft. It looked like we'd have a good position for our 100-foot cable hoist to drop between various masts and antenna. Ken's silver lapel bar glistened in the sun as we made a circling right hand sweep to re-approach from the rear. I looked at my shiny gold bar and was thankful my lower rank would let me observe a senior man at work. Things looked okay so far. With the cruiser's fifteen knots and a wind reported by the captain at twelve knots, the twenty-seven knot relative wind would give us ample rotor lift for the pick up. Our hoist operator, hanging out his lower cargo door, vectored us by intercom for pickup. Passing over the fantail, the deck team slipped beneath our nose and view. I noticed additional seamen coming topside seeking vantage points on decks and stairwells to see their comrade evacuated. Ken had our helicopter centered between two masts. I was to keep an eye on the left front while he quarter-turned the aircraft to watch his side. Our hoist operator lowered his cable to the deck men. "They've got him secured," our operator downstairs called.

Without hesitation, Lt. Ken responded, "Bring him up!"

I gulped, "How about . . . ?" Too Late! With a two hundred pound man, anchoring us below and without applying additional power . . . our hoist operator was merely reeling us ONTO THE SHIP! "You're loosing rotor RPM!" I shouted to Ken while tapping my finger on the Main Rotor Tachometer. He responded by applying up collective pitch (a bigger bite with the blades) WRONG! Much like starting a drag race in your Corvette locked in fourth gear! Finally, he applied additional throttle with the motorcycle style twist grip in his left hand. Again, too late, he was behind the engine/rotor power curve, we kept settling and couldn't get the rotor RPM back up. We continued to descend and the main rotor was now within a foot of the whip antenna rising from the mast to our forward left.

"Ping-Ping-Ping –", the blades sang out as they severed the antenna several times per second. At each whining impact, we could hear the rotor slowing down. The old flight school axiom ran through my brain, "Thy Rotor RPM Is Thy Staff Of Life, without it you will surely DIE!" Our staff was getting shorter! Now we were dropping fast. The ship's mast was telescoping as BIGGER sized pieces were being cutoff in a continuous stack of silver dollars. "Wheeer-eer-er . . ." the main rotor screams became more intense as our metal blade pockets were being ripped loose in their breeze. Now our craft started humping in vertical motion as we continued to sink. "The next section of mast should surely rip the blades off," I thought. From this height, we'd crash on our side or go inverted. This Kamikaze Helicopter was going to take out the WHOLE SHIP!

"Bang!" We stopped falling. Either Ken or our crew chief finally fired the 45-caliber cartridge, shooting a guillotine knife through the cable. With the helicopter shaking violently, Ken slowly moved us sidewise to the right and pogo-sticked our way toward shore. While our crewman downstairs was moving our life raft into ditching position next to his door, I considered the abandoned seaman. Our ride was wild; his view must have been awesome. A floundering dinosaur, snorting exhaust and defecating metal shrapnel, while diving to eat alive . . . the prey it came to "save"!

Proverbs 15:33: "The fear of the LORD teaches a man wisdom, and humility comes before honor."

We didn't see our fearless 1st. Lt. on the flight line much after that, he was assigned more important jobs on Terra Firma and I had learned a lot!

Churches Have Problems, Too

Our first church attendance after we settled in the hills at Oxnard AFB, California, was at a little Methodist Church across the street from our house. Attendance there was obviously one of convenience for me . . . and Sharon's observance of her Grandmother's Methodist faith. After a couple week's attendance, when the two of us swelled the crowed by 4%, Sharon worked as part-time secretary. I guess they didn't want to lose us! This was Sharon's first shot at clerical work and we felt ashamed to take the few dollars pay, we knew it was probably more than the pastor received. I wasn't a Bible scholar, had only heard a few chaplains speak but it was easy to tell the church had a big problem. The preacher's messages confirmed he WAS probably adequately paid. We needed a different church.

The next Sunday, we headed down our orange-tree lined road, turned into lazy Camarillo and found two old churches, a Catholic and a Baptist. I was told my father may have directed me sprinkled Catholic but I was never in a church until my mother and stepfather dropped me off at a Protestant church a couple times . . . they knew I needed help from someone! While most of my shirttail relatives were Catholic, I'd never heard much except excommunication, drunkenness, adultery, confinement for unwed pregnancy and discontent. Since Sharon had been saved and

48

baptized at thirteen, washed feet as a Mennonite and I'd accepted Christ through the preaching of a Southern Baptist Chaplain . . . we choose the Spanish mission-styled Baptist Church.

I cannot remember much about the preacher but we were welcomed into a young couple's Sunday School Class taught by a mild mannered Naval Officer, Dick Hukel. We were thirsty for God's Word. Dick and his wife, Gertrude lived out the Bible through their family and marriage. I was baptized at this church and Sharon was dunked, too, as she followed obediently to support me. The whole class wrapped us in their lives and we learned to reciprocate that fellowship and love. We spent two wonderful years with them and they became our family, as we were 1700 miles from Toledo. It was difficult to leave the group. Later we learned this first close fellowship would never be repeated the same way . . . God had prepared a special place for us as newlyweds.

John 14:2b " I am going there to prepare a place for you"

First Solo Rescue

The Flight Operations Alert Siren screamed through the ready room. I grabbed my crash helmet and Mae West while running for the latest weather briefing sheet. This was it, the first time I would launch as solo pilot in one of our two Sikorsky H-19B rescue helicopters. A small fishing boat had just sent a distress call near Santa Rosa Island, 40 miles offshore from our base in the Pacific. The Coast Guard asked us to respond. This was not a drill.

Our standby crew chief had the ship readied for startup. I donned my helmet, scrambled up the footholds in the side of the fuselage and slung my body through the window cockpit door. Both hands were already involved in priming the engine, adjusting the throttle and engaging the starter switch before I hit the seat. The old reliable Wright 900hp radial engine turned over a couple revs and fired off immediately as the magnetos were energized. When the engine warmed up to the proper RPM, I nodded for the Flight Mechanic to release the rotor brake. I had already established the process of training our maintenance crews to handle the controls and be able to fly these beasts back to the ground if I became incapacitated . . . at least to a controlled crash! This shared survival instinct was a first for our small group and set well with our enlisted crews to bond us in training and hopefully now, in action.

49

A second flight mechanic jumped aboard below and would become the hoist operator if and when needed. An extra set of eyes were always an advantage during any sea or ground search sequence and, since there were only two fishermen reported on the craft, we had ample lifting capability to bring them aboard with our extra crewman.

Our ninety mile per hour dash speed seemed like snails pace during the trip but we were assured to be faster than the Navy HUP-1 Helicopter, probably launching simultaneously from Port Huneme NAS at Point Magu. What's more, if they did get there first, they'd need help as the HUP could only carry one other man on this warm day. The Navy also had to throw in the towel on any land operations much over 1,000' in elevation. The surrounding hills ranged well over 12,000 foot. Effectively, we had responsibility for over 80% of all air rescue operations between San Diego, Monterey and Edwards AFB in California.

A clear day! Good! We could spend time with our GCA (Ground Controlled Approach Radar) to get an update on new information. The Coast Guard had not heard from the distressed vessel since the first call, quite unusual since we had relatively docile weather, only a 2-3 foot sea and crystal clear visibility. Within 6 minutes we crossed the shoreline at Oxnard, California; our first two boys would be born in the hospital directly below. "Take up a heading of 262 degrees," Oxnard Radar called. "They last reported their position to be just a couple miles off the eastern tip of Santa Rosa Island".

Once I turned the ship over to the eager hands of the crew chief, I yanked the weather sheet from my right leg pocket. Previously, only giving it a quick scan as I ran from the ops room, it showed our current pristine conditions. But I hadn't noted the "expect costal fog thru the day" in the BOTTOM remarks column. Sure enough, about five miles off shore, cruising at 500' we slid over a solid bank of clouds . . . now racing by just below the wheels. Everything was perfectly clear above, with the twenty-five hundred foot peaks of Santa Rosa Island silhouetted in the sun some 35 miles further out to sea. The question was, "Should we stay on top and trust the water to be open around the island?" To answer that, I relieved the crew chief of the controls, pulled aft on the cyclic stick and climbed to 2,000 feet. The picture was unsettling; Santa Rosa looked like a mound of chocolate floating on an endless sea of marshmallow.

One of our secondary missions at Oxnard was to support the Early Warning Radar sites surrounding the Los Angeles Basin. These sites were located on the 150-mile long chain of Channel Islands starting at San Clemente, to the South of Santa Catalina, and extended northwest to San

Miguel, just West of Santa Barbara. PT boats running out of Port Huneme or Long Beach normally supplied the islands; however, many times during the year they were not able to make the trips for several weeks due to high seas. During their down times we would handle emergency or VIP crew transports ... and that included the Chaplains on Sundays. The seas we typically flew over looked like we were auditioning for the movie, *"The Perfect Storm"*. Today, except for fog, it looked more like the peaceful cove *of Gilligan's Island*. We called a couple of the sites and found that all of the locations were reporting the same surface water observations, "Less than a quarter mile with fog". Two options remained, abort or try underneath.

I called back to Oxnard's GCA Radar to take one final fix on us as we spiraled below the Eastern edge of the fog blanket. We'd try to sneak in underneath. Slowing down so we could maintain visual contact with the water, we were sandwiched in less than 25 feet above the waves. Oxnard Radar advised they lost contact with us below the ground clutter. "Santa Rosa Radar will be able to track you to within five miles of their shoreline", they assured. It was great help to have the crew chief change radio channels and handle other cockpit duties. With only two or three waves in sight at a time, it was necessary to maintain a visual reference. Our ground speed had dropped to a mere 10 - 30 miles per hour, as we slipped in and out of translational lift. Anything below 18 mph required more power than when going faster where cleaner airflow over the rotor created more lift. It was important that we not slow to an actual hover as we could become enveloped in salt spray and lose all vision. If that catastrophe happened we would be left with only a pure instrument climb and departure, something practiced in training but never before accomplished by this pilot. Our helicopter didn't have SAS, Stability Augmentation System, or autopilot . . . features only under development for helicopters.

Scooting along the water at this altitude was nothing new; we'd sometimes cruise along the beaches waving at the bathing crowds. It was good to know we could now count that in our training syllabus rather than just raw buzzing. In less than forty minutes from takeoff we were told by Santa Rosa Rader, "Radar contact lost. Good luck finding them, give us a call outbound".

"OK", I responded, hoping we could do just that, "But we'll stay tuned to your frequency." Beyond Santa Rosa, the next stop was China! The old parable started drifting thru my mind, "When rescue goes down, who rescues rescue?"

Jaws

When cruising higher on sunny days, it sometimes appears as if you could walk to the islands on the "big whites" sunning themselves. Today with the fog, flying low and slow, we surprised a shark that came up below us as it did a slow roll to suck down a piece of garbage from the surface . . . a snapshot of things to come. If bathers saw a picture of those dudes huddled at the continental water runoff line, where the surf looses its silt, waiting for innocent fish darting into clear water . . . swimmers wouldn't float there, TROLLING with dangling arms and legs!

A few weeks earlier, I had taken a crew of oceanographers on a trip around all the islands. These cats went wild for two hours filming the coastline and rocks where seals were gathered. They would go home, play back the film in slow motion and count seals; next year we were to do the same thing and check the population shift . . . we dubbed it "The Crazy Seal Census". Right at the end of this year's census we came upon a seal and a shark dueling it out. I learned from this scene and film crew that a sizable seal could be a formidable enemy to a shark. We started circling and the crew began filming. We could even hear the photographers roar of orgasmic excitement over the noise of our engine and transmission. A blood patch began forming; occasionally hiding the seal, then the shark and sometimes both as they made lunging thrusts to determine who would deliver the killing blow. The red circle expanded to a couple hundred feet and then I noticed other visitors circling, relatives of the shark. They weren't attempting to help their buddy; they were just waiting patiently to clean up the debris, whoever lost. Right then I realized, with fuel running low, "If we lose our engine . . . we'd land right in the bloodbath". Announcing that we were not adding to the aquatic food chain that day, I headed back to base with a frustrated film crew unable to win that year's National Geographic TV Documentary, enough reflection.

As we approached the probable location, determined by time and speed calculation, my thoughts turned from sharks to the equation at hand, finding the fishing boat and crew. Our hoist man dropped a floating smoke signal and then we set up a right hand expanding circle search pattern, dropping dye marker at every North and South compass heading. If we could keep the dye marker on the right without seeing the smoke signal again . . . we might be able to expand the search without repeating or getting totally lost. Our enemies were now time and ships. At our speed and visibility we would never see a sizeable ship before impact.

"Go back", shouted our topside mechanic without use of the intercom. "There was a floating piece to the left!"

After gingerly rolling the ship into a left turn for about 30 seconds, we saw the first man, then the second, frantically waving while clinging to separate sections of the boat. We slowed and kept circling, never to fully stop and pick up that dreaded salt spray. We didn't want to lose them now. They looked okay, in fact, quite elated. We dropped one final smoke signal. Good, it looked like five knots would keep the spray aft. The hoist operator called to drop the hoist into the water. "Roger", I replied. We didn't want the poor guys to reach up and ground out any static electricity from the ship, it can be shocking enough to knock them unconscious. Then I cleared the mechanic who found them to unbuckle, standup, raise his seat and drop below by ladder to assist with boarding.

Hoisting each one up fifteen feet was uneventful. Once on board, I stabilized the ship, dropped the nose and started an instrument climb into the formless fog. As we broke out in just a couple hundred feet, the sun shining through the canopy above produced a vertigo induced strobe effect, probably the most taxing portion of the trip. Now cruising on top, we could see the ring of hills and mountains surrounding our base. Then a call from down below, where they were comforting the crew, "You know what happened to them, Lt. Schweibold? They landed a 10' shark in a 19' boat, and the shark won!"

With an easy flight back, I could relax and reflect on God's goodness . . . that first prayer I prayed after my salvation was answered. I wasn't stuck as a pure fighter pilot or crowd killing bomber pilot. He let me have a wide diversity of aircraft experience, allowing me save and help my fellow man. I learned a lot this day; God answers prayer . . . in His best timing!

PS 5:3 In the morning, O LORD, you hear my voice; in the morning I lay my requests before you and wait in expectation.

7

Seeds of a Test Pilot

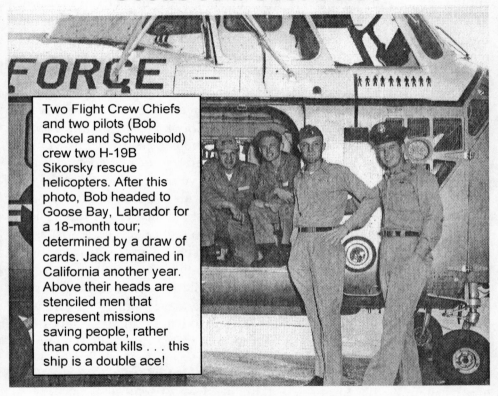

Two Flight Crew Chiefs and two pilots (Bob Rockel and Schweibold) crew two H-19B Sikorsky rescue helicopters. After this photo, Bob headed to Goose Bay, Labrador for a 18-month tour; determined by a draw of cards. Jack remained in California another year. Above their heads are stenciled men that represent missions saving people, rather than combat kills . . . this ship is a double ace!

"Let me show you one more maneuver . . ."

Back in aerobatic training, learning to recover from inverted flight, my instructor flunked my feeble attempts. He gave me a chance to go back out to learn the maneuver or kill myself. Obviously, I'm still alive, so I must have exercised the first two steps in FAA's "Learning Process". First, learning by ROTE or mechanically memorizing the procedure to roll level from inversion and second, eventually being able to UNDERSTAND and repeat the maneuver. There were still two additional steps to learn, APPLICATION and CORRELATION. Three years later, I took my Base Commander, Joe Fry, up for his first helicopter ride. "I'm scared to death of copters Jack," he finally said, "But I trust you. Let's go!" By the time we got finished with an hour in our Sikorsky H-19B rescue helicopter, he could hover within an area the size of a tennis court.

"Pretty good, Joe . . . but let me show you one more maneuver," I quickly added. To impress him with the agility of the ship, we climbed up to 1,000 feet, waited for the XKC-135 out of Edwards AFB (the prototype for the civilian Boeing 707) to make a low approach over our base. Then I brought our ship to a stationary hover over the end of the runway. "We'll cut the engine and autorotate right to the spot below us." Out of the corner of my eye, I could see him start to pucker . . . it's not natural for a pure fixed wing pilot to sit suspended over the end of his runway. In fact, it's much like standing atop . . . then being pushed off the Empire State Building!

I had practiced this activity many times, an engine out spiral from a thousand foot hover . . . with recovery to a three-foot hover over a predetermined spot. Today should be a textbook repeat of this training activity; except for the discovery of wake turbulence and wing tip vortices remaining from the heavy jet making a go-around at 500 foot with gear and flaps down. From the engine and collective pitch reduction at the top, through rolling the nose over, to diving in a right hand spiral to gain airspeed . . . everything went well for the first 180 degrees of turn. Then I started to lessen the bank, bring the nose up to reduce speed . . . just as we hit the jet wash! All of these conditions created high main rotor blade loading, causing the retreating blades to fully stall.

As the ship pitched up vertical, the craft did its own reverse right snap roll . . . right onto its back. As the old aircraft adage said, "There we were upside down, at 500 foot!" We were starting to hang from our safety straps and the flight control hydraulic fluid fell out of the reservoir, sending the cyclic stick violently ripping my right hand around the cockpit with every revolution of the rotor! I knew the blades would be coming through the upper canopy as the blade pitch links lost contact with their mechanical swash plate following device . . . this aircraft was not designed for negative G's!

Instinctively I increased throttle to maintain rotor RPM and rigidity on the blades, increased angle of attack or upward lift, now sucking us toward the ground but reducing negative G's while simultaneously rolling the aircraft to the right with opposite rudder. We rolled out at 50 foot above the ground. A textbook recovery from inverted flight, just as my first Squadron Instructor had trained! With his tyrannical approach to get my attention, he had given up his right to train me . . . so that I could now save our lives by what he taught. I had experienced the third step in the *Learning Process*, APPLICATION. I had instinctively put into practice the training maneuver, recovery from inverted flight.

Rolling level, we found ourselves aimed at our tie down spot on the ramp. I held the ship as steady as possible and let it slip to the concrete in a running landing, making a taxi turn to its spot. On setting the brakes, I looked over to my commander. Joe sat slumped, covered with blood. "He must have been thrashed around the cockpit while I was trying to hold on to the controls," I thought. I shut the engine and rotor down, he unharnessed, scrambled down the ladder steps and fell to his knees on the concrete, bowing with outstretched arms while kissing the ground. When my feet hit the pavement, I was shaking so I couldn't standup . . . had to sit on the right side of the cargo door. Then my commander came around the front of the helicopter, blood dripping from his nose. I stood as best I could, to a point of attention. He reached for me, I figured he was going to rip the wings off my flight suit . . . instead he gave me a big bear hug for saving his life. The blood was from my shredded knuckles that ripped knobs off the instrument panel. I began to understand what it meant to be "In the Safety of His Wings".

Ps 57:1b "I will ... take refuge in the shadow of your wings until the disaster has passed.

Vacation Times Were Special

Our first three years of marriage were one continuous honeymoon; we were away from home . . . alone together, first in Texas and then in Camarillo, California. The disadvantage of this, of course, is that we loved our families in Toledo and would spend all annual leave and saved monies to travel back home. Our first trip would come when Scott was just two months old. I was able to hitchhike back by military aircraft. I checked by phone with local bases and then stood in line for the next empty seat heading in my direction. I put Sharon and Scott on a National Airways, Non-Scheduled Airline out of Los Angeles for Chicago; the ticket cost $39.95. As the plane started up it belched so much oil it disappeared . . . I prayed Sharon and Scott wouldn't disappear, FOREVER!

They beat me home and we spent a couple of weeks with our families. When returning, we decided it would be cheaper to buy an old car in Toledo and sell it on the West Coast where cars were in demand. Mom and Dad Crouse lent us four-hundred dollars to buy a 1954 Ford Fairlane.

We loaded it with our luggage, strapped two-month old Scott in a rear peanut seat and headed west toward Denver in mid-April. We turned NW out of the Mile-High City, entering Estes Park. I had always thought that US 40 was an all weather highway. Not so! Entering the east edge of the Park, we came to a twenty-five foot wall of snow; this was the END of Route 40!

I should have known better, I trained in the high Sierras near Reno and often looked down at Donner's Pass . . . it was still covered with snow at this time of year. Some of the first settlers to cross Donner's seventy-five years before had survived by cannibalism. We still had plenty of time, gas and heat to make a detour south to Route 6 and enjoy Aspen, Zion National Park and Death Valley. On reaching California, we were able to sell the Fairlane for $450, almost paying for the gasoline and loan (with interest) to Mom and Dad. God was just beginning to open His goodness and vistas to us.

Our first real vacation wouldn't come for another year when we left son Scott for the first time; just before our second son, Mark, was born. We lived 30 miles NW of Los Angeles, so we took a big trip to the exotic island of Santa Catalina, 19 miles from the Long Beach harbor. It wasn't a long trip but a big step for a woman that would be delivering a baby in a month. Even though the island was less than fifty miles from home it was like taking a time warp one-hundred years earlier into a small Mediterranean seaport.

After we walked all the beach streets, we took a longer stroll inland up a canyon road to a bird sanctuary. It was in a jungle-like setting, quite empty since we were well ahead of the tourist season. Our mode-of-operation is still to travel in low cost, low-pressure periods.

We were engrossed with each other; actually, I was enjoying necking with a pregnant woman. Suddenly, we were startled by a crystal clear voice, asking . . . "What's your name?" We looked around . . . thought we were alone, where was the peeping Tom? Couldn't find anyone; have to admit we were frightened; we were a long way from town with night shadows starting to lengthen. "What's your name?" the person repeated. Finally, we found him, a Myna Bird in a nearby cage. That little bird was good for many laughs and gave us a fond memory . . . much better than the one of another midnight Catalina trip, by helicopter, to evacuate a pregnant woman . . . and baby, born enroute to the mainland. Although we treasured our family times, our motto became, "Come away . . . or come apart!"

"Snakes Alive, Men are Never too Young to Die!"

During bivouac at Survival Camp in the desert, the instructor who made daily rounds to see if we were still alive . . . or AWOL, challenged us to add Rattlesnake to our diet. So-o-o, we thumbed through the survival manual packed in our parachute kits and found the page on how to trap the Sidewinder. The challenge actually amused us. We had months before lost interest in the daily roundup of Texas Scorpions crouched to pounce from lairs in aircraft tie-down ropes; so we vowed to take on these poisonous serpents, little knowing that this combat experience would help launch the nation's space program!

The directions made it sound simple; a number of volunteers formed a search party for the elusive rascals. This, of course, reversed the tactics we had developed to avoid them. We soon found that the rattlers were interested in staying out of OUR way; sounding their warning rattlers to scare us off before we found THEM. The first man to find a long stick with an appropriate "Y" fork would become the "Pinner". At first we thought no one really wanted lead position on that task until we learned that the manual didn't tell us where to find that special branch . . . in the treeless desert!

This was to become one of my first practical uses for "prop tape", a special super sticky variety that aircraft mechanics use to balance propellers; its flimsy civilian counterpart is duct tape. Today in real life, each of our male grandchildren receives an abundant supply of various types of duct tape for their 13th Christmas. While the first grandson looked questioningly at the present, the ensuing young men looked forward to their rolls as a celebration of Schweibold manhood. The prop tape secreted in my pack quickly made the required fork out of a tent pole and ration can.

While I didn't get the lead slot, I did get the "Gunship" position. With the rattler targeted, the formation moved forward . . . with great caution. The manual author had sensed this timidity, and added an encouraging tidbit of text, something like … "Don't be overly concerned as you approach the prey. Rattlers do not see well . . . especially if they are molting. They strike at heat." We soon learned that meant OUR body heat!

Creating our own tactic, a formation approach of massive body heat, hoping that the critter sensed a closer then actual target would precipitate a premature strike, it worked! When the critter fell short of the "Pinner", it would hit the ground outstretched providing a moment of vulnerability before recoiling for a second strike. The fork man then pounced and secured the snake to the ground and called for the gunship . . . me, with an axe. Although we had an endless number of kills, we probably ended up with a light load of meat, severing the head WELL behind the poison glands. The first day or two of lengthy cooking turned their carcass to rubber before we learned a lighter cook meant lighter meat. Our team completed training with an impressive row of fangs adorning hats, like kills painted on the side of cockpits.

What does this all have to do with *space*, not much . . . except that two years later, when assigned to Oxnard AFB as an Air/Sea rescue pilot, an early mission was to combat snakes. The task was to cleanout rattlers and un-detonated artillery shells on a site 80 miles north, at what would become Vandenberg AFB. Our job with two pilots, a crew chief and an old H-19 Sikorsky helicopter, would be to burn off several thousand acres of California coastland mountain brush, trees, snakes and shells. This area had been an offshore practice gunnery range for our Navy ships during WW-II. Now, they were losing construction crews to a multitude of venomous snakes and shell explosions as earthmovers leveled the region.

It looked like a David and Goliath task . . . and we weren't David or even Goliath, we were the **slingshot**! Our first pebble would be a phosphorous hand grenade, thrown from our chopper by an explosives expert. WHOA! What happens, if the guy fumbles a pass out the door . . . our ship is made of magnesium . . . same stuff as a 4th of July sparkler. We would burn even underwater! Having a safe flight and long life demands sensible risk management. As captain of the ship, I hung the "expert" on the rescue hoist 50 feet below the ship, cutting potential loss through a fumble by at least 75%! The ordnance man thought it was great sport. They have a crazy, crazy job.

What a joke! Lobbing these babies into this miniature rain forest was like throwing a match in the ocean . . . nothing happened. We failed, even with bigger shells strapped to cans of gasoline. Military's answer? Call in the Marines! The project commander climbed aboard and we became the airborne command center, vectoring Marine fighters to drop napalm bombs on the mountain and valley foliage. Again, little was accomplished . . . except a 50' x 200' swath scorched through saturated foliage. This should have been a foreteller of our inability to conquer the Vietnamese jungle by air. The Air Force and Marines surrendered. The Seabees assumed the fight, hand-to-snake and hand-to-shell combat with bulldozer and shovel, a credit to their skill and tenacity.

A year later, we saw the inter-continental missile silos that rose (actually submerged) at this facility when we flew the President and Vice-President of the United States to view the first operational Atlas. This IBM (Inter-continental Ballistic Missile) would propel our early astronauts. Lt. Bob Rockel flew President Eisenhower in one H-19 and I flew Vice-president Nixon in the other. While we were on the ground, we joked with later-to-be President Nixon. On the flight back, I would fly President Eisenhower and found him not so jovial. As he approached the ship, the blades were already turning. After giving me a quick glance, Ike sat on the edge of the doorway and pointed first at his shoes. A multi-starred accompanying general immediately fell to his knees in the mud and wiped Eisenhower's shoes clean with his handkerchief. Ike turned his head up and pointed a finger up at me, yelling something over the engine roar to the general. After returning to base, I asked the general what Ike said. His reply was, "Is that kid old enough to wear those gold bars?" After D-Day, General Eisenhower should have known that in the military . . . men are never too young to die.

At Oxnard AFB, some of Jack's first Allison Engine time was flown in the squadron's F89 Interceptors. These ships were on constant alert readiness in defense of our nation.

Our Three Sons

"My Three Sons" was a 1960's TV sitcom. At least by title, it could have named our family well; however, their show never measured up to our trio. That program only played once a week for a few years, "OUR Three Sons" became a daily highlight our entire life . . . and now with ten grandchildren, our tribe's show should continue until the Lord returns. Sharon and I never talked about marriage before engagement. We first started dating regularly when I was 17 and she was 14 but we never trapped each other in an early commitment of "going steady". I don't think

61

we needed to. We both knew in our hearts that we belonged with each other. We met, well actually my mother advertised for her . . . when Mom needed a baby sitter; as I prepared to leave for college. Mom owned a couple of shoe stores at that time and needed backup help at home. An old axiom says . . . "A babysitter is experienced when she knows which kid to sit with and which one to sit on." Showing her experience, she chose to sit with me and let me sit on my brother, Rob and sister, Barbara. I ended up turning her off after one date . . . or maybe it was my room that turned her stomach. After a few months, she gave me another chance and we continued to date.

I headed off to Ohio State University at 17, knowing we each needed to be free to enjoy our high school and college years. Actually, she didn't lose me to much action at OSU. I pledged a fraternity for a short time but was too limited on cash and confidence to chase the female set. We continued having fun with other friends as I later returned to Toledo University and then went into the military, while she attended Bowling Green University. While we never talked about being husband and wife, we discussed the features we would someday like to see in a family: a home, children, church and family values. Never did we imagine the joy and ACTION three boys would bring.

On the morning our first son was to be born, Sharon calmly commented from the bathroom, "I'm going to shower and freshen up; the time may be getting near." I heard the shower spraying . . . followed by her frantic yell, "Help, help me, I can't get out of the tub!" We had an unforgettable drive to the hospital some 12 miles into Oxnard. It was only a mile to the 101 Freeway and things went smoothly. We alternated between enjoying seeing miles of varied colored stock, not animals, but pink, white and blue flowers and . . . focusing on her increasing labor pains. To break the cycle, I checked her vision by asking her if she could see the cloudless mountains. I heard from her friends that she required them to read the large overhead interstate signs which she couldn't see without her glasses. "Yeah," she answered defensively, "the mountains are still there!" Glasses were her last thought at this point. Right then, at 80mph, she braced her back on her door, placed her feet on my thighs and tried her very best to shove me out of the car!

We hit the entrance hospital door as her water broke. Was this one going to delivered as a waif on the doorstep? Fortunately, a nurse recognized Sharon's dilemma and shoved a wheelchair in place . . . "Nice job", I breathed in relief. They zoomed around the corner and out of sight as I parked the car.

Finally, she was wheeled to a bed in the labor room. The same nurse escorted me to the waiting room where I met the doctor who was heading to the cafeteria for coffee. In a few minutes, I heard them paging for him to return to the Maternity Ward. I stood at the doorway hoping to see him going past. To my surprise, he opened the door as I got there; to tell me we had a son, both were doing well. I wondered who actually delivered Scott . . . and *told* the DOCTOR! "Wow, only four hours of contractions, that was close; my girl was going to be a true baby machine!"

Steven Scott was awesome, she had delivered a kid but I knew he couldn't be ours! He was all red and had a full head of coal black hair, ready for the barbershop. Good grief, they must have switched him with one of those itinerant stock field workers, no birth certificate, just a Mexican Passport. I rushed into Sharon, but she proudly testified he WAS ours and together, we praised God for a healthy son . . . and wife.

God's moving

Gregory Mark was a moving experience from beginning to end. We thought Scott was Speedy and were concerned the next may try to beat the starting gun. Sharon called the doctor on Sunday, her due date to discuss a problem she was having with water retention and swelling. He suggested she come in for a check and recognized it may be best to induce labor. Mark was born two hours later. No fuss, no rush . . . "I shouldn't have even moved the car," I mused. "At this rate they will be asking me to take them home soon."

Moving continued to cross my mind during the delivery; I was going to be moving more than a car. I was up for base transfer as my three-year assignment in paradise was ending. A few months earlier, an assignment had already come down for a helicopter pilot to Goose Bay Labrador. I cut cards with Bob Rockel since he and I arrived at Oxnard the same day. I drew a king . . . and won a year extension. "How long would my luck hold out?" I had to think about Sharon raising our bigger family alone. Goose Bay, Labrador or Thule, Greenland would mean 18 months without the family or 36 months with them. Having only the Officers Club or sculpting icebergs with chain saws for entertainment, it was a prescription for AA, Alcohol Anonymous!

As I arrived upstairs, I couldn't find her in the labor room . . . they'd moved her right to delivery, I think her doctor was in position for this catch and grabbed Mark on the first bounce. Sharon was a precursor to the now-famous Japanese "just-in-time-delivery". We sat there together

63

enjoying another son. I saw him before he reached the crib; this one had a US Passport tucked under his chubby cheeks. Our rejoicing to God included a prayer to get us out of a far north assignment. He moved our spirits right then, to leave the Air force and raise our family in America.

Having completed my six-year active duty and reserve commitment, I resigned my commission by letter the next day . . . joining the Navy at seventeen wasn't a bad choice after all. Two days later, the suspected assignment came down for Goose Bay, Labrador, requiring a support pilot for the DEW line (Defense Early Warning) Rader Sites on the Artic Circle. We didn't have to go. "Thanks boys! I never would have made that decision without you, Mom and the Lord." Brad would show up a few years later in stair step fashion.

8

Barnstorming
to
Brainstorming

Hired and Fired

God may have called us out of the service but he had in mind that we would spend a couple of years maturing in the desert wastelands of Chicago; they were to be difficult times. I accepted a job with Chicago Helicopter Airways, an airline running between Midway, O'Hare and Meigs airports, with a couple of flights a day all the way to . . . Gary and Evanston. Midway was at its zenith but was losing traffic to O'Hare, which could accept the Boeing 707 jets, like the XKC-135 that flipped me over with its jet wash. The helicopter was the ideal answer to shuttle passengers from the commuter prop aircraft at Midway to the intercontinental stuff only thirteen miles north. I was pilot number fifty-four, one of two hired to replace a crew that had gone down in a cemetery with a full complement of 12 passengers; we heard it had lost a main rotor blade.

What was the appeal of this opportunity? Well, just as my military flight instructor promised, "After the Korean War, pilots will again be worth only a nickel a dozen." I hadn't realized what a prophet he was. The big jets carrying one hundred seats or more were displacing smaller equipment carrying fewer bodies at half the speed . . . a cycle that has continued to repeat itself about every ten years. Of course, fewer pilots were needed. I remember a decade later when the first 747's came out, being a passenger in this double-decker, SEVEN of us riders were pulled up front with the twelve stewardesses. We all ate food and drank beverage for the other 400 empty seats. Starting pilots in 1959 were not even worth a nickel a gross; I just needed a job . . . now!

Chicago was not our choice of locations. It was presently the only one available. Fortunately, I had logged a lot of early rotorcraft time. The lines of heavy metal applicants for this job had not. I was hired! Chicago Helicopter Airways (CHA) was one of three airlines in Los Angeles, New York and Chicago approved as an experiment by the US Congress. They were subsidized by airmail for a set number of years (much the way fixed wing airlines began in the 30's) to determine if scheduled intra-city passenger helicopter operations were feasible. Whenever possible, all airmail was picked up and transported by small three-place Bell 47 Helicopters. These ships were equipped with containers next to the pilots and saddlebag compartments above the side landing skids.

Over 400 heliports had been built in the greater Chicago Area. Most were concrete circles surrounded by 50' diameter chain link fences. Some were on rooftops or the parking lots of post offices and cooperative office buildings. Where it wasn't possible to land, the post office installed telescoping poles that would lift the mailbag to the hovering helicopter. The pilot would slip the ship sideways under the load and lift it off with his saddlebags, a modern day version of the Pony Express!

New hires began as copilots on the bigger Sikorsky S-55 & S-58

passenger ships, civil versions of the Air Force H-19 and Marine H-34. We shared cockpit duties making every other take-off and landing. This was to be my position until seniority raised me to rank of captain, then I would downshift to flying the Bell mail mules before returning to passenger service. Our airline uniform was medium-blue with dark stripes, looking just like the Windy City bus drivers . . . but making 1/2 their starting pay! The Airline Pilots' Association didn't bill themselves as a union, but as our bargaining unit I placed them on a level equal to my affiliation with the Teamsters when in wholesale hardware. Air Line pay for a pilot was scaled to aircraft weight, passengers and speed. NOTHING ranked lower on the pay scale then our starting copilots. In those days men weren't candidates for stewardess or I could have doubled my pay serving food on a 707. I blended into the airport scene well, whether in the terminal or on the bus ramp. The only difference, I carried a brown bag; the bus drivers could afford a lunch pail, complete with thermos.

We'd already decided to leave the big city environment of Los Angeles; so, not wanting to live intercity, we headed to Oak Forest, 12 miles south of Midway. At the edge of the city hubbub we found a one-year-old empty tri-level for $125/month, half of our pay BEFORE taxes . . . this was not a good omen. We had a deep lot that was adjacent to the last four empty plots. We were soon to find out why they were empty; they were swamp!

Our house had been empty, too; sent into foreclosure by the original owners gambling habits. He abandoned his pregnant wife and several small children in diapers. The house told their story. The upstairs portion of the attic had doors opening to the hall. Months of trash had been thrown there after the contract trash service had stopped. Sharon said she must have been a very tidy person by nature; all of the baby food jars and cans were well washed before disposal. Strange, BIG men started coming to the door after we moved in . . . looking for the previous "Welcher". Fortunately, Sharon learned how to handle them . . . or hide and I must not have matched the pictures they carried! We tried but never fit into this Lithuanian neighborhood, even at their local Baptist Church. We were beginning to learn how the ethnic areas of Chicago and New York developed, for family survival, when one only had the barest of means . . . of DEFENSE!

This house would become a LIVING nightmare. The lower basement, half underground and well windowed to the outside, was also open to the crawl space under the living level . . . and all its living creatures, BIG SPIDERS! They must have been Vampire spiders, only coming out at night . . . but we knew they were there, waiting for us! Coming downstairs after dark and turning on the lights, they would be there in a black blanket. All big ones; black, silver dollar sized! As defender of the family, it was my job to attack with two claw hammers in hands. Smat, smat, smat . . . would continue for months, finally dwindling to a handful per night going into winter.

Warm weather brought its own hazards, snakes! Sharon encountered her first one trimming around the downspout, coiled up waiting to strike

... I heard her yell over my lawnmower! As trash dumper, my job was to take the paper trash to a 55-gallon drum and burn it. From the back door to the barrel was a NO-man's-land, covered with snakes of all types, colors and lengths. At this junction, I traded hammers for a hand axe; going forward with waist-bending calisthenics, ripping through their bodies warming in the sunlight. On a good day I could take vengeance on 6-12 before the rest slithered back to the swamp . . . waiting another sunny day.

The one highlight of this period was that we were back in the Midwest, closer to home in Toledo. Family roots were reestablished after five years away in the service, holiday activities were exchanged with our parents, brothers and sisters. Sharon was building our portfolio of family traditions.

Improved family relationships couldn't hide the pit into which we were sliding. We were eight months into our year lease; savings from service were running out, Sharon and the kids were isolated, and we were depressed. While flying, I long ago memorized all of the landmarks on the eleven minutes between Chicago and O'Hare, thirteen minutes between O'Hare and Meigs Field and the seven minutes between the Loop and Midway. The only excitement came half way through the day . . . we'd reverse directions! Sitting above the passenger compartment didn't provide interaction with the passengers; noise was so bad, we couldn't even harass them with spastic messages on the intercom. Out of boredom, a captain circled a downtown building ONE time and was disciplined excessively for an unauthorized flight leg. Finally, it happened, complacency in the cockpit. Another, probably our highest time pilot, sitting at the gate waiting for passengers . . . SNEEZ-ZE-D . . . pulled aft cyclic and cut the tail boom off with the main rotors!!!!

I knew I was next. This job was mundane and boring, right up there with tollgate attendants and the guy that sits in the middle of the Holland Tunnel waiting all his life for an accident to report. On top of this, for the first time, we were going to have payroll cuts. Midway was starting to lose flights as O'Hare was taking the load, our revenue was down. Six or eight other pilots had been hired underneath me. So I thought I was sitting pretty cush! After all, I was up for my formal ALPA membership that would protect my slot. I was called in for that review . . . and CANNED! I'd been graded down in everything. My attitude, feelings and performance had been read well. Ed Packer, my Chief Pilot was right on the money . . . that day I was on the street! Funny, you don't always recognize when you are in the safety of His wings.

Barnstorming to Brainstorming

Being canned was a real kick in the rear . . . or in the can, as the terminology must imply. That was one of the hardest days in my life. It seems like Sharon held me in her arms through the night. The best thing about being broke was that I had to start knocking on doors the next morning; I began at eight a.m.

Chicago Helicopter Airways (CHA) was on the Southside of Midway Airport, the only other helicopter operator in the city was right next door at Butler Helicopter Airlift (BHA). I had talked to Bob Richardson, their Chief Pilot before signing with CHA but the glamour of being aboard an "Airline" got to my ego. Suddenly, their little operation looked appealing to my now shattered pride. Although less than a tenth in size, Butler had the world's largest fleet of executive transport helicopters, seven Bell 47's. Their President, Hal Conners was a visionary, becoming the first Executive President of the Helicopter Association of America. Bob Richardson eventually became their Second Executive President, advancing it to the current Helicopter Association International.

I was nervous waiting to see Mr. Richardson. It could only bring more rejection . . . I'd have to tell him I was fired. "Well, Jack . . . " he started, "you lasted a few months longer than I thought."

"Er-r-r . . . what to do mean?" I sheepishly asked.

"You had too much against you. Most of those guys were Navy and Marine drinking buddies. They don't fit our profile or probably yours. Our pilots need to take interest in the passengers and **business** . . . not just fly to pick up a paycheck. I think you might have the personality that fits better with us . . . but we don't need a pilot right now. As you know we also lost a ship due to rotor blade failure. Business is still down. However, I've got to fly a Bell up to O'Hare for drop off. If you don't mind riding back by car, I can at least evaluate your flying." I smiled and nodded yes. Sometimes it's best to remain silent. He'd said it all. By the time we returned by car . . . I was on the payroll, at least as a temp!

I soon learned that my best asset was not my flight skill or looks . . . but my light one hundred forty pound weight. In those days, the little Bell 47H was under-powered as a true three-passenger helicopter. To make it look more like an airplane and appeal to the public, the manufacture enclosed the tail boom and added interior carpet and cosmetics. An old-timer drawled as he climbed aboard (according to a parody) "They add pretty carpet to cover da flaw's".

The Stewardess said, "Don't you mean **floors**, Sir?"

"Naw, I mean **Flaws**, Ma'am, they cover the **FLAWS!**" replied the old-timer.

The "H" Model and Bell 47J's were eye appealing. The "J" model was the first to fly a President, Dwight Eisenhower. Helicopters had only been certified for passengers 12 years earlier; these ships did have "executive" eye appeal in an embryonic industry.

I was assigned my first tool the next day; a one-gallon can of sand. Being lightweight, I would need it placed in the nose behind the instrument panel. Eight pounds doesn't sound like much but it would give me just enough center of gravity shift forward so the tail boom wouldn't strike the ground when lifting to a hover. When there were two BIG passengers up front, I could move the can to the rear baggage compartment . . . so we wouldn't fall over on our nose; and if too heavy, I could leave it behind (rather than off load baggage) and still get airborne ground. My skinny frame was finally worth something other than growing acne!

Nearing the end of my 30 day trial, their business conditions didn't appear to be improving. While Mr. Conners was the primary sales generator, he was extremely busy handling a public relations campaign and remotely engaged in getting the Helicopter Association off the ground. I saw the place really needed help selling aircraft contract time. Flight time was offered in blocks ranging from $70/hour for 100 hours/year to $85/hour for a sample 12 hour block for the three place ships; hourly rates were also available. "Why couldn't this twenty-five year old sell so he doesn't get booted again?" Plaguing answers kept gnawing in my mind, "Jack, you have always thought salesmen were the scum of the Earth. You'd always run from helping in your parents shoe stores! You are too young, look too young, have never sold and CAN'T sell anything!"

"Well, that's not totally true!' I mentally rebutted. "You can sell yourself, Jack." So, I walked into Bob Richardson's office and asked to do just that. "Rich, I know you don't have enough work to keep me busy. Thanks for the try . . . how about letting me work part time in sales. Maybe I can generate additional sales to keep us busy. . . I really enjoy my work here!"

At first I think he, too, thought it ludicrous but suggested, "Yes, we can tell you are working out well and would really like to keep you, but we can't; however, you do see our business needs sales. Let's try it for a month and see how it works."

"Wow!" I replied feeling brave, "That's great but I need to move further north, how about a raise and/or commission after that period."

A quiet pause followed, Rich could see our mutual problem, money. Finally, he closed, "Jack, it sure sounds like you CAN sell . . . but let's see how things go after a month."

The next month was a new equation in my career. I remembered some good sales training I received while selling mutual funds for Hamilton Management Corporation in California. I never figured that I could depend on my health sustaining a medical flight physical indefinitely. I found I could sell things I believed in. I believed in saving through monthly investments. I also believed in the future and use of helicopters and had confidence the world needed them and would buy the service . . . besides my job depended on it! The major element of this sales equation would be prospecting.

Butler Aviation, our parent company had been formed by Paul Butler. Legend was that Paul had landed his Twin Beech aircraft at Midway Airport one night, blew a tire and couldn't get it fixed. He figured aircraft maintenance and fueling operations were needed in Chicago and went on to establish facilities at the three major airports . . . eventually obtaining sole fuel rights. Try imaging a few cents profit from each gallon of fuel pumped into every aircraft from a J3 Cub to the jumbo jets flying out of Cook County. You have the picture, mega-cents; just one B747 holds thousands of gallon/cents worth! While Butler Aviation was more than solvent, our small helicopter entity had to stand on its own financial legs.

Being part of Butler Aviation was a door opener in the area, but I also found that Hal Conners had done his job well and canvassed most of them. Coupled to a scale down in the general economy, efforts were not immediately productive, except for one new "Bluebird" 12-hour contract. Brad, our son in Computer Software Sales now tells me that a Bluebird is a sale that just flies in your window and sits on your shoulder by chance;

71

this one fit the bill. I flew the potential customer on a demo flight and within a week signed for 12 hours. I made certain to fly him on every flight the next week. I learned about the importance of customer service and he upgraded to twenty-five hours. Bluebird or not, it looked good to the boss. I was granted monthly employment extensions . . . ultimately they were able to keep all of our staff.

Operations to date included: Station WGN, one of the nations first radio copters, small corporations transport, blowing frost off tomato crops at night, photo missions, delivering Santa Claus and the Easter Bunny, giving rides at fairs, towing banners, dropping football queens at stadiums, etc.. With over 400 heliports available, we could cover the five county area with ease . . . but I was running into resistance and decided it wasn't me. We needed fresh meat.

Moving into the summer season, we had two or three small county fairs to attend and sell rides. The other junior pilot was assigned to check me out on these activities. They normally sent two pilots, one to sell tickets and one to fly. On one of his flights, he took off low over the horse arena and spooked a young rider. On landing, he was punched out by a husky father. I observed, again, the need for good community and customer relations, realizing we were employing the techniques of early barnstormers during the 20's and 30's. We were generating interest by landing/take-offs, selling a few rides, and educating the public . . . all while paying for equipment and putting food on our table. In the aviation industry, it's called SURVIVAL!

"Why don't we do more of this?" I asked on returning, "It appears very profitable".

"Yes, it is sometimes profitable if we don't have to fly too far . . . but not many fair boards call us." Rich responded. This captured my attention; I had always been interested in the amusement industry. Sharon reminded me she saw that spark of imagination during our dating when I showed her a sketch of a roller skating rink. I'd designed it with indoor/outdoor paths and ramps to attract new interest to a dying sport . . . a shade before inline skates permitted kids access to streets and walks. A brainstorm, this might be an un-mined source of revenue . . . and why not try for a state fair?

Praise God, we didn't lose one day of pay after getting fired, got a $50/month salary increase and we were still eating!

An Affair in the Air

After writing to a number of the county fair boards, I sent a couple of letters to the state fair boards in Illinois, Ohio and Wisconsin. Meantime, a handful of county and 4H fair boards responded. Bob Richardson was right, if they weren't too far away, they might be profitable.

On location, the ventures resulted in a lot of sitting and waiting for peak customer time. I learned about the amusement business, like why the merry-go-round has always been a winner . . . once in place, it can haul fifty to one hundred people at a time. In an hour they can turn one-thousand riders while we flew twenty to forty, the big difference . . . we were knocking down three to five dollars each while they were getting only ten to twenty-five cents a head; however, their overhead and maintenance was much lower. Finally . . . I lined up a STATE fair, seemed simple!

"Our State Fair is a Great State Fair . . ." the song played through my mind as I flew toward the State Capitol. This was a sleek ship; the pilot sat in a single bucket seat up front with a bench seat for three adults across the back. I had strapped in my luggage, a couple of folding chairs and a card table, I would hire a ticket seller from the temporary employment trailer when I landed. Finding the fairgrounds, I parked far out in the center of the parking lot . . . didn't want to be punched out for spooking some cowpoke before the show started.

I posted our insurance certificates with the office and was given authorization to hire temporary employees. Arriving at the employment office, I found dozens of applicants milling about, from clowns to laborers, waiting for announced positions. "Who'd want to sit out in the middle of a hot parking lot selling tickets for ten days," I speculated. "Probably some con artist that would rip me off!" To my surprise, at least ten people ventured across the line to be interviewed. I didn't have all day for this, offered a buck over minimum wage and took the first kid in line. He was attending school in the fall and needed some quick dollars; besides, I figured I had at least an even chance if he tried to wrestle me for the night's bankroll, providing we did make a sale. He turned out to be a great choice; youthful, energetic, honest and excited about being part of aviation.

I'd brought along four-foot stakes and a bundle of carnival flag rope. We staked out our fifty-by-fifty foot claim right on the main drag about three hundred feet from the entrance. This provided a blacktop walk right to our ropes, gave us reasonably safe approaches

(FAA considered driveways and aisles between cars as acceptable emergency recovery areas) and funneled a great percentage of the crowd right past us. Centered in this location we had three cardinal directions for departures and landings . . . without transient directly over the fair, wind direction would not be a problem. From the start, we began loading people aboard at seven dollars for adults and five bucks for kids; my young man needed help to juggle everyone, money and close ship doors. I sent him back to the hiring booth for an associate.

He already sold out the next hour's worth of passengers, so I really didn't miss him. Riders had enough sense to stay outside the ropes until I motioned them in, using hand signals to keep heads down and stay forward . . . out of the tail rotor. The first month or so working at BHA, we had a mechanic killed when he was standing in front of a ship during a test run-up after maintenance. The Chief Mechanic was at the controls and got light on the skids; the tail whipped around and decapitated his fellow worker. I saw it happen only a few feet away . . . and today, wanted that stuff left to the midway's Chamber of Horrors!

He returned quickly . . . "He had his girl friend with him!" I thought, as I squinted through salt stained eyes. "Look, he's got her selling tickets!"

When he came to load the next group, he grinned, leaned in, and yelled in my ear, "Pretty good, don't you think, boss?"

Not wanting to offend him, I nodded in agreement, "Doesn't look like she qualified for the freak tent!"

"Just like me, she was first in line!" he inserted. Never did ask him how deep in line he really went to get this eighteen year old that seemed to out work us both. Soon we saw that at the half fuel point, we could squeeze four adults or six kids in the back; with two ground helpers, they could load from each side and push the doors simultaneously to squeeze, latch and launch. We ran about three hours between fueling, which would be my break time. On about the third trip for fuel, our gal leaned in and said with joy, "I got double price from these guys, since they get twice the trip!" The young man hadn't done such a bad job in hiring; besides, I think the two of them had such a good time together for ten days . . . they would have paid me.

We worked from a nine am takeoff at the local airport to a midnight return. I sent the boy to the hardware the first night to get battery lanterns to mark the heliport. The other pilots used the old cannon ball, black oil flare pots for heliport night markers. I had the picture of a crash or roll over dousing them in fuel. I've never been a proponent of the "Big Bang theory!" Each night we would have pockets, bags and envelopes stuffed with bills, about $3,000 cash a night. In those days, that was BIG money and we could imagine every thug in the area crouched to jump us in the dark. Nearing midnight we would have everything ready, five minutes earlier each night so hoods couldn't time our departure. We'd stop taking money except for each load . . . and then unannounced, the two of them would jump aboard and we'd all escape to the airport!

After five days, the Board Manager I dealt with came out as scheduled for a halfway point settlement on proceeds. I shelled out a couple thousand dollars and he screamed, "That's not enough, we've been watching you and you've been taking in three to four grand a day . . . and we get 50% from every amusement ride on the grounds!" I was stunned.

"When I talked to you on the phone, I thought you said fifteen percent, not fifty," I squeaked. "Wait a minute; I have a copy of our contract in the back. Let's check." Sure enough, the agreed on commission WAS fifteen percent. No wonder they were fan-faring our location on the loudspeaker system at least once an hour.

"Well, have a good stay this trip. You'll NEVER be back!" he retorted, angrily stomping off with his security guards. Seeing those toughs at his side, we knew our concerns at night were not unfounded. We never again heard, "Have an affair in the air at our great State Fair", over the public address, but our traffic held. After making our final installment to his squad and paying off my two great employees, I picked up a check from the bank where we had made night deposits, just short of thirty thousand dollars.

Returning to the office after eleven days on the road, the check in today's economy was equivalent to about a quarter million dollars; enough to pay for one of our ships or twice our whole pilot staff's annual payroll. Needless to say, there was no question of permanency as sales manager . . . and pilot, of course. Now salary was based on flight hours sold and personal hours flown, about a 50% total increase . . . we could afford to move out of "Lower Lithuania".

9

Hold on to the Bed!

It's Heading to Indy

A housing upgrade let us move seven miles closer to Midway and likewise O'Hare, from 180th street south to 108th in Chicago Ridge. We found a fairly new flat, the second story unit on a low traffic cul-de-sac since the boys safety was primary now. In a two unit building Sharon would have a neighbor in my absence. The only question we had was the frequency of trains on the three or four tracks running behind the unit, "Oh, only two or three a day, and they're not a problem." landlord Charlie was quick to respond. We grabbed it!!

The first night we only set up the beds, as typical with most self-movers. Sharon was still a little miffed at my poor packing job, coming down Cicero Ave at 55 miles/hour (she'd told me to slow down) two of her treasured end tables entered solo flight from the trailer and were shattered to smithereens. We fell into bed exhausted; she was silent. We lay there in a bare room, except for the bed, the silhouette of a lone telephone pole sat poised on the left wall. Then it began to very slowly drift across that wall and when reaching the center wall, another pole materialized to the left, soon there was a pole on all three walls . . . continuing to accelerate at a faster rate. As one pole disappeared to the right, another would appear in full Cinemascope fashion as a shadow from the train's headlight to the left. Soon we could hear the faint whine of a diesel engine spooling up, then we began to feel a low rumble, like your stomach growling . . . poles were moving faster, now we could see the power lines drooping and rising in a symphony. The bed began vibrating and then shaking, at first lightly and then . . . violently. "Hold On to The Bed!" I yelled over the thundering engine. Like a mighty steed rising to defend the ramparts, in a vibrating gallop the bed raced across the hardwood floors and went aground on my wall. Every passing car extended the tymphonic concert for several minutes and eventually faded in the distance; once more, eerie quiet settled over the flat. We lay laughing hysterically, not holding the bed . . . but each other. Funny, the

77

damaged tables didn't matter anymore and in a couple of weeks, we never heard the trains only seventy-five feet away. This helped pattern us for life's crises and Satan's attacks . . . hold on to each other . . .

"Because the One in you is greater than the one (Satan) in the world"
John 4:4 NIV.

A Snowball Fight from Hell

The summer was over, ending, "What's next?" was the question shooting around the office. The new Sales Manager was tasked to fill the coming slow winter months. Yes, there were fairs in the sunshine states but with so many helicopter operators already in those areas; it wouldn't be possible to profitably compete. Besides, when we took equipment out of the area it depleted our assets to address peak activity in Chicago.

With Christmas coming, I focused on delivery of Santa Claus. "Old stuff," most all shopping center associations replied. A set back? Not really, a salesman should be a good listener. I didn't hear them say, "We don't want to use helicopters". They said, "We want something new!" They'd had Santa delivered by copter, fire engine and squad car for years; I needed to dream up something, NEW!

The fairs had convinced me that barnstorming was still in vogue, "How about giving away a few free rides?" I considered. A couple of November contracts were signed but we still had a lot of equipment sitting on the skids. "What these centers need is a COMPLETE advertisable PACKAGE," I determined. My presentation to our management . . . "Let's provide a gimmick, a Gigantic Snowball Drop and Santa Delivery. We'll give away six free rides (or helicopter models) identified by six out of three hundred Styrofoam snowballs dropped over the shopping center . . . at three times our normal charge. Hal and Bob said, "OK, give it a shot!"

It was the shot in the arm we needed. The centers loved it. I sold two out of three centers visited. Sharon contracted stuffing the three hundred, two-inch Styrofoam balls with 2 x 4 inch tags advertising the individual center and noting the winners. A further stimulus was added permitting individual stores to offer extra gifts, they could advertise dozens of winners and . . . unload a bunch of dead merchandise otherwise scheduled for the Salvation Army. Sharon stabbed tags in balls, making sixty-four thousand snowballs that would pinwheel down (like falling Maple leafs) over eighty shopping centers during the six weeks before Christmas.

I made sure to pilot the first drop. Coming in low, about five-hundred feet over the center into a twenty-five knot blustery wind, Santa unzipped the modified side window and readied the first of three paper grocery bags full of tagged snowballs. This slow flight around the center brought out excited kids and parents. An appropriately roped and guarded area designated the drop zone for the balls and then Santa.

We lined up for the second pass, dropping down to 300' and going beyond the drop zone to let the wind drift the balls back to the crowd. Santa dropped the first bagful, then the second and third. One complete bag was sucked out of his hands but exploded open as it hit the rotor wash. I pulled up and started a left hand climbing turn to evaluate the effect. It was beautiful, not a great number of balls, but enough to create the effect of a descending cloud of snow. The balls hit the target, but wait . . . they struck the ground, blowing at 25 mph! A bigger cloud of thousands of kids was running after them, we'd NEVER considered this! Zigzagging through rows of cars, in front of others, kids were even crossing the divided roadways oblivious to oncoming traffic. Then, with sportsmanship observed only at international hockey matches, there were real snowball fights. Every ball caught was torn to micro-shreds; sometimes 6 kids on a ball, as they looked for prizes INSIDE the balls.

Gritting my teeth in fear for the kids, I pulled around to drop Santa. No one was in sight around the landing pad . . . they were all a quarter mile downwind. Since then, I have seen the TV sitcom, WKARP, where announcer, Wes Nesman, reports the similar delivery of turkeys at Thanksgiving. "Here comes the copter," he reports, "they are opening the window and dispatching the turkeys . . . the turkeys are starting to fall, Oh heavens … they are in freefall! We forgot turkeys couldn't fly; there goes one through a windshield and another. I can't look . . . !" The writer of that show must have seen one of our drops. Eighty other drops were made, augmented to better hit the zone; with no incident reports, it was an eventual success with greater profit margin than the state fair.

The next year continued to expand with more Easter Bunnies, rides from secondary shopping centers, carnivals and additional charter contracts. Soon I was approached by Ed Goshorn, Eastern Sales Manager for Bell Helicopter to candidate for his position as he moved to Boeing. After I agreed to attempt that, he asked for a private dinner meeting. He suggested, "Jack, I know you are a family man. You need to know this job has responsibility for all states east of the Mississippi. I'm never home! Should you be considering this position? There is a strong company down in Indianapolis that needs a Test Pilot for a new little turbine they are building for the Army; I think you might fit the bill." I agreed about his job and to contact Allison Engines, General Motors Corporation. Thanks for the heads-up, Ed!

Dejavu

"Test Pilot, again?" kept flickering across my mind, I'd already turned my back on that opportunity in the Air Force. This time it might be better than selling helicopters 27 days a month. "It may not hurt to apply in Indianapolis, just for the experience," I rationalized with Sharon. She had already concurred with scraping the Bell job, at least in Chicago I was home nearly every night.

That weekend I flew Paul Butler to one of his local polo games. He owned at least one team and several players. I guess this assured HIM a spot on the team. I had never witnessed an entire game before and I was amazed at its intensity. Paul was riding his prize horse, goading him and racing to get shot after shot. The next mallet impact, WHACK, was adjacent my seat on the sideline. Suddenly the horse folded its front legs, head down, and skidded in a death roll right in front of me. Paul slid off over the horse's neck and, without loosing a stride, boarded another mount and returned to the fray. The horse laid dead at my feet the rest of the game.

I waited eagerly for the finish, to see Paul come over and salute his faithful friend. He never even glanced toward my side of the field as his team headed triumphant for the showers. The dust settled and a tractor finally appeared. Yardmen roped the rear feet and dragged it unceremoniously toward the stables; they said its heart exploded. That horse and I had been fellow employees with identical contracts, to carry the chief. It was time to call Allison Engines in Indianapolis. God permits us to see His will, sometimes just one blink at a time.

Gambling Men

A standard form letter arrived from Allison after I returned home, acknowledging the interview in Indianapolis and stating they had other candidates to examine. There was no reply to my note of thanks expressing further interest. Weeks went by in silence.

The good life at home went on but things at work were deteriorating. A few months earlier, the federal mail subsidies ended for the three helicopter airlines in Chicago, New York and LA. Unexpectedly, the heliport system within the city became subject to Mayor Daley's political machine. His administration announced a one time levy on every existing and future heliport PLUS an annual licensing fee. The helicopter operators and owners within the area couldn't have sold all of their aircraft, buildings and other assets to meet the initial levy.

A new law and edict effectively announced, "It is illegal to land aircraft within Chicago except at city approved airports except in an emergency." Aircraft included helicopters! Being gambling men we continued to fly and meet our contracts; we considered every flight an "emergency". If we didn't fly we were out of a job and business . . . that's a real EMERGENCY. We held our breath, continued operating without incident until several of us were called to heliports and met by . . . men in blue, police officers! Hundreds of heliports, shopping centers and businesses became off-limits. Daley also tried to close down Meigs Field, the city's lake front airport but it took his son forty more years until Junior personally bulldozed its runway. How would you like to be in business with "Friendly Administrators" like these?

The handwriting was on the wall. We'd gambled and lost. I should have tried for that position at Bell in helicopter sales. Then I received a letter, seemingly from heaven, containing an offer for an eighteen month contract with Allison Engine Division, General Motors . . . that's almost the same time we'd been in Chicago on TWO jobs. "You have one week to accept this offer, Mr. Schweibold," it read as if from Mission Impossible. I was to learn what "GM" meant. They too, were **G**ambling **M**en, masters in the game of employment poker. Like a hungry amateur, I folded on the first hand and accepted the contract. I found out later that they had been wooing Charlie White, an experienced Bell Helicopter test pilot, for those past three months but he had been holding out for three times my salary offer!

In moving, we'd leave behind good and bad:

Bad:
- Snakes
- Spiders
- Poor Pay
- Traffic
- Pollution
- Crime
- Corruption

Good:

- Business friends and mentors.
- Playing cops and robbers with Irv Hayden, Airborne City Policeman broadcasting aloft every weekday morning and evening, at times circling low or landing to review and report accidents . . . I believe we may have caused more than we prevented, all legal . . . WE were the cops.
- Picking Eleanor Roosevelt off the Merchandise Mart and hearing her respond to seeing, "God's beauty!"
- Flying comedy acts like Arthur Godfrey, he used to be a helicopter pilot until he buzzed a control tower, the men in the tower were terrified but they got the last laugh . . . and had him grounded, permanently. He always enjoyed getting at the controls again.
- Delivering Bob Newhart, he was so popular in the Windy City; Mayor Daley dropped the helicopter embargo just to land Bob, complete in pinstripes, tie and tails at his favorite intersection on the Southside.

Our family was blessed; we received a new job, better pay, and escaped the political heat and decay of the Chicago Desert! As you can see, we did hold and play out the best poker hand. You never go wrong with cards that read, *"Proverbs 3:4, 5 & 6"*.

Trust in the LORD with all your heart and lean not on your own understanding; in all your ways acknowledge him, and he will make your paths straight. Do not be wise in your own eyes; fear the LORD and shun evil.

10

New Breed

Last of the Big Ones

My office at Plant 10 Flight Research Center was remotely located as the only building on the Southside of Weir Cook International Airport. It was a single structure, hangar/shop/office combination. The hangar could handle a combination (two to four at a time) of their two Air Force YC-130's, a four engine Lockheed Electra, two Convair 580's, one B-45 a F-84 and a Army U23 . . . looked like a neat array of test vehicles to me!

It was an impressive facility finished by the government at the end of WWII. They had their own self contained departments: machine shop, welding cribs, wood shop, instrumentation lab, radio repair, sheet metal shop, parts department, photo lab, fire truck and ambulance, data reduction, walk-in vault, engineering bull pen, administrative offices, locker rooms, oxygen pre-breathing center for flight crews and a pilot's office. At its peak it housed about one hundred fifty personnel; upon my arrival we sat at seventy-five . . . on a rapid scale down!

I moved into one of ten desks in the Pilot Center, a large office on the second floor just off the main center engineering bullpen. I was given a front unit position, probably so everyone could keep an eye on me. Apparently the old timers sat in the prestigious rear row against a giant flight planning map of North America.

My task for upcoming months was to "fly" this desk, read and learn everything I could about my engine and aircraft program. "We'll get you the material," said Senior Pilot, Vern Ford. Little was offered. This covey of pilots was not anxious to have this new twenty-five year old . . . on **their** block. To say I was ignored or shunned would be an understatement; there would be little typical pilot camaraderie.

Whenever I was introduced in the other plants, I'd get the same response, "You don't look like you are twenty-five or . . . a test pilot!" This really set me back until I also heard, "You are the first new hire around here in eight years." The company had been spooling down, ever since the Korean War, so there was a void of personnel under thirty to thirty-five. My baby face stood out like a monkey's rear spotlighted on a blackened stage!

The pilots would come in late and leave early. They encouraged me to enjoy the same work life. They also appeared overstaffed in the cockpit and didn't invite me aboard. Instead, being a hands-on learner, I saturated myself in available raw technical material. I volunteered to do the unthinkable, plot data and run the photocopy/blueprint machines; otherwise, I'd have gone crazy with little to do all day. Everyone was amazed. Pilots never stooped to that stuff.

Near the end of the third week, a big meeting of ALL employees was called in the main conference room. Robert Hicks, the Chief Test Engineer over all the plants entered the room last to address the group. As he passed, he recognized  having interviewed me. He stopped at my chair and said curtly, "Jack, you are not invited to this meeting. Please remain in your office".

I remained alone and dejected. . . .

A New Breed!

The meeting room emptied. I hadn't moved from my desk but I could see everyone come out and head to their locations. The pilots filed past me without a look or comment, then left; their day was over. "What's the matter, guys?" I thought, "No one have the courtesy to tell me I'm gone?" My contract did have an evaluation clause.

Last to exit was the Chief Test Engineer, Mr. Hicks. He turned left for the exit stairway, then reversed course directly for my office. I snapped my head down. He entered the pilot's office and closed the door. "This is it," I figured, "another pink slip and I didn't even get a check ride!"

"Jack, may I sit down," he asked coolly.

"Of course", I replied, he owned the place.

"Please excuse my abruptness in asking you to leave that meeting; you were not invited as it did not pertain to you. Have you heard this place, Flight Test, referred to as the Country Club?"

"Yes," I nodded.

"Well," he continued, "effective this hour, memberships have expired. Over the past decades, we have enjoyed funding by the military for our engineering flight research programs. Since Korea, there has been a cutback in all military services. The armed forces test activities are shifting resources to sustain military test facilities at Edwards and Patuxant River. Even the Army, who is funding your program, is developing a new flight test capability at Ft. Rucker, Alabama. What I told the staff was that things are going to change out here. Most personnel will be gone by year end ... and beginning with you, we are going to have a new breed of competitive and cost-effective staff at this facility. It will no longer be called a Country Club. We had the option of hiring other "seasoned test pilots", but we believe you are trainable to the new system we desire to establish."

"The Army scrapped their twin-engine airplane program downstairs. They determined it would become a turboshaft helicopter engine first. We have intentionally hired you a year before our first engine is ready for flight to give you time to learn the ropes around here from the ground up and we have already seen you are not afraid to get your feet dirty. I have assigned you to the Engine Test Department as an engineer on the test stands, to learn about and operate your engine. On occasion, you will teach a class on helicopter operations as it applies to the engine. Six months or so before first flights, we have arranged with Bell Helicopter Company for you to work with their Research and Production Flight Department to assist in developing our helicopter flight test procedures. Are you willing to help instill this new work ethnic?"

"Yes, Sir!" I responded . . . now I understood why I was treated like a half-breed in a bag full of bigots. I was to be the NEW BREED!

Quiet Pilots

When they announced a scale down at the hangar . . . they meant it. I was alone! Bob Hoover had quit a few years before I came aboard, Bob went on to become Vice President of North American Aircraft and spent years mesmerizing the air show circuit in his twin engine Shrike and P51. Rolly Martin and Bill Gibboney were absorbed into the big engine Service Department and came back to the hangar only occasionally to fly the Electra, C-130's and Convair Turboprop. Vernon Ford transferred to Hawaii as a Service Engineer in Customer Support. Dick Peterchef moved to the Test Cells and continued to fly in the Terra Haute National Guard. I guess Mr. Hicks was right; it was best not to get involved with the old time clan.

Allison's Electra was sold to LA Dodgers, note flying baseball.

It had been hinted that if I became a member of the "Quiet Birdmen", a secret society of the area's elite pilots; it would enhance my flying career and advancement. While I had profited from being a member of DeMolay in my teens, a junior Masonic group, I never gravitated toward further secret organizations. I believe the Bible addresses this matter directly by stating,

"No one can serve two masters. Either he will hate the one and love the other, or he will be devoted to the one and despise the other" MT 6:24.

I had enough trouble serving my employer and God; to throw in secret alliances would only complicate issues. Besides, when I was home I desired to be with my wife and growing boys, not a bunch of frustrated airplane jocks pumping egos with a whisky bottle. I already had enough trouble with ego.

When I wasn't in the pilot's office, their society must have worked. It was absolutely QUIET . . . and empty.

Margaritaville

The engineering staff at the hangar and main plants did accept me, they were curious about rotorcraft. In turn, I was eager to learn about their engines and test operations. Two fine young engineers took me under tow and mentorship, Bill Long the Flight Test Engineer on my small engine program and Bob Joeston, a Test Projects Engineer who knew all of the nooks and crannies in the Engine Test Stands. Bill and Bob invited us into their families. Bob even invested a Saturday night introducing us to the Meridian night club strip . . . not knowing that Sharon and I didn't fit the profile of what they were led to believe test pilots enjoyed; i.e.: Bebop bars and nonstop drinking.

The truth was, I had been exhausted from that routine in flight school and never could choke that lifestyle down my wonderful wife, one of the reasons I married her. I'd seen enough bar floozies. While training in B-25's at Hondo AFB, Texas and long before I would help Jimmy Buffet learn to fly his Allison Turbine Bonanza, I spent a weekend chugging Tequila, salt & limes in Mexico. My buddies must have dragged me back into the U.S.A. and poured me into the barracks shower. Monday morning, I woke up on the shower floor in a pool of blood and soggy taco chips. The taco chips turned out to be sections of my stomach lining . . . I'd poisoned myself! Fortunately, I had a compassionate Flight Surgeon who put me on a diet of strained food and milkshakes for six months, instead of drumming me out of the corps.

Bill and Bob did share our family values. By chance, we moved into their general area of Speedway. I can still remember driving Sharon up to our new rental house. She didn't say much as we walked up to our mass-produced aluminum cracker box ranch in a high-density neighborhood. My bubble of pride in moving her out of Chicago burst as she broke into tears seeing the inside. "It's ALL painted speckled Easter egg!" she choked out. "The walls, shower, ceiling, window sills, doors, woodwork, switch plates . . . EVERYTHING!!! It's horrible!!!" She was right; the speckles flowed into a dirty purple-gray puke color. She cried for days, until we got it repainted: each room a different bright color: yellow, blue, orange, purple, etc... In looking at photos today, it's a hoot . . . but we were happy and tickled PINK! The thing we most enjoyed was rain on the metal roof; it had only rained a couple of times during our three years in California. One of those days we painted, it rained all day. We surrendered to intimate times listening to the liquid symphony. Today we rejoice . . . Brad was born nine months later!

11

The Promised Land

Out of the Desert

We had just spent two "Desert Years" in Chicago: location, jobs, isolation, marital strife, etc. before being led into what would become our "Promised Land", Indianapolis. As we crossed the border of Indiana, our shoes weren't worn out but we were flat broke; all assets depleted. We were sitting on the floor under the tree; it was Christmas Eve when Sharon started her tears. "What's wrong?" I asked.

"What are we going to do if it's a girl?" she continued to cry.

"I thought you wanted a girl," I responded in bewilderment, "we've got two boys".

"Not now, we only know how to raise BOYS . . . and besides, I don't want to be in the hospital on Christmas!" Fortunately her weeping didn't send her into labor and she made it through Christmas to our Anniversary on the 27th. What a neat Wedding Anniversary present Brad was! And of course, he was a wonderful tax deduction. Knowing how fast things moved with Mark, we'd already made practice runs to Methodist Hospital and had her bag pre-packed. Methodist was my kind of hospital; it had a rooftop heliport. The actual run was clear, no snow, we made it by car in record time! Once Sharon was safely upstairs, a receptionist waylaid me at the desk for "sign-in". I'd never had time for that routine before.

Racing upstairs, I figured to meet the baby on arrival. "Stop!" the nurse pleaded, "She's in the Labor Room". Having been in the Teamsters and Airline Pilots Association, I always thought that was where labor contracts were settled. I soon learned I was not in the bargaining process. This was her show and the settlement she wanted was PAIN KILLER! All she got was a whiffer mask, with what seemed to be only a 1% solution of diluted chloroform scent. She would suck on that mask so hard and long she would fall asleep from exhaustion. I think the whole thing was a test of some demented doctor . . . and she got the placebo! Suddenly, all of the intimate times we shared together weren't worth the suffering she was undergoing.

91

In conscious moments between contractions, she would lie there in her beauty, look up and say, "Isn't this wonderful? I love you" . . . she was formatting the way she would handle pain all her life. I think they had her on ice until the doctor decided to get to the hospital. Then I was fortunately shooed to the waiting room. Today they chain the men to the stirrups, with one hand free to hold the video camera. In all honesty, I believe men who go through the full birthing process make the best fathers . . . I was a wimp!

She was to spend more time here than she spent in total for the first two kids. "Another boy", she breathed with a smile.

"Who is Spencer?" I bravely questioned, having already seen "Spencer Brad" on his crib, "We never talked about a *Spencer*."

"Well", she courageously replied, "I was so afraid we'd get a girl, I never thought about boy names. YOU try coming out of anesthetic and have YOUR mind straight." She was right then, and now, when she refreshes my mind on these deliveries, for some reason her recall is more vivid! The one thing we agreed on, our three sons were the greatest blessings in our new "Promised Land". Thanks for the perfect landing, Brad & Sharon!

Our First Business

"You bought what?" asked a concerned Sharon.

"A helicopter," I nonchalantly squirmed.

"I thought you went to the Amusement Show at McCormick's Place to meet with Shopping Center Managers," she continued to interrogate while we still lived in Chicago; "we can't afford a helicopter!"

"Well I did meet with them and contracted a few bunny deliveries . . . and I think we CAN afford this one. Let me show you its pictures. I haven't really bought it yet, let's talk!" We talked, as she looked at the picture of the "Whirlwind Helicopter" amusement ride. A self-contained 8 x 20 foot trailer sitting four and a half feet high held a small helicopter on a hydraulic piston lift. The pilot sat in the front with four-axis controls; collective pitch in the left hand for up and down eighteen feet; cyclic stick in the right hand fore/aft and left/right bank; and rudder pedals for left and right rotation. It functioned just like a helicopter without ever leaving a hover, complete with rotating rotor blade. She agreed with the potential of operating it in shopping centers with our real helicopter rides or as a stand-alone amusement. Besides, it looked like we were heading to Indianapolis and we'd get exclusive sales rights to Indiana. We bought it.

Fortunately, their company was well-structured and had financing available; our dealer's discount was the bank's $800 down payment on a $4,000 purchase price. While established businesses and crime syndicates pretty well had coin-operated vending machines tied-up, nobody wanted to mess with the one-of-a-kind operation. Initially it was a hit.

While placing our real helicopter rides in shopping centers or fairs, we would trailer this little jewel to the landing area; it worked great to help draw a crowd! Kids who couldn't afford the real thing could hit mom and dad for a quarter to ride in the look-a-like, letting parents off the hook. People who did fly the real thing wanted a crack at the simplistic controls. It could even pull a crowd on its own at centers or single stores. As we left Chicago for our new job in Indy, we sold our first machine to Charlie our landlord, hope he did well. Maybe I just got even for all the trains.

Once in Indy, we continued to operate the ships in local centers on weekends. Our boys probably don't remember their early entrepreneurship; they would run the ship up and down as shills to attract business. Bob Reed was my new Manager of Flight Test. I'll never forget Bob slipping up on us at Eagledale Shopping Center, right in front of Sears. He stood for an hour counting the quarters coming out of pockets and clenched fists before he let me see him. The next Monday at work he called me into his office to acknowledge I was a P.T. Barnum and asked, "Why do you even bother to work for Allison?"

"It's the only way I can afford to fly my own aircraft!" I faked back; little did Bob realize he hit my only busy hour all day. He didn't know the principle of the Merry-go-round. I never told Bob otherwise. The only money we made was from quickly selling this and four other machines before the market collapsed. We netted about four thousand dollars that put us back in the black. A couple of the units we sold put two families of kids through college, making generations of life-long friends. Bob never failed to give me the maximum available raise each year while working for him. We were in the Promised Land.

Mr. Allison's Speedway!

Bob Joeston knew his way through the test facilities like a rat in a maze trained to find cheese crumbs. He started with GMI, everyone I talked to said that meant Guaranteed Monthly Income. General Motors Institute was GM's corporate school to train their own engineers. Men and women started college with the institute in Detroit; six weeks at school and then six weeks working on the job at one of company's plants, which agreed to underwrite that student for the five-year term. Normally that division tendered fulltime employment upon graduation. It was not a bad arrangement coming aboard a company right out of school with five years seniority, already knowing the corporate ropes and politics. I can see this is the same opportunity Allison by offering . . . investing in me and bringing me aboard a year early.

My first day as Test Engineer was spent touring dozens of test cells at various plants scattered around the Westside of Indianapolis. Some were for individual components, fuel systems, vibration, altitude chambers and others were for complete engines to be exercised across their environmental spectrum.

I hadn't walked that much in years and Bob was still racing ahead. The first thing he taught me was, "Jack, you can do anything or go anywhere in this company you want . . . if you carry a handful of papers and walk FAST!" It was the most profitable corporate advice I ever received . . . it also works just about everyplace else!

 We were in the Town of Speedway. Mr. James Allison was a prime mover in auto racing beginning in 1909 when he, Carl Fisher, Arthur Newby and Frank Wheeler formed the Indianapolis Motor Speedway. They purchased the farmland that saw the first race in 1909. The little industrial community to spring up around the track became the backbone of the eight-cylinder engine. As WWI hit, engines quickly stretched to a 12-cylinder design. The "Liberty" powered US and allies airpower in Europe. Responding to wartime directives, Allison produced one hundred twenty-five more than its levied quota, with numerous automotive companies delivering a total of over 20,000 of these "monstrous" powerplants by war's end. Jim Allison's refinement of his Liberty evolved to the Allison V1710, powering P38's, P40's, & P51's to WWII supremacy. After recounting this local history and leaving Plant 2

in Speedway, Bob received a call, which he relayed . . . "Jack, our 250 Engine just BLEW UP!"

There She BLOWS!

There it lay, as if a dead whale washed up on the beach after being torpedoed by a passing submarine. Its scorched carcass was still hanging in the engine mounts with strands of countless hose and instrumentation lines streaming from its gutted body. It was not a pretty sight, like having just paid for your new Cadillac and blowing the engine the next day; the Caddy may be under warranty but it sure puts a crimp in your vacation midway to Florida. Likewise, this would set the program schedule back several weeks, a critical delay since we were in competition with another engine company.

The turbine portion of the compressor, turning nearly 50,000 RPM, had failed. I can remember in high school the traveling science professor who demonstrated spinning a paper disk until it exploded and catching in on camera. The paper shattered with a BANG . . . in pieces; and because of their light weight, the particles were harmless. The heavy turbine casting exploded in just a few chunks, the biggest cutting through a 10" ceiling I-Beam, the rest severing anything in their way. It was easy to visualize this eruption taking apart a helicopter's tail rotor drive shaft, fuel tanks and lines . . . or even a main rotor blade. Engine flight test was suddenly sobering!

First Solo Test

95

Norm Parshall, Bob Joeston's supervisor, dropped me off for my first solo test program. No, it wasn't at the Flight Line; it was at the Fuel Test Laboratory. The disconcerting elements that commanded my attention passing into the lab, were the hundreds of 2' to 3' square metal panels covering the cell blocks. "What do all of those geometric designs represent?' I questioned Norm. "Those are pressure sensitive blowout panels." Norm coyly responded, "If you foul-up your test ·. . . hopefully they'll reduce the concussion before bringing the whole building down on the rest of us."

The little engine was a new concept for turbine engines . . . a reverse-flow design, short and compact to fit small wings or helicopters. The normal turboshaft engine was a straight through flow, starting with a compressor, fuel/ignition, thrust/power and exhaust; in lay terms, the air entered the front and exited the back.

Our reverse flow engine:

- Sucks the **air** in at the front with the compressor (Intake/Compression)
- Ducts it to the REAR and turns it 180 degrees to move forward into a combustion chamber where fuel and ignition take place (Ignition/Combustion),
- Expands it through a compressor turbine that turns the compressor at the front end, then passes the air into a power turbine that turns the output drive to the helicopter rotor or airplane propeller (Power/Output)
- Dumps the balance into an exhaust chamber and turns the remaining airflow to exit the aircraft up, down or sideways (Exhaust). This whole procedure has the same cycles as a reciprocating engine: Intake, compression, power, and exhaust.

Well, like every "newbie" on the team, I got the butt end of the engine, from front to rear; the fuel nozzle is the last piece. Beyond a shadow of a doubt, Norm picked the Fuel Nozzle because it was the part I could least destroy and a piece he knew I really needed to understand before starting his prize engine. This test would involve securing a fuel line to a newly designed nozzle structured with a multitude of small holes for the fuel to exit and placing it above a clear plastic measuring container sectioned like a pie. Running the fuel pump at different speeds would produce varying spray cones and precipitation rates. My job was to measure the spray cone angle and volume of fuel collected in individual pie quadrants at various pump speeds. In several days the results painted a vivid histogram of just what that pattern looked like with fuels of different viscosity/temperature, varying engine speeds and temperatures . . . a picture I would have never seen from the cockpit. Months in these labs and running the engine on the test stands were designed as my graduate school in engineering; my thanks go out to a patient company of mentors.

During my years at Allison I credited survival, not only to the Lord, but also to absolute trust in three men; Bob Joeston, Norm Parshall and his counterpart, Bill Stiefel. These men were the most knowledgeable of the entire engine system . . . and their professional integrity was without question. My normal response was, "If Joeston, Parshall or Stiefel approve the system, I'll strap it to my back and fly it!" If I ever suggested, these men would always fly WITH me if a seat was open. That's mutual respect!

12

Wild Bull Riding

Bell bottoms to Bell Helicopter

In eight months of working in engine test and flying our C-130's, Electra and Convair 580's, I gleaned a thin understanding of Allison flight test procedures. Allison's Air Force Contracts Colonel arranged for me to fly with Bell Helicopter Company in Texas; first, for two months on production acceptance flights of the Army HU-1's, then, for a month in Experimental Flight Test to observe final assembly of our test aircraft.

Strangely, the ship was designed in Navy colors, funded by the Army and administered by the Air

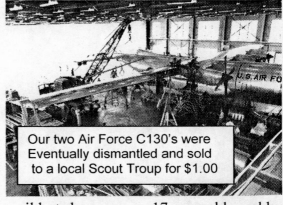

Our two Air Force C130's were Eventually dismantled and sold to a local Scout Troup for $1.00

Force. I never imagined in my wildest dreams as a 17-year-old swabby jumping into my first bellbottom trousers (with 13 button fly, one for each of the first thirteen colonies, you learn to unbutton fast) that I'd move from fueling to flying a Navy Aircraft, yet alone fly for all three services simultaneously!

Two pilots, Smith and Hartwig, took me under their tutorage. Smitty was infamous for holding the World's Distance Record, having flown non-stop in a Bell-47 from Fort Worth to Buffalo, NY. I was able to shadow them as they prepared for the first flights. Bell's contract with the Army was to build two new ships as close to a military production model as possible; install two new experimental turbine engines, one by Continental and one by Allison and then deliver them to Ft. Worth. The closest model they had available was a Navy version of the Executive Bell 47-J that I flew in Chicago. The Navy had bought a quantity of these a few years earlier as trainers and equipped some as anti-submarine aircraft . . . an effective tool when launched from a destroyer. The Air Force used them to fly the President.

99

This was a single pilot aircraft, sitting forward with three side-by-side seats behind. During the first start sequences, I sat in the rear seat until adjustments permitted normal operation. Tied to the ramp the first few hours, the ship completed full power and control cycling. Smitty took the first few flights, accepting it for the Army and in turn passing it to our control. Once we had completed ten hours of local flight (an FAA requirement) it could head to Indianapolis, not in flight but by truck. The program was worth hundreds of millions of dollars and was cloaked in secrecy. The competitors (Continental for the engine) and three different airframes building competitive helicopters (Bell, Hiller and Hughes) were

breathing down our backs. We couldn't chance seven flight hours flying home. Expected life of the hand-built engine at that time was only 50 hours! Three days waiting for the truck in Indy felt like three months. Once it arrived it would be MINE. The comforting element in the meantime was that Continental was just delivering their competition engine to Bell for installation. The race was ON and we were one lap ahead!

Wild Bull Riding

The heart of the turbine engine is the fuel control system. In this first design, it was a hydro-mechanical unit. Two flyweight governors sensed mechanical speed of the two turbines and governed the fuel flow automatically, depending on pilot inputs through a network of pneumatic bellows and air chambers. If the system was too sensitive it could be disturbed by outside forces, such as rotor passage or turbulence, and become torsionally divergent and could destroy the helicopter in a few cycles . . . three to four seconds! Alternatively, if it were too sluggish, the engine slowed when reacting to acceleration and deceleration needs, creating the peril of slow response.

The engine entered service extremely aggressive . . . too sensitive! As it picked up airspeed, rotor vibration increased due to differential lift on

the advancing blade. To fly faster increased the problem. Pneumatic pulses were created in the fuel control, resulting in plus or minus 100 horsepower (hp) per cycle, at four diverging cycles per second; meaning the hp differential got higher with each cycle . . . much like wild bull riding. If one didn't kill the engine quickly, the ship disintegrated!

Engineering's initial answer was to add more volume to the air chambers to slow the engine down. They started with a one cubic inch metal chamber but ended up with a forty-two inch hose rolled up around the engine like a garden hose. This equated to the acceleration and deceleration characteristics of a single diesel engine pulling a one-hundred-car coal train. Our job was to balance these characteristics while proving other altitude, speed and starting capabilities of the engine during the first fifty hours of flight. By the time we were finished, the Continental Engine was just taking to the air. The Army decided to come to our hangar for a final demonstration flight, sending the Secretary of the Army and his staff.

Bleachers were set up to hold the small contingent of evaluators and observers. The Secretary of the Army stepped to the aircraft. As a civilian it was all I could do to hold back a salute. Together, we performed a walk-around inspection then eagerly boarded and strapped on the ship. I talked incisively, a beautifully choreographed briefing of the entire process; hit the starter button and the engine roared to life. The crowd waved intently; they were eager, too. Then they came running, giving me the cutthroat signal. I figured we must be on FIRE.

I cut the throttle and pulled the fuel shutoff valves closed to terminate all fuel. Looking over my shoulder, I didn't see any flames, only my red-faced Chief Program Manager. Jack Wetzler was untying our tail rotor. My mouth had been rattling so intently it had not engaged the brain, and I forgot to untie the rotor blades on the preflight.

Gathering my wounded pride, I explained to the startled Secretary, "We've just passed the first rotor brake demonstration . . . six months ahead of schedule!" I watched out the corner of my visor for the frown. It was a GRIN, then a laugh. We had a great flight running my White River, Nap-Of-The-Earth combat course, simulating an air and trench battle, ending with a maximum performance zoom climb, engine shutdown and airstart during a spiraling descent. Within a few days, his team determined we were the demonstrated winner. Our program would continue and so did my employment contract.

We also won the Continental helicopter for spare parts and were given the green-light to extend the engine life to seventy-five hours. That's the way the engine matured, hour-by-hour until it completed its 150-hour test target. The engine would ultimately go to production and would power all three aircraft companies' competition helicopters. We had tamed the bull!

Hi-jinx to High Jack

During these trying test periods, a little levity always broke up monotonous periods of endless data reading and report writing. At this time we were still filming twenty-five-gage photo panels and running film speeds at an average of ten frames per second, meaning we would read a hundred frames of film for a ten second hold of the trigger finger. Then we would select several parameters to record against time. For accelerations/decelerations, we would typically read fuel flow, turbine outlet temperature, turbine speed, main rotor speed, and collective pitch and throttle settings. Otherwise, six readings every tenth of a second, or sixty pencil points/second generating six curves from six-hundred hand plotted points on a graph . . . for a ten second maneuver.

A long length of the record wasn't a crisis; it just meant we would have miles of extra 35mm film to develop and reel through to find our ten inches of data. Since I was also doubling in the photo lab, I soon found that winding yards of useless film on racks of doweled drying spools got tiring. I think this was one of the advantages of getting involved early in the engineering side; I became programmed to be precise and short on the recording switch. That's not to say we didn't have to repeat a few flights because I missed the trigger by a millisecond while attempting to get conservative. Boredom in these tedious plotting periods became too tempting not to get slaphappy! Bill Long and Lou Esenwein became cohorts in this sport and we all ended up being the butt end at times.

The Bright Engineer - Lou was the new Flight Test Engineer on the block, direct from Sikorsky Aircraft and he WAS sharp. Bill assigned him to a project away from the film readers, a darkened area with 3' x 4' glass panel, back lighted readers for 35mm film. In his absence, I strung a couple dozen Speed Graph photoflash bulbs behind his glass panel and wired them in series to the machines 110v on/off switch. Bill darkened the whole room and gave Lou a reel of film to examine. We patiently waited . . . FLASH !!! You got the picture, Lou SCREAMED and the only thing that saved us from immediate reprisal was that for a half hour . . . he was BLIND!

Boss has Sense of Humor - Bill played his best one on himself. He was delayed at home on a morning he was to give an important presentation to our Director of Engineering. He called me to bring him his needed items. As we arrived, Bill was huffing and puffing from the rush up to the second floor . . . just in time for him to step forward to give his synopsis of a flight sequence. With sweat dripping from his forehead, he pealed back his suit jacket and rolled up his sleeves to a roar of laughter.

103

He turned to look at his jacket and there was even greater hilarity. Above his white dress shirt pocket his wife had written in BOLD black ink pen on an old frayed dress shirt, "BILL'S WORK SHIRT"; meaning work around the house. On the back was also written in bigger letters, "BILL'S WORK SHIRT". As he recoiled with red face he finally saw the sign on front, backed to a mirror and saw the bigger letters. Gordon Holbrook said, "Well, Bill, its okay . . . I guess you are at work!

Why Rush? - Always jittery, Lou rushed out of the hangar to take a visiting flight crew to a restaurant on their short turnaround. But wait, we had jacked his rear wheels a half-inch off the ground with small axle jacks. No matter what he did, nothing happened, the engine just roared. Rushing back into the hangar frustrated, he found us working at our desks. "My transmission's out!" he said in a dismayed rush, "Someone lend me their keys". We tossed him a set of keys and he was on his way . . . and we removed the jacks. On his return he handed back the keys and headed for his car. Nothing was wrong, he was perplexed. Finally we told him he was just too tight to use his own gas. Lou went for a week, expecting his transmission to go out! I guess we shouldn't have wondered how Lou got so jumpy.

Broken Window or Broken Mind – The real coup came with a five-inch cast iron steel ball we used to slowly roll down the length of the second floor engineering center. The building was now almost vacant and rolling the ball that had a raise bead around its circumference caused a low frequency rumble, THUMP, rumble THUMP . . . to be echoed eerily throughout both levels of the building. It used to drive our remaining secretary, Jean Brown, out of her mind. One day she said, "I've had it with you men, you're driving me nuts!" That's all the encouragement we needed.

Her office was located between other empty rooms with upper windows looking into all of them. Bill and I staged a mock quarrel, as to who was to blame for harassing her. Finally I said, "That settles it, I'll just throw the ball out of the building and get rid of it!" To which I picked up the ball in the outer bullpen area, threw it through her adjoining office and the outside window glass. The smash was mind shocking, Bill looked at me and shook his head in disbelief and walked off. Jean just sat dumbfounded. "Well, Jean, you started it all; it's up to you to call maintenance and get the window fixed," I mused as I stalked off. After a few minutes, she called maintenance.

While she was calling, Lou had been lying out of sight in an adjacent office and crept beneath her side windows to remove a big cardboard box where we had laid a large pane of glass . . . that's where I actually shot-put the ball. He merely pulled it silently across the carpet into another office. When Wally Walters arrived, completely oblivious to the situation, she told him what the office clowns had done. He stood at the window in the next office shaking HIS head. "What are you trying to pull on me, Jeanie?" he said in dismay.

"They broke the whole window out!" she retorted, heading for the office and the "broken window." They both stood now scratching their heads. Then Jeanie started shaking. "What has happened?" she demanded.

"What are you talking about?" Bill questioned. "You said you were going nuts; you must have lost you mind." We just walked off and watched while we worked from the pilot's office to see her pace back and forth between the two offices . . . in the Twilight Zone.

Top Secret

As they tested their new aircraft, Bell, Hiller and Hughes all made the same call … "Allison, your engine is SLOW." Allison was an Engineering company and one of the first things I learned was that engineers don't like anyone to say something derogative about their pointed head, one-eyed genetically handicapped child . . . or product. While I didn't appreciate the criticism either, I'd been complaining about it for so long that I was hoarse; maybe the three customers could get management's attention where I'd been out-gunned.

"Okay, Jack", Gordon Holbrook started, "we have received Army clearance for you to be the first person to fly all three helicopters and teach their pilots how to fly our engine!"

"I'm going to teach THEIR pilots how to fly?" I thought. "Sir, I'll do my best," was all I could come up with.

"You have been right about most things in this program regarding the flying. I count on you as my final conscience in these matters," Allison's Chief Engineer finally stated in front of his staff. "Now go out there and bring back a report on just what the problem is, theirs or ours. If we have to improve acceleration, it will cost millions. Remember, other than a formal test report to us, you will be signing papers of confidentiality with each company and the Army regarding disclosure of any detail of their aircraft until the competition is over." I felt I had just been deputized as a

U.S. Marshall and was heading west to take on the bad guys, alone . . . without a posse.

13

Final Judgment

I'd only been to San Francisco a few times and most of those trips had not left fond memories. The first time was to attend Letterman Army Hospital just before I left the Air Force. Diagnosed with ulcers, I was there for an upper GI bore-a-scope. My arrival fan-fared a Dr. Frankenstein experiment, staged for fifty students sitting in circular bleachers on an overhead balcony. As I lay on the operating table, I felt like roast Guinea Pig perched on a platter to serve the entire peanut gallery. To ease my anxiety, they strapped a sodium pentothal needle to my arm and pumped it to keep me on the edge of the Twilight Zone. The pig vision became more realistic as they rolled me nude on my side, tucked my legs into the fetal position and skewered me down the throat with the optical tube. For the next hour I rotated on the spit while each of the overhead poachers took their turn to view a hiatel hernia in my esophagus, a restriction just before it enters the stomach. Many "O-oh's" and "A-ah's" were heard as each one seemed to find a new gold vein to view at the end of the mineshaft. Whenever I winced they just pushed the plunger on the hypo.

After the table examination, they carted me into another assembly room with all of the students watching and sat me up for interrogation. Two of them held me upright; I thought they were the Gestapo. Questions took me back to the first time I recognized problems swallowing . . . I could never remember a time I didn't have difficulties. I always had trouble at Christmas or when swallowing under high excitement or pressure . . . like eating food I didn't like and had to choke down. Spanked for not eating it, things only got worse. My step-dad said I was neurotic and convinced me he might be right. I really didn't want to tell this roomful of medical officers that I vomited in closets, shoes or whatever was around to escape harassment. I learned three things from this; I had swallowed bleach as a kid or had a birth defect and . . . I couldn't standup against truth serum. It's going to be even more embarrassing to stand before a living God in final judgment.

After the interview, they directed me to put on my uniform and head back to base, 400 miles south. As I hit the street with dilated eyes, I was blinded by the California sun, could hardly see to stagger to the bus for the airport. As I stepped aboard the city bus for a downtown connection, the lurching start ignited a churning bomb in my stomach. Blurred vision still let me see that every seat was partially taken. About half way to the back, the stomach finally exploded; fully erupting in front of 25 onlookers viewing a drunken Air Force Officer in dress blues, holding on to a pole and barfing into his hat. Suddenly, I had full seats offered wherever I moved. I staggered to the back and took the entire seat . . . no one bothered me! Disembarking downtown, things were no better; I had four hours before my flight. I hit the first darkened movie theater, flushed my hat and crashed. My grandkids still play dress-up with that now dry-cleaned hat.

Hiller YOH-5
Palo Alto was just over the hills from San Francisco, a decade in advance of becoming Silicone Valley. This trip was not for ulcers and could be viewed with new eyes . . . and stomach. The competitive aircraft for this competition were the Bell YOH-6, Hiller YOH-5 and Hughes, YOH-6. "O" stood for Observation, "H" for Helicopter and the military puts "Y" in front of all of their prototype models. Each company had three prototype ships to accomplish a year of tests, ending in a championship winner-takes-all competition at Fort Rucker, Alabama.

Hiller and Bell had a monopoly of the small observation/training helicopters in the Army; Hughes Aircraft was a renegade entry. I was impressed with Stan Hiller's design. It was clean cut, of conventional construction with a standard two-bladed main rotor. For us engine people, a sleek engine cowling pulled easily aft over the tail cone for preflight inspections and maintenance. In flying the machine, it demonstrated a slow engine response in abrupt recovery from autorotation and quick stops, the same complaint I'd voiced about our own test ship; all other characteristics appeared normal, it looked and flew like a winner!

Another Spruce Goose?
I wouldn't meet Howard on this trip but it was still inspiring to walk into Hughes Aircraft Company, his own private "skunk works" at Culver City, California. Fairly close to MGM's studios, his airport . . . running from the beach at the Pacific to the expressway, appeared to be his own private movie set. A giant, long-bladed, heavy lift helicopter stood high on pogo stick gear; it must have been his effort for the flying crane market

won by Sikorsky. Spotted here and there were various abandoned projects that came off Hughes's personal drawing board. It was easy to picture his Spruce Goose parked nearby in an air-conditioned preservation hangar, a plywood Goliath that he piloted to ten feet over the bay . . . against the military's wishes. "BARROOMM!!!" Regularly punctuating this nostalgic setting was the startling, explosive firing of a Gatling gun, one of his production pieces soon to mow down the Vietnamese jungles. The YOH-6A would be one of Howard's last projects of personal involvement.

Stepping into the Flight Test Section, a small WWII type shack, I met my old acquaintance, Bob Ferry. Bob had observed my inverted flight maneuver in the H-19 at Oxnard five years earlier. After several hours of pre-briefing, similar to the preflight at Hiller, with the exception that you had to be a trained midwife or proctologist to examine the engine located in its lower rear-end, we took to the air in "The Egg". Ferry reassured me as we walked to the ship, "An egg is aerodynamically perfect and effectively crush-resistant". We proceeded to the helicopter in crash helmets and Nomax flight suits; if that was true, why did we need these? Ferry continued to expound on the design philosophy, "An exceptional light weight concept maximizing speed, high payload and agility . . . that's how we made the competition. Bell and Hiller are old heavyweights. We're the new kids on the block". I wasn't convinced!

The ship looked like micro-thin tinfoil wrap . . . with toothpick structural members. The main rotor had four mini-blades, a light-inertia concept that left a lot to the imagination and raw skill when making power off autorotation touchdowns. Similar lightweight rotor designs, which previously equated with hard landings and broken backs, were never popular with instructor pilots. Once we were in the air, it was shake, rattle, and roll; however, my job was to evaluate engine response, same as Hiller, slow. My departing critique held no punches on the heavy vibratory flight loads. I figured since they asked me, I'd tell the truth. They confessed their findings were parallel and tried to assure me they were "working on it"; a phrase I would soon hear often and would occasionally use myself. I couldn't say yet that we were "working on" our slow acceleration but I did assure them I would report it as an unacceptable problem. It's "Jack" that will be unacceptable returning to Allison; in time of battle, agreeing with the enemy is treason. In reality, these companies and pilots became friends not foes, as they supported my previous reports.

Bell Knows Best

The last evaluation on this ten-day whirlwind would be the YOH-4 at Fort Worth. We'd heard the "slow" complaints first from Bell; their ship was of stouter technology. They had already experienced structural fatigue in tail booms on existing HU-1 gunships. Even though its little brother, this LOH, was tagged as an observation helicopter, they knew full gun pods and rockets would become permanent fixtures on these sporty ships; therefore, Bell figured heavier would be better. They built a bathtub structure they "knew" would be the BEST. Well, at least it would become the *best-heaviest*!

It was good to be sworn to secrecy. Everyone casually pumped me these ten days . . . even the Army. It was hard to keep my mouth shut. Instead, I remained open to criticism and suggestions regarding the engine and was able to impart valuable information on our own test experience that might enhance their installations effectiveness. Each manufacturer extended an open invitation to return; the problem was . . . would mine welcome me? I was going to report that our pointed-head, one-eyed bundle of power was S-L-O-W. I hope our Chief Engineer was ready to listen to his conscience and ready to open the corporate pocketbook. I was starting to get a vision of how the Bible prophets felt during travels to tell the Israelites about their shortcomings.

Chug-a-Lug Contest

Entering the conference room to debrief the engineering staff was similar to visiting a Mexican bullfight. Jack Wetzler, Model 250 Engine Program Manager, was the matador and the various Component Managers stood ready with swords. You guessed it; I was El Toro, the Bull. I'd attended one bullfight in Mexico but never a second; the bull is slaughtered before your eyes. Now enter El Toro. Did you ever see a praying bull? The staff unknowingly did.

I stepped boldly to the head of the room and gave a verbal and graphic synopsis of each airframe's flight. The presentation ended with a colored ink pen graphic depiction of what I perceived the engine's problem. That chart would remain in the conference room for a number of years, as it became the solution to understanding the dilemma. The engineers failed to figure certain aerodynamic and kinetic energy loads, which delayed an acceleration signal to the fuel control. Fortunately, the Lord had given me a clear and convincing delivery. Sadly, the engine would have to cut 1 to 2 seconds off its 0 to 275hp acceleration time.

110

Since the engine was already accelerating at maximum fuel flow rate, additional fuel would only send it into compressor surge or stall. This is similar to chug-a-lugging a root beer. When you drink too fast, it comes back up. Likewise, the compressor chokes when accelerating air too fast. With the safety features in this engine, it's a self-recovering situation but slows the acceleration. The engineers developed a solution, now that we had a PROVEN problem. A bleed valve to dump the air midway down the compressor would permit the engine to run faster during the initial part of the acceleration. This is much like putting a dump valve at the bottom of the esophagus . . . to relieve backpressure during the drinking process. We could likewise improve our acceleration rate and win the compressor air chug-a-lug contest. It would require an additional engine test program, extend my contract another few months and lighten GM's profits for the year. Each of the manufacturer's flight test teams also required additional testing; soon I would become a commuting member of each group. I wasn't carried out of the arena in matador fanfare but at least "El Toro Jack" wasn't served on the grill that night . . . and continued to be counted as a portion of our Chief Engineers' conscience.

The Winner is - -

To balance what sounds like a very prideful preceding scenario, once home, I was pressured to forecast the airframe winner. I picked Hiller Aircraft with Hughes as last. In fact, I suggested Allison might get a different pilot if Hughes won. I didn't want to fly their aircraft. You have it; Hughes straightened out their vibration problems and underbid the competition, at $19,000 per airframe. The engine first came in around $7,000. Hughes won; the total aircraft package came to only about $26,000. Today their new commercial model sells for more than $700,000.

In the end, Bell Helicopter demonstrated they were the master of market research. For the first time, they turned an artist loose with the direction to sketch a helicopter that would be a public pleaser . . . the

world went goo-goo-eyes over the resulting "Jet Ranger". Since they lost the military contract, Bell and Hiller could sell their commercial models. Hughes couldn't sell commercially until they produced their military orders. My prediction didn't hold a drop of water, but few remembered since we would soon be testing them all in our own stable at Indianapolis!

14

Hazards

Howard Hughes

Once Howard was officially crowned as winner, I began frequent trips to Culver City to fly our engine in their YOH-6A's. The "A" was to designate our new T-63A engines with the faster accelerating bleed valve. On one of these early trips, Bob Ferry, their chief pilot, asked if I'd like to meet Mr. Hughes, we were in the flight shack. "There he is, standing on the ramp," Bob said, pointing out the door to a man standing in tennis shoes, slacks and sweat shirt.

"He doesn't look like one of the richest men in the world to me, but yes, I'd be pleased to meet him," I reservedly replied. We strolled out to where he stood at the rear of the ship we would fly. I was introduced as Allison's Chief Test Pilot. He had numerous, intelligent questions regarding performance and operations, letting me know he had been intimately involved with his ships design and progress. After the 15-20 minute conversation, he walked off with another man standing nearby.

When we got back inside, Bob asked, "Do you know who the fellow was standing with him?"

"His body guard?" I flipped a guess, "That's probably a breakdown machinegun he's carrying inside the black case."

"No," Bob said, "that's his food taster. Mr. Hughes has *germaphobia* or whatever you call it. He has all of Mr. Hughes tableware and condiments in that case and *pre-tastes* and checks all of his meals."

"Not much to live for," I thought. Even though I saw him only occasionally, he continued to remember me as "Mr. Allison", better than the courtesy I extend most people since I'm not too great with names. A few years later Howard died a recluse . . . alone with his own fears.

1TImothy 6:6 But godliness with contentment is great gain. 7 For we brought nothing into the world, and we can take nothing out of it.

113

Hangar Bugs

Open hangars in remote cornfields attract lots of strange insects, birds and animals; ours was no exception. Trying to get rid of birds was an ongoing process. Exterminators applied poison to the girders, then material to burn their feet. Defenders of the fort shot from the ramparts with BB guns and scared them with frightening lights and sirens. All remedies seemed to be worse on workers than on birds; eventually, we learned to live in the aviary . . . and wash aircraft.

Animals were the most interesting. As we closed the upper engineering area and moved to the lower level, we noticed that mouse population picked up dramatically in the fall, as the critters moved in from the fields. The entire staff baited traps nightly in all out warfare. Each morning we would find a pile of mold that appeared to consume the bait overnight. Later we noticed a number of grease ants were feeding on the mold; then I closely examined the mold and found a miniature BACKBONE! These ravenous ants were coming up from cracks in the concrete after the mouse was caught. They digested the victim overnight, leaving only a lump of moldy looking fur. Nobody must like mouse hair in their food. After that ominous find, we didn't see many noontime "power naps".

Strangest of all wildlife to visit the hangar came seeking the security of our remoteness, the only building on the Southside of the airport. We offered safe haven to many visiting dignitaries and VIP's, including congressmen and presidents. One day the airport manager notified us that a VIP flight would arrive on our ramp for police protection. Beforehand, crawling out of fully-tasseled cornfields came teenagers suffering from insect mania . . . "Beatle Mania". Within minutes the Beatles did show up, their appearance and their aircraft interior left little for anyone to admire. The young people who arrived, hot, sweaty and covered with cobwebs, departed disillusioned . . . when they saw a beetle crawl out of its natural environment.

We also became "last resort" for trapped beasts, dogs, cats and deer finding their way into the fenced airdrome. One lunch hour, a stray "Tabby" cat sauntered across the hangar, and singled me out of a dozen men. It headed straight for my leg, rubbed at my pants and managed to beg some of my milk. She hit my heartstring, and that's something . . . since my two favorite cartoon books are: *"1000 Ways to Kill a Cat"* and *"Another 1000 Ways to Kill a Cat"*! Our friends, Dick & Marie Miller once permitted their "attack cat" to bite me, for years I retorted with comical letters and gifts; a page from the cartoon book or a can of "poison" for the kitty from France; fish.

John Orr, our Maintenance Supervisor headed for the phone to have the airport police terminate the invader. "Wait!" I interrupted, "I'll take it home for the kids." Quiet prevailed; everyone knew my feelings about cats.

Overnight, "Cat" shredded a new davenport and drapes. Even compassionate Sharon asked to read my books. I tossed "Cat" into my backseat and drove for work . . . I'd call the airport police to handle the execution. Halfway to work on the expressway, I looked in the mirror and "Cat" was sitting on my seatback. Within a couple of minutes it moved over and rubbed its back on my neck. That did it! Down came the window and out went the cat. At lunch, our Instrumentation Technician, Bill Stevens asked, "Jack, driving in, didn't I see you with a cat on your shoulder? I thought you hated cats!"

"Oh, not me!" I immediately fibbed. We continued our Hearts card game. Within fifteen minutes in sauntered "Cat", walked right up and rubbed against my leg. That stupid feline had found its way seven miles back down an Interstate highway, through a security fence, and across two runways . . . just to brand me a liar! I had to fess up and admit I'd lived out one of the pages in those books *"... And catapulted pussy cat off the aircraft carrier deck into a 65 knot headwind!"* I called the police, sat back and happily visualized the cartoonist's expression on that cat . . . as it road the steam catapult off the flight deck. I trust that Gods mercy extends for acts to cats.

Flameout – In a Pigs Eye!

Everything pilots ever train for . . . the engine quit! I can't remember why it quit but there at a comfortable altitude of 4,000 feet, just south of Indianapolis and within our legal test area . . . silence. The military and FAA assigned us a twenty-five mile by eighteen mile by twelve mile tri-angle to stay within for our first 150 hours of testing. We couldn't always comply because of winds, but at least I was legal now. This would be my first real engine out landing!

Immediately, I entered autorotation by lowering the collective pitch, reducing the main rotor blade angle. In descent, the air moving upward through the rotor moves the center of lift from the top of the blade toward the front. This provides a tractor or pulling force on the blade (much like blowing into a child's pinwheel) increasing RPM and providing normal control maneuvering in a descent. This is the way autogyros land on every flight. The only difference is that everything needs perfect timing to hit a spot, at near zero airspeed for landing, necessary because we didn't have wheels. By increasing collective pitch and main rotor blade angle just a second or two prior to touchdown, we could momentarily break the 1200-1700 foot per minute descent . . . the ultimate event for which we've practiced.

I attempted three airstarts, believing we had lots of time, but each start failed halfway through the sequence. Bill Long, my test engineer, just sat there as quiet as the engine. I checked the altimeter . . . only 500' left; better look for a landing area! I turned into the prevailing wind, immediately in front of us sat a BIG white Indiana farm BARN! A house to the right, trees to the left, I was committed straight ahead. I pulled aft on the cyclic stick, tilting the rotor back to make a flare climb over the barn . . . airspeed fell off. We just cleared the lighting rods and dropped straight down on the other side. What would be there?

Clearing the peak, I closed the firewall fuel shut-off valve and turned the battery off to help with fire suppression. Next, I pulled collective pitch, increasing blade angle to trade kinetic rotor blade energy stored as RPM for momentary lift to brake the fall and cushion a higher than normal final free-fall to touchdown. At ten feet, I saw them, pigs, sows and piglets . . . hundreds of them. We settled abruptly into a wet, muddy pigsty. Those pigs were screaming before we hit the ground; we had no trouble hearing them with the engine out! As the skids slowly sank out of sight in the mud while the rotor slowed down, those pigs stacked themselves against the fence three to four deep. My final concern as the ship came to rest on its belly in the pig slop was "I wonder if they suffocate like the four hundred turkeys we killed flying too low during Texas training.

It took four minutes for the rotor to stop. Bill and I continued to sit in amazement. After discussing the sequence we realized our weight was . . . helping sink the ship, Bill's alone was near 300 pounds. We deplaned and sank to our calves in the goo. Now, I knew why we always wore high-laced flight boots in the military, so we didn't lose shoes when the parachute opened. I lost my low quarters in the first two steps. Once to the rail, the pigs scattered as we crawled over the fence into the hands of a waiting farmer and his wife.

"Never saw anything like this", he drawled.

"How about the pigs?" I asked.

"Our son is opening the barn door and they'll go in . . . those pigs never seen anything like you either," he assured. "Ya know, I was in the

116

Navy during the Second World War, but I never would have guessed the Navy would land here," as he observed the markings on the fuselage.

He was right, old "Navy" was a sorry-looking landing craft. It eventually took a lot of shovels, a crane and a flat bed truck to extricate the helicopter. We learned several things that day. First, we had discovered a serious problem. Second, our ground rescue team was invaluable. I had transmitted a radio call to the tower announcing our position as we went down, but it was our own company ambulance and fire truck who found us thirty minutes before the sheriff. Third, always keep a landing area in sight. Fourth, and most importantly, that God's gifts come in unusual packages; wallowing in a pig lot was better than violent impact with a barn.

Altitude Hazards

As we progressed in our test program, higher thresholds were examined. The engine was to be certified for 20,000', which meant in a single engine aircraft, we'd climb to 23,000-25,000', shutdown, permit the engine to stop and still have time to initiate and complete a start before descending through the 20,000' certification altitude. Simple? Consider some of our problems with helicopters at altitude. Retreating blade stall occurs as a helicopter flies faster or higher; therefore our airspeed envelope shrinks beneath 30 knots. This resulted in going places I didn't really want to go. In a climb at 50,40, or 30 knots into the wind, with wind speeds up to 75-125 knots when climbing into the jet stream, I could take-off from Indianapolis heading west and end up 100 miles (behind me) east in Ohio before reaching 25,000. While going BACKWARDS at 50-100mph, various radar controllers would perceive me heading East (not West) and give vectors for seeing my traffic or directions for me to turn . . . 180 degrees out of phase!

Initial climbs were reasonably rapid but even on a warm, 80 degree day on the ramp; with a temperature lapse rate of 3.5 degrees F per thousand feet, I'd pass through the freezing point by 16,000'. Since the air had been pretty humid back on the ground, EVERYTHING inside the aircraft would suddenly turn to FROST. . . including the windows. The heater at that time utilized bleed air from the engine, reducing horsepower and limiting altitude; therefore, I learned to leave the heater off and keep the windows open all the time . . . even in the winter at minus 45 degrees. At that temperature Fahrenheit and Centigrade are about the same! Learning to keep the windows open permitted exhaust of most exhalation moisture and reduced some of the fogging and frost. In addition, open, even frosted windows, gave at least an occasional peak at the ground or rogue aircraft if I was not in a cloud. If the attitude gyro crapped out, a helicopter wouldn't fly well on simple instruments of needle, ball and airspeed; it has no natural stability like a fixed wing airplane. I dressed warm. In the summer, the converse happened . . . I was a sweat box hitting the summer ramp, putting on weight at this point in life was not a problem.

On one of our earlier flights, I checked in with Air Traffic Control (ATC) coming up on Flight Level 180 (18,000'). "Indianapolis Center, Experimental Helicopter 839 with you at Flight Level 180, going up 230 (23,000')."

"Got you, Helicopter 839," Center replied, "Report reaching Flight Level 210, we've got a TWA ready for lower once you are out of 210."

"Roger, Indianapolis, Helicopter 839 report reaching 210", acknowledging my clearance.

Then a strange voice piped in, "A helicopter up HERE, at WHAT altitude???"

"It's one of Allison's Test Helicopter's on way to an eventual Block 190 to 230," (meaning once cleared, I would have unrestricted flight within 19,000 – 23,000' on a specified course) replied Center.

"Indy Center, this is TWA XYZ. Where is he? We've got to see this!"

"He's just beneath you at about 1 o'clock, at 3 miles," Indy Center responded in a sporting voice.

"We've got him, that's awesome!" responded TWA, "Indianapolis Center, this is TWA XYZ, we are running a few minutes early. How about a two minute left holding turn here, the passengers have to see this!"

"OK with you, Helicopter 839?" asked Center.

"839 appreciates the company," I happily called back.

"TWA, this is Indianapolis Center, you're cleared as requested, maintain visual separation."

"We'll do it!" replied TWA. This was the only company I'd ever have nearby above 20,000 feet. I could never afford the extra weight of

118

passengers. As he banked above and around me, I could imagine dozens of noses pressed against the windows. I guess I should have waved.

Once in the clouds you are on raw instruments, this is a Sikorsky S76.

15

Going Hunting

Get Your License

"Jack, the Army and Hughes both called and they have asked you to go hunting!" our Program Manager phones.

"Huh," I gulp, "The last time I went hunting with the military . . . they bagged ME, for six years! What are you talking about?"

"No," he replies. "Hughes just received permission from the Army to use one of their prototypes for a month, to break as many Aviation World Records as possible. Hughes will fund the operation and the Army will support it out of their Test Detachment at Edwards AFB. We will provide technical support on the engine . . . and the Army and Hughes have offered you a seat for the distance record."

I'm flabbergasted. I haven't even heard about this in the rumor mill. "Well . . . I guess so-o," I stammer.

"We don't know much about it ourselves yet," he continues, "apparently, it's something Hughes Sales and Engineering Departments dreamed up, and while it's against government policy, the Army says Okay. They must need a shot in the arm, too. Everyone feels you should be on the team. Someone will be contacting you regarding a Sporting License needed from the Federation Aeronautic International (FAI) in Paris. You are cleared to do whatever is necessary to represent Allison."

Shortly after this conversation, Bob Ferry, Hughes Chief Pilot and Phil Camack, one of their young Flight Test Engineers called. I believe Phil is the real driving force in putting these attempts together. "We think a handful of records are already in the bag and there are several others we have an outside chance at landing," Bob and Phil relate. "The Army pilots at their Edward's Detachment will fly everything below 10,000' and we

121

civilians will get the tough stuff above 10,000' . . . or over ten hours."
Most army helicopter pilots never receive Physiological Training, altitude
tank experience in non-pressured atmospheric conditions or instrument
training, flying in the clouds. "Three of the marginal records will be
Weight Class for Altitude and Unlimited for Distance. Our Jack
Zimmerman will be shooting for altitude, Bob will be going for a good
wind on Unlimited (All Class) Distance in a Straight Line and you'll get a
try for Unlimited Distance in a Closed Course. Since your flight is in a
circle, you'll get no help from wind. You and Zimmerman will end up at
the highest altitudes and have drawn the short straws because you're the
lightweights."

"Hey, being the 99 pound weakling in High School finally pays big!" I
quip . . . and then continue, "I'm honored, men. How can I help?"

"I'll send you an application package you'll need to submit for your
sporting license," advised Phil. "FAI is the longstanding agency in Paris
that began keeping Aerospace Records with the first balloon flights. They
run this thing like a Duck Shoot. You apply for a hunting license through
the National Aeronautics Association in Washington DC and we'll pay a
fee for each record you want to challenge. They issue you a passport type
license with your picture. Inside are stamps for each record attempt that
are good for a certain sanction period, normally ninety days. So for the 90
day period, you will be the only eligible candidate for the record; and of
course, we'll go armed only with the Allison powered YOH-6! Not to
dampen your hopes but we only have a few day window, maintenance or
weather can scrap any or all of us."

Bob adds, "Your job will be to just show up Edwards . . . when and IF
we can get their SPORT (Spatial Positioning and Orientation Radar
Tracking) scheduled. They will track you over the two-day flight for
validation, and it's hard to get priority that long. . . ."

"Not JUST to show up," Phil jumps in, "But show up programmed in a
sleep pattern to depart bright-eyed and bushy-tailed at midnight, targeting
lower temperatures for enough lift to get ·you off at almost TWICE
maximum allowable weight. We'll be in touch," he concludes. I always
had trouble sleeping when contemplating a good fishing trip with the
family. This will be no exception.

Go For Gold

I'd flown into Edwards many times in support of rescue or test
operations but this is my first trip by ground. The drive from Lancaster
reminds me why this location was picked . . . the expansive salt flats give

plenty of self-sealing runways; every time it rains the ground cracks fill in, for a natural healing process, giving a relatively smooth landing area for miles.

Reaching Army Flight Ops, I arrive in time to see Army Lt. Col. Richard Heard fly a 3 km course record to set the Light Weight Helicopter Speed Record at 171 mph. This is established by flying a short, level run at maximum speed, turning 180 degrees and returning over the same course with speed measured electronically. Once three round trips are completed, an average of the three runs validates the new record. During the previous week, several other records had been won by the agile helicopter. "If the ship and engine hold together, Jack, your flight will launch at midnight tomorrow night. You'd better hit the pad and get in sleep sync," advises Test Engineer Phil Camack.

I'd already been getting up at 1 a.m. Indy time, 10 p.m. Edwards time but this afternoon I just couldn't sleep. Phil hands me fresh target altitudes for the different weights to optimize engine power vs. fuel burn for best true airspeed. This matrix, rather than sleep, streams through my mind.

The alarm buzzes at 9 p.m. as I wake from just a few minutes light snooze. I roll onto the base on schedule at 2200 hours, 10 p.m., dressed in a summer flight suit. I pull my flight helmet and oxygen mask from my crew bag and tuck the Sporting License in a leg pocket. Walking to the ramp, the maintenance crews are securing the ship; we are scheduled for liftoff in less than two hours. Suddenly I don't feel ready. I continue with preflight of the aircraft. If something can be found wrong, maybe we will lose the launch window. "Stop that thinking," I say to myself. "You know you really are READY for a shot at this record!"

As I finish my checks, it is fueled with pre-cooled JP-5 fuel. JP-5 is a heavier Navy type fuel, effectively No. 1 Diesel Oil. Army/Air Force standard fuel is JP-4, which has a percentage of lighter weight gasoline. The gasoline mix provides better ignition in cold weather. JP-5 or heavier fuels are dictated by the Navy for shipboard safety, but their aircraft generally utilize fuel pre-heaters. The advantage of utilizing JP-5 for this flight is that being heavier; it produces more BTU's per gallon. By pre-cooling and shrinking the fuel, we squeezed in a few more cups of BTU's. If this is going to be a win, it will be marginal. As they finish fueling, the fuel is already warming in the tanks, evidenced by expanding vapor exiting vents. The "Egg" looks like a miniature spacecraft silhouetted in the night lights; proportionally, it is.

Getting a final physical check by the Base Flight Surgeon, I ask him for some No-Doz pills. He slips me a box and says, "Take two as needed." I don't need them now, I am geared to GO. Just as they close my door, the doctor sticks his head in and asks, "What do you have for a snack?"

"Nothing," I reply, "We're going at minimum weight!"

"Try this tube of apple sauce," he adds, slipping it through my closing door. "We designed it as high energy protein for astronauts on the Apollo Missions." The ground crew subsequently closes my door and seals it, as are the others, with propeller (duct) tape. This cuts parasite drag and hopefully, will pick up one or two needed knots in speed. While I strap on my parachute, I wonder if I could actually break the tape seals on the door to bailout if the ship became a falling coffin.

A final cross-check of fuel and oxygen shows all systems ready. I give a spool-up signal by rotating an index finger over my head. The crew chief responds likewise, I hit the starter and the engine is on its way. After a short one minute run up, I began to lift the ship off its skids into a hover by raising the collective pitch lever in my left hand. The main rotor blades take a proportionately bigger bite of air and the engine responds automatically to increase power to maintain rotor rpm . . . but we are too heavy and sit there on the skids. I look at my buddy in the left seat; they'd painted a smiley face on the black fuel bladder fixed in the seat straps. "You and your brother in the back are just too heavy", I think. "Maybe we shouldn't have pre-cooled your fuel!" They had built a full ceiling-to-floor, form-fitting fuel tank for the back seats. It too, is full.

Holding maximum power, I nudge the cyclic stick forward, trading vertical lift for forward thrust; still no movement. I push the cyclic forward to the stops. The vibration of the rotor hitting the stops break the ground friction and we start sliding forward on the sandy concrete. At fifteen knots, clean air over the rotors produces slightly better lift; I can feel the ship getting lighter on its skids scraping along the ground. I neutralize the cyclic and we begin to lift off at 20 knots, barely skimming the ground a few inches.

35 knots, good, I initiate a shallow climb . . . have to get over the first range of hills just a few miles away. With all this fuel, we are set to be a fiery napalm bomb if we hit anything. If something happens to the engine at this weight, there will be no recovery!

"I eagerly expect and hope that I will in no way be ashamed, but will have sufficient courage so that now as always Christ will be exalted in my body, whether by life or by death." Phil 1:20

Where's The Hill?

The slow climb is agonizing, we gain only 100' the first two miles down the runway,. I don't remember my trig tables, but this has to be less than a two-degree climb angle. The course is 60 kilometers in circumference and in 20 km I have my first range of hills to scale or it will require orbiting a turn or two before proceeding. We can't afford that luxury. The course is laid out by a set of twelve pylons and if it were daytime, I was told, I'd be able to see the marker on the ground . . . but not tonight. "Army 49213, this is SPORT. We marked your time as you turned from the taxiway down the runway, Good Luck!, we'll call your turns for you; suggest a 30 degree turn on the first few until we can help you with the winds."

"SPORT, Army 213. Thanks, I'll take all the help I can get!" I respond with enthusiasm now that I am on the way.

"213, SPORT, get ready to turn on my mark, 3, 2, 1, turn." I turn my rough 30 degrees. The runway lights start to drift from immediate view. I am running just a couple hundred feet over the salt beds and need to increase the climb angle. I slowly bled a couple knots off the airspeed with a very slight amount off aft stick. The climb rate almost doubles to 300' per minute, but not for long . . . finally settles out at 200' per min. "213, SPORT. Get ready to turn, 3, 2, 1, turn 30 degrees. Suggest you come back left 3 degrees."

"OK, thanks, SPORT, 213." I am now staring into BLACK desert and must force myself to raw instrument flight this close to the terrain. As I leave the dry lake bed, I know the hills will be rolling upward. On the next turn I lose sight of all land lights, even in peripheral vision. "213, you are drifting inside the next marker, make an IMMEDIATE LEFT TURN or you'll cut the corner!" calls SPORT.

"Turning, SPORT, 213," I turn 90 degrees . . . and I know that doesn't help altitude. "Where's the hill, SPORT?" no answer, then . . .

"213, this is SPORT . . . you just cleared it by 40 feet."

"Thanks a lot," I think to myself. They always say a miss is as good as a mile. This banter continues for a couple of laps until I settle in and they become accustomed to my turn rates . . . and the ship has enough air underneath to comfortably clear all obstacles. These first two laps take almost an hour each. As fuel burns off, airspeed increases to a couple of laps/hour. In a high speed aircraft, I imagine they just hold the ship in a light bank, clipping the pylons; in reality, they have much bigger courses for the fast guys.

As weight decreases with fuel burn and speed increases, Engineer Phil instructs a climb to optimize fuel burn and engine performance. To determine the best airspeed at altitude, I momentarily accelerate above V_{ne} (Velocity Never to Exceed) for that altitude until I hit V_r, (Velocity of Main Rotor Roughness) and then back off 1-knot airspeed. This gives us the least amount of drag for speed in the rotor system without slipping into retreating blade stall. Fuel management is simplistic. The rear tank filling the entire aft passenger compartment, gravity feeds into the lower main tank. They had installed a hand wobble pump next to my left arm for me to pump out my bladder tank strapped in the copilot seat. Right now I need him full for proper fore/aft balance.

Four hours into the flight and I'm already climbing through 10,000'. To keep my night vision crisp, I strap on my oxygen mask swinging from my left helmet strap. It's 6 a.m. Turning Eastbound, the faint rays of morning appear. It is going to be a glorious sunrise. "A good time for a cup of coffee", I relish to myself. No coffee but I do have that box of caffeine No-Doze pills. I pull them out of my chest zipper pocket, drop my oxygen mask to a side strap, chew and swallow two of them with a sip from a small thermos of water.

I remember the tube of applesauce. It is still tucked under the copilots fuel tank restraints, kind of tucked in his left armpit. I unscrew the cap and slowly squeezed down a family-size tube of breakfast. Not too bad, at least it doesn't flow all over the space capsule in a weightless environment; it heads right for the stomach. Kicking back and relaxing, now fully off instruments, I enjoy looking around. I even find five of the twelve ground pylons! At fourteen thousand feet it is time to buckle on the oxygen mask. The air is getting thin. I have at least another ten hours to go, time to get rid of some fuel up front. A little exercise on the hand pump mounted between the seats empties the buddy bag. His painted smile sags to a frown; that is good. He is empty.

"Army 213, this is SPORT. Good morning, sir. The airspace is yours; you are cleared as able to Flight Level 190."

World Record Attempt

"Army 213, Army 213, this is SPORT, do you read?" I faintly hear the controller call. "You just cut inside that last pylon, enter an immediate left turn 270 degrees . . . or you will blow the mission!" I hesitate to respond, hadn't slept for over two days. I'm exhausted. Reluctantly, I slowly roll the ship into a lazy left bank. The forces on the cyclic control stick at these altitudes are so heavy that I wrapped an elastic bungee cord around it; fastening ends of the cord between doorframes, to help relieve the flight control steering pressures. This reduced some of the left lateral force but I hadn't taken another wrap on the cord since passing 20,000 feet over an hour ago. Fatigue is setting in.

Juggling the cord to take up another winding, I slump slightly forward and Howard Hughes' experimental helicopter slips higher in speed; it only takes another two knots to enter high-speed rotor stall. The violent shaking rattles me back to a minor threshold of alertness. I neutralize the controls and allow the speed and angle of bank to drop back within a safe flight envelope. Terminal rotor stall will flip the craft inverted . . . and at this altitude with little, if any, expectation of recovery. Once upside down, bailout through the rotors is not an option; the only hope is to be thrown clear if the aircraft explosively separates.

"Continue the turn!" yells SPORT, forgetting the formality of radio call signs . . . they know I am hurting. "You've got thirty-five degrees to go yet." I apply a shallow bank to the left. "We'll call your rollout assuming you hold a constant rate of turn . . . good we see you turning. Get ready to roll level on the count . . . three, two, one rollout!"

I struggle through the next three laps of the sixty kilometer speed course, in the Army's attempt to capture the Unlimited Class World Helicopter Distance Record for the United States.

"Mr. Schweibold! Listen up!" the flight surgeon calls curtly to get my attention. I know his voice. He had called several times before, but now I can sense his growing concern. "Check your oxygen supply again."

"It's still half full and turned to Emergency, 100% safety flow," I respond. I'd been flying fighters and bombers for years, pressurized and un-pressurized, trained in altitude tanks, the works . . . physiological altitude equations were nothing new, but I still can't analyze what is going wrong.

"How are your nails?" he replies on queue.

I pull my left glove off and stare through a fogging visor to inspect my finger tips, "Rosy red!" I say softly, hoping for some other reassuring direction. Silence, he is still looking for some sign of hypoxia that might be contributing to my exhaustion. "How about taking a couple of those No-doze capsules I gave you?" he finally adds.

"Took several over the past few hours," I admit, to turn off his interrogation. Don't want to tell him I had already choked down the whole box of twenty-four tablets hours ago, lack of caffeine is not the problem.

"Can you hold on for two more laps?" the Engineering Project Manager asks comely, "It might be best to bring you in now. You've already set the Light Weight Class Record." However, I understand nobody really wants an early termination. Months and years of effort have gone into designing and building this ship . . . but half-a-pie might be better than none at all.

Air is leaking from my mask; I reach up and pull the mask straps tighter with my still naked but now cold hand . . . leakage stops as the mask seals in raw crevices of cheek. Two more laps feel marginal and fuel is already bumping on empty. Softly I reply, "We're, we're . . . going for it". I can only listen now, no vocal resource left. I can't understand, four miles high, but I'm drowning. . . .

The Final Lap

Someone seems to be talking through a watery mist . . . "This is the Final Lap, Jack . . . hang in there!" called Phil. Phil sits with a secondary microphone in the control center and can transmit to me on a separate receiver in the ship. Everything seems to be happening in slow motion. I don't really think I can "hang in there".

In fact, I can "Hang" no longer. Suddenly, to my immediate front right side, I see a white robed arm slowly uncoil out of the dark violet sky and open its hand toward my door. I move to eject my door and step into it.

128

His voice is low and astonishing, "No, not yet," the hand and arm slowly retract and disappear. This gets my FULL attention. I yank my oxygen mask off, at 22,000', I don't care anymore. If I'm going to die, I'm not going to be strangled by the mask!

"Army 213, turn 30 degrees on my mark . . . 3, 2, 1." As I struggle to make the turn I experience a rush of energy . . . but turning, I'm staring at a giant thundercloud forming. It towers thousands of feet above; it drifted into my track since the last semi-conscience circuit. I can't fly through it at these altitudes, especially in my state of alertness and its internal turbulence. I'll just make a wide turn around it. With only a handful of gallons remaining, I have to chance the detour. I turn back left twenty degrees. Skirting it, it just keeps growing bigger in height and girth, like an ugly Genie expanding out of its bottle!

"Army 213, we've lost radar contact with you. Reply please!" SPORT called. They couldn't hide it any longer, now I could sense in them the concern I'd felt for the past few hours.

"SPORT, 213, I've turned left to go behind this thunderhead in front of me, can't fly through it and don't want to clip inside a pylon now. 213 is descending out of Flight Level 210."

"Army 213, reply; we've lost contact with you!" SPORT continued several times and . . . even they fade out. At 19,000' and several miles outside my course . . . I'm feeling GREAT . . . even without my oxygen mask! I should be unconscious by now. I recheck my nails, still good and red . . . plenty of oxygen. I've been unconscious before at 18,000' without supplemental O2. What's going on?

Once through 16,000' I turn back and parallel my last course assignment as I tuck under the cotton candy swirls of moisture forming around the cavernous cloud. Continuing to turn as the fringes of the churning caldron permit, I clear its base at 4,000' and make a call to delight all. "Sport, 213, clear of the cloud a half mile outside the final marker!"

"Roger, 213, we've got you in radar contact again. We must have lost you behind that thundercloud. Good to have you back; we thought you were GONE!" I drop the nose for maximum speed on the remaining descent and will hold it to the finish line. Less than a quarter mile to go now, it's good to be only a couple feet over the runway again!

"Jack, PULL UP, PULL UP!" Phil shrieks over the secondary radio. "You've GOT to finish HIGHER that you started!" I immediately pull aft cyclic and zoom UP several hundred feet and cross the Finish line.

I make a high speed turn and head for the ramp. The crew is waiting and waving. It has been a long night for all. As I land the ship, it is hard to wait out the 60-second cool down requirement. I hope it will just use its last fumes and run out of fuel. The engine stops, I lock the controls, unbuckle my chute and hop out; in fact, I keep hopping for several hours. Twenty-four No-Doz pills have me running at full throttle . . .

Years later, in looking back, besides setting the World Unlimited Class Helicopter Closed Course Distance Record at 1700 statute miles, one that still stands today; I had tested a new element of aviation . . . the food tube. On the flight Surgeon's examination of my oxygen mask, still hanging from one strap on my helmet, and the applesauce tube, we found a major structural failure had occurred in flight. While pumping applesauce into my mouth, it squirted out one end of its ruptured seam into my hanging oxygen mask, sealing both EXHALATION ports while I enjoyed the morning sunrise. My parents had always yelled at me for squeezing the center of the toothpaste tube rather than neatly rolling it from the bottom. I should have learned!

At the lower elevations I didn't notice the blockage. At higher altitudes where supplemental oxygen pressure automatically kicks in, I had perceived the problem as mask leakage and tightened the straps. Well, it WAS leaking. It couldn't hold the pressure, and I just kept exhaling HARDER against the pressure. In all, it was easy to suck in but . . . but like blowing against a sealed hand forced over your mouth . . . for eight hours. No wonder I was exhausted! When I took my mask off at 22,000', it didn't matter; my blood was so oxygenated I probably could have stayed alert quite awhile!

As for the arm, hand and voice; I never said anything for years or hung my salvation on it (that comes the moment we trust only in Christ to take us to heaven) but chalked it off to my pastor's message that visions were from eating too many hamburgers. However, I am now convinced that my wife and children's prayers at that very moment had a lot to do with this supernatural rescue. Even if it was a nitrogen narcoses reaction, I'm thankful that my heart and mind tuned to thoughts of Christ; the picture is engraved there . . . of being *In the Safety of His Wings.*

16

Award Ceremony

What, No God?

We were on our way to the National Aeronautics Association's Awards Banquet in Washington DC. The other part of the "we" was Allison's Director of Public Relations. Suddenly, I needed a babysitter on Trans World Airlines! It took me some time to gauge exactly why he was along. I assumed it was to keep the corporate nose clean and see to it I didn't insert my foot-in-mouth.

Upon entering the banquet room, I was stripped from his protection and given a seat with others who would receive awards. By chance, I had the opportunity to sit at one of two tables for eight in front of a lustrous head table that included: Vice President Hubert Humphrey, Charles Lindbergh, General Jimmy Stewart and Bob Hope. Oh, they weren't there for us helicopter jocks. They were there to hear and honor our guest speaker who was also sitting at my table, Col. Neil Armstrong. Neil had just completed a two week quarantine being the first man to set foot on the moon. He would be making his first public appearance since returning to Earth. I noticed Mr. Public Relations, seated toward the rear, seemed to be drooling in his meal.

This was an outstanding opportunity; Madalyn Murray O'Hair had just badgered the US Supreme Court into throwing prayer out of public schools. Now she was back on her broom, petitioning the court to kick Bible reading out of space. The first Apollo Mission to orbit the Moon occurred last Christmas Eve and found the crew quoting Scripture, "In the beginning, God created Heaven and Earth. . . ."Part of her thesis was supposedly that Neil Armstrong was believed to be one her fellow atheists. Discussion at the table was already lively; I could hardly wait to hear his presentation!

133

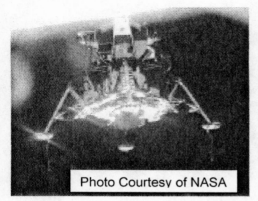
Photo Courtesy of NASA

Col. Armstrong described his descent from the Orbiter Vehicle as one continuous series of problems and wasn't able to look out either of his two side windows until the landing module was righting itself in the automatic mode. "I glanced out and saw giant boulders . . . the size of cars and trucks," Neil vividly painted. "Realizing I was on the edge of a crater, I elected to utilize my God-given right and take over in the manual mode to hover to a clear area." He continued, ". . . The final seconds fuel exhaustion warning sounded, I don't know who landed the ship!" Col. Armstrong concluded.

I still don't know what Neil's religious beliefs are but that certainly didn't sound like an atheist to me! I never again heard Madelyn take on NASA; in fact, a few years later, NO one heard from HER.

A Corporate Offer

I can't remember exactly where in the ceremony our bunch stood to receive our 19 records. My two were for the Lightweight and Unlimited World Helicopter Closed Course Distance Records. Howard Hughes had us each presented with a beautiful Atmos trophy clock, mine still sits on our fireplace mantle. With all the accolades floating around, my PR man was anxious to get enroute toward home.

The night before the presentations, to impress me, he took me to the Rotunda Restaurant. On entering, he showed me how to get a good seat in the best place in town. "I'm DOCTOR _____", he told the Maitre de. We received a prestige seat . . . next to the restrooms, right alongside all the other "doctors". On departure Mr. PR, who suggested I join the health club with his fellow "executives", flexed his prowess to the doorman when asking for a cab. As the door was opened, four other guys piled in and pulled the door shut. Mr. PR stuck his arm through the window and grabbed one of the rowdies, who immediately rolled the window up, jamming his muscular arm in the cab . . . that dragged him several feet before discharging him. I have to admit, it was VERY impressive.

Once more on TWA, the PR man made a surprising offer. "Jack, the Corporation would like you back in school to obtain your master's degree. What would it take to get the job done?"

134

This was the height of one-ups-man-ship; he was certainly a master of that game. "Well, I only have two years of college (that was pushing it), I could probably get credit for my aviation ratings and test out of a few aviation courses at Purdue, possibly one year for my Bachelor's . . . and then whatever it takes for the Master's." I concluded.

"In your case GM might be willing to foot the bill for you being gone. Can you do it?" he baited.

"Probably, but I proved to myself years ago I'm not interested in becoming a pure engineer." I hesitantly responded, "If flying folds here at Allison, I'm ready to sell real estate."

"OK, we can move you to ARGONUT, our real-estate department in GM, or how about in our own Sales Department?" Mr. PR added.

Allowing a significant time for considering the travel potential and propensity of heavy drinking in corporate sales, I concluded the conversation with, "No, thanks, I don't think I can be trusted there. I passed up the Air Force Test Pilot School once to stay with my family. My family still comes first." A book entitled, *The Peter Principle* was written about advancing on the corporate ladder one rung above your true capacity. I was probably already standing on that rung . . . and didn't want to fall off!

The rest of the trip home was quiet. Apparently the PR man still went back with a good report and the company must have held me in some esteem. Two months later I was bannered, full page, advertising in dozens of magazines around the world, from National Geographic to Reader's Digest . . . as an example of "General Motor's Mark of Excellence." That's a heck of a title to emulate.

Jack's Had!

Everyone knew Jack was in trouble. The hangar was almost empty now. During lunchtime, for over a month, I had been starting tomato seedlings in old file trays . . . arranged by category in empty file cabinets during their incubation period. Once they sprouted, I moved them up several flights of steel stairs, across an open catwalk the full length of the hangar bay and up two more flights stairs into our abandoned control tower. Man, what a green house! It was complete with table space, three-hundred-sixty

degrees around beneath twelve-foot high windows. I even installed a garden hose for running water to feed the 4,000 plants. What a production facility! Then, in walked the Chief Test Engineer to examine the tower, Bob Hicks, the man who hired me and said I was going to be the start of the new Breed. Instead, I just became a full-fledged member of the old Flight Test "Country Club"!

The only thing that probably saved me from being canned that day was that I had just been touted internationally as "General Motors Mark of Excellence" in 57 different magazines around the world (Ha!) and a fact I learned later . . . Mr. Hick's hobby may have been raising African Violets. On his dramatic departure he said, "Get that mess out of here today, and . . . they need more light!" I don't remember any more hi-jinks, I'm wondering if one of my cohorts squealed! God has ways of keeping us humble.

PR 16:18 Pride goes before destruction, a haughty spirit before a fall.

Management Stress

I soon learned the trauma in dealing with two types of management stress; the first from working with no direct supervision and then working under direct adverse management. Our staff at flight test was cut to a dozen. John Orr became superintendent of maintenance, Bill Long and Lou Esenwein became equals in engineering and I was put on a like level as pilot. Four of us left as "friends" on the same footing in a hangar isolated from whomever we individually reported to miles away. I always thought we were established as someone's thesis project in demented psychology. When we queried the head-shed about the matter,

management just replied, "Supervision will rise from your ranks." sounded a lot like cannibalism to me.

Within a couple of months we managed to work out a mutual relationship. The four of us pretty well stayed out of each other's way. Then, along came "OPERATION PACE". One of Allison's

136

sixty-some Prop-Jet Convair aircraft conversions suffered a serious accident. One of its two massive propeller systems failed and exploded through the cabin of the fifty passenger aircraft . . . maiming several before the plane recovered to the ground. Operation Pace would find our little crew removing two engines and propellers for repair at the main plant, reinstalling two a day in another aircraft while inspecting and flight testing a third . . . effectively turning around one full aircraft per day, a massive project!

In sixty days every one was exhausted. One man even gave his life for it. At the program's tail end, I arrived home from work when we heard an ambulance siren wailing up and down our side streets. It sounded like it was searching for a ghost ship lost at sea. The phone rang. It was Bill's wife. He had just suffered a heart attack and was lying unconscious on the floor . . . she'd already called the rescue squad. I didn't tell her we had heard the truck but they were lost. We only lived a few blocks away. Sharon and I got there before the ambulance. They arrived a few minutes later confused in their search for a street address that was split by the Speedway Park. There was never a thought that an earlier arrival would have helped. Bill hit the floor with all of his near 300 pounds and never moved, a "massive heart attack". Everyone at the hangar knew Bill had worked his heart out and we knew what killed Bill . . . stress. It took eight of us to move him to the ambulance. Sharon had the biggest job, to comfort the children; I had one I couldn't handle.

Following the vehicle to the hospital, his wife asked me a stabbing question . . . "Jack, is he in heaven?" I couldn't answer her. After all, I had been pitted by management as one of his stress risers and had been a very poor witness of the gospel. I'd let them down. She expected me know his relationship with the Lord. I trust this incident changed my life message to become outgoing for Christ. I began by placing a small 12-point typewritten label on the cockpit panel of the company's next aircraft, reading, "This flight may be terminal. Do you know for certain you would go to Heaven? John 3:16". More later. . . .

17

Stable of Aircraft

Management Stress - Advanced

With the advent of Bill's death, my renegade tomato plant crop, my rejection of school and grooming for a management position, we continued to operate without onsite supervision. Until . . . the appearance of "The Big Major". He showed up on the ramp one day and told some of the maintenance people, "I'm going to run this Flight Test Center soon". As accurately as the Bible foretells the future, he reappeared in a few days to be introduced by our vice-president as, "You're new Manager of Flight Test". Big Major was one of our Army team that had set the OH-6A records at Edwards. It seemed that, the corporation put more value on those awards than I had considered. Suddenly I was inducted back into the military. I'd made the rounds, starting in the Navy, to the Air Force and now sucked under Army command.

No, he wasn't in the military anymore; he swapped it for General Motors but treated us all like "boots". He ordered the plant Security Guard to answer all phone calls as his receptionist, a job not in their union classification . . . management wouldn't give him a private secretary, a perk reserved for executives; he wasn't one. This little action started a steamroller against him. I learned early why he had resigned from the Army; he became emotionally unstable in the air. On an early flight, we were to go to 10,000'. When reaching 6,000' he suggested we go back for a meeting he had "forgotten". I replied, "We can keep going up on the way back and record our 10,000' point without losing much time".

He responded, "MR SCHWEIBOLD, I'm ordering you DOWN, NOW!" I headed down immediately. It was only a few minutes flight. He ran from the same type of ship he had set a low level record in . . . and tossed his lunch in the grass. No wonder the Army assigned all record attempts above 10,000' to the civilian test pilots. He never flew with me again and he would only take short low-altitude administrative flights. Big Major began screwing our thumbs in a vice by imposing severe rules on all classifications in the hangar. At the same time, he expanded his arrogant behavior, such as having his personal lawn mower repaired by maintenance and having them build his wife's nursery school projects.

One day, Lou and I were ground-running an airworthy helicopter on the far side of the ramp. Instead of having a mechanic push it back to the hangar door, we air taxied at 3' high across to the hangar. After shutting down and walking in, each of us dripping sweat from sitting in the sun for an hour, he bellowed over the hangar speaker system, "Schweibold and Esenwein, report to my office at once!" We stepped into his office and were dressed down like recruits for a half hour on the seriousness

Lou Esenwein was a crack engineer and good friend

of our "Unauthorized Flight". Afterwards Lou and I were both in the washroom and found to our dismay, we were standing looking at each other . . . urinating in the round mechanics sink . . . not the urinals! The "Major" had so completely managed to unnerve us that we lost control of our senses. What would we do wrong next . . . in the COCKPIT?

We vowed this would have to end. I don't know what Lou did but I went to prayer. Mathew 5:44 states,

"But I tell you: Love your enemies and pray for those who persecute you, that you may be sons of your Father in heaven".

I claimed that verse and learned to live it out. I soon saw the frailty in this shallow man as Sharon and I prayed for him and began to see him in a new light through Christ's eyes. I was suffering one of the worst summer colds and was grounded for the first time by my flight surgeon . . . for a week. We had been scheduled for a 20,000' test flight in a Bell Oh-58, the Army Scout. Big Major said he would take the flight but kept delaying it. Finally, I was told later, management ordered him to make it, "We hired you as Schweibold's back up, now back him up!" they said. I wasn't even at work, but home with an upper sinus infection. I'd never said a word about Big Major's fear of flying. That would have been sour grapes . . . maybe I should have.

140

A few days later when I got back to work, the men told me he had trouble with the flight but without detail. I felt shut out. I immediately completed the flight and the necessary airstarts without incident. Big Major was as flamboyant as ever . . . even while removing a welding project of oil drums for his kid's jungle gym play yard. Then one morning, he didn't come to work. I was called later in the day and directed, "You are in charge until further notice."

Then the maintenance men told me about his 20,000' flight. "He launched with oxygen mask on, was gone only 20 minutes and he came back at high speed and low level", Murray Griggs told me. "He touched down on the skids at about 25 knots, bounced along the concrete and came to a stop sidewise . . . FROZEN to the controls. Once shut down, we pried him out of the cockpit," he continued. "What happened?" they asked him.

"Well, I was nervous and breathed 100% oxygen, with extra safety pressure from takeoff. At 10,000 feet, I ran out of altitude, oxygen and GUTS . . . all at the same time," he reluctantly admitted.

"Jack, we know you were dealing with this for months," Murray continued. "So-o, we took it in our own hands to report things as we saw them, doing his personal work projects and what he told us on landing. Sorry, but you must stay out of this process." Murray ended.

In a couple days I received a call at home from Big Major. He asked me to intercede for him. I really had compassion for his situation but when attempting to mediate, management ordered me to stay out of the equation and not speak to him again. He was gone, in less than ten days . . . after I had gotten MY heart right. Two other managers were later removed in similar fashion. God answers prayer and is in control, even when all else fails. His power is awesome!

PS 66:3 Say to God, "How awesome are your deeds! So great is your power that your enemies cringe before you.

RO 8:28 And we know that in all things God works for the good of those who love him, who have been called according to His purpose.

Aircraft Stable

By this time I had my own stable of aircraft, five helicopters, a Cessna 402 twin engine . . . and if you can believe it, a little L-19 with 420 turbine horsepower, which only took a couple hundred feet for near vertical take-off! The corporation effectively left me as the lone pilot at the airport . . . until the Blue Ribbon Program came along. We bought Bell Helicopter's 98th production Jet Ranger and moved the engine's time between overhaul (TBO) from 500 to 750 hours. To fanfare this new engine, containing many improved features and parts, we flew the ship 12 hours a day, seven days a week until we hit 750 hours.

Obviously, I wasn't going to keep my feet in all seven aircraft and fly around the clock; even Carleton Heston didn't ride that many chariots as Ben Hur. Therefore, we brought back three employees who had worked ten years previously as pilots during the "Country Club Era". Rolly Martin, Bill Gibboney and Colonel Petercheff; all were eager to get back in the cockpit and happily submitted to the helicopter transition, even trained by the newer kid on the block. While they were excellent pilots in fixed wing aircraft, I don't believe they were ever totally comfortable in the helicopter . . . but we were able to get through the 750 hours quickly and without incident.

To break up the monotony and subject the engine to various operational environments, we covered almost all 48 states and landed at all

registered airports in Indiana. Bill was probably the most excitable of the crew. He appeared to continuously toy with his pipe to cover it up. One fine late summer day we headed to a Hughes helicopter for a training flight. On the way out I told him to preflight the ship. I had forgotten an item. He was ready for startup when I came back and threw a handful of gunny sacks in the backseat. "What are those for?" he asked.

"Oh, the sweet corn is coming in, we'll find a field and pick some," I casually replied.

"We'll WHAT!" he sparked back.

"We're gon'na pic sum korn," I drawled back.

"We can't do that!" he defensively replied. Bill was a good man.

"A'h duz it avery yeah!" I continued to twang as we started westbound, scouting the cornfields at low altitude. "Se, dat stuff beelow, tit'z feel'd co'n."

"How can you tell field corn from sweet corn up here?" he responded in amazement, starting to look in earnest himself.

"Ah'z trained mah eyez ov'ah da seasons." as I finally spotted my quarry, "we'z land'n now fo dat zweet gold stuff!" Bill didn't want to land, so I took us down.

"We're too close to town," Bill argued. "We'll, be caught."

"Naw, we won be kaught, we'z be FAZT! Here, grab a couple of bags and start pick'n." I directed as the rotors were coasting down. "Work from inside rows out so you don't have to carry the bags so far to the ship." We worked diligently and in just a few minutes we had both of our bags full, at least I did. Bill was doing more looking than picking.

Then he hollered, "THE FARMER'S COMING! Look, he's got . . . got a GUN!" I finished topping my bag while Bill opened the door; he'd dropped his bags in the stalks.

"GO get your bags, I'm not leaving with half a load," I shouted while stuffing my bags in the back. I'll crank her up while you load yours."

Bill scampered back into the rows, wishing he'd brought them out the first time. I looked over my shoulder as I heard him open the door. It wasn't a gun the farmer was carrying; it was a pitchfork.

He grabbed Bill by the arm and asked, "What do you have in that bag, it looks heavy?" Bill was terrified as he turned and saw . . . our old retired aircraft mechanic, Gene Fouch. Bill quickly transitioned from scared to MAD to uncontrolled laughter. We all had a good laugh as we thanked Gene for my annual supply of corn. This year our three boys would get their first sales training . . . selling it door-to-door for a buck a dozen.

Old Pete had the most unusual landing in Indiana. He touched down in the center of a remote grass strip and lit up a cigarette to relax for a minute. While the engine and rotor were still running, a girl came out of the woods, walked up to the door and motioned to talk. Pete, not taken back by much, opened the door but turned down her invitation to meet her group . . . she was standing stark naked! He had unknowingly landed at Roselawn Airport, a nudist colony, home of the Annual Miss Nude Pageant. In Pete's daily Pilot Report, he noted he made a speedy departure.

After two short months, these pilots returned to their jobs within our other plants. Rolly and Bill retired. Col. Pete went on as a weekend warrior to become the commanding General of the Indiana Air Guard. He gave his life for his country . . . killed when landing his F-100 on a snow-covered runway. Gene Fouch continued to supply us with corn until his and Ruby's 40 acres became a housing development. I was privileged to preach his funeral, as he had become a fellow believer in his later years. Gene had planted many seeds for us, but he became God's harvest.

Making Snow

Who ever would have thought that our old shopping center Snow Ball Drops would escalate into the real thing? About this time, just a couple seasons after Bell, Hiller and Hughes began delivering Allison turbine helicopters, a few of these ships started falling out of the sky; akin to Chicken Little running around in circles on the ground . . . clucking loudly, "The sky is falling, the sky is falling!" Yes, we had blacked the sky with helicopters but now part of that sky WAS falling.

One of the first candidates for examination was the Hiller FH-1100. During test cell certification, the engine was subject to water ingestion and inlet distortion duplicating the heaviest known water flow in the atmosphere. In real life, water injection is even provided as an option for some turbine engines to reduce inlet temperature and create more horsepower. Shouldn't snow give the same advantage?

The challenge was to produce snow on the hangar ramp. Hiller, being in sunny Palo Alto, California, sent us one of their test ships. All we had to do was tie it to the concrete and feed it snow during our colder Indianapolis winter. As the engineers invented new delivery methods, we'd test them.

The first test rig was pretty crude, a series of conveyers running up from a shaved ice truck into the front of a large electric ducted fan. The engine inlet sat above the cabin near the main rotor, large flexible ducting directed the shaved ice flow into and around the engine inlet. An onlooker might have conceived the picture of a charging, fire-snorting dragon attempting to be quenched with a Rube Goldberg ice-spitting wagon . . . operated by the Keystone Cops. It choked the dinosaur alright, but it was determined shaved ice was not a representative testing element.

How about visiting a ski slope? Our closest one was at the "monstrous" 300' high Mt. Paoli in Southern Indiana. We flew into the slope but they couldn't help us. It was too warm, but they would rent us the nozzle to make snow on our ramp. Our first lesson learned, snow nozzles just made fluffier ice. At least it wasn't clogging up in massive ice chunks capable of doing physical damage to the thin compressor vanes. Soon we were able to produce an occasional flameout. A set of small viewing windows were installed just in front of the engine compressor, directly behind the aircraft screen. As the screen became blocked, a camera filmed ice melt as it passed through the screen, freezing on its rear side … eventually breaking off and entering the engine to produce a FLAMEOUT!

This was the first proof snow/ice particles in chunk volume could quench the engine. Until now, they blamed the engine but in real life, the airframe was throwing ice particles and snowballs at us. That was a no-no. The engine was to be furnished clean, ambient air by the aircraft inlet. The company was very liberal in helping test the helicopter manufactures final design, not on the ramp but in the air! That didn't mean the managers who volunteered would do the flying. It meant who? Just me and Engineer Lou!

Finding Snow

The basic cure for keeping snow and ice chunks out of the engine was to install a reverse baffle in front of the inlets during recognized or forecast snowfall. This baffle effectively caused the inflow air to pass behind the airframe inlet, to be turned 180 degrees, entering the inlet from the rear. By turning the air abruptly, the heavier water/snow/ice continues aft and is augmented away from the engine inlet; this proved fairly effective. The final proof, however, could only be proven by flight in actual snowfall . . . easier said than done.

I was soon to develop a nose for finding snowfall . . . initially, we zeroed in on International Falls, Minnesota. Other test crews would become friends there, testing products from aircraft to cars and Die-Hard batteries. We met many border Americans,

While snow sometimes piled above our ships in Indy, Harry Sutton and I still needed to hunt it!

Canadians and Alaskan Americans, finding all to be a generous and hospitable group living a rigorous life fueled by hard work and a good measure of natural wit.

Waiting for snow was a headache. Even with the best in forecast capability, the difference between no snow and heavy snow only needs to be a degree or two in temperature or dew point. And just what was

146

suitable snow? Over the years we proved it to be when the visibility in falling snow was less than ¼ mile and not too cold, somewhere above 20 degrees F. When it was very cold, the snow normally stayed in its freefall state, chunks didn't build up anywhere ahead of the engine . . . the engine happily ingested it.

The quarter mile visibility in falling snow was the real show stopper. That's pretty heavy stuff. We had to wait a long time for that window and on many trips we never found it. When we did find the quarter mile snowfall, then the chore began. It didn't generally last long. Visualize flying in blinding snow at cruise speeds up to 160mph with cloud bases squeezing us down to just fifty or a hundred feet above the ground . . . that's right, we couldn't see a thing. The ground is covered with snow, the air is full of snow, and we'd be in a WHITEOUT! Nighttime, fortunately, was better than day. In the winter they only had a few hours of daylight. Our cruise speed dropped to 40-60 miles/hour . . . and we still couldn't see.

The remedy was that we flew along the runway, groping for each runway light. In addition, we lit dozens of oil flare pots set a couple hundred feet apart in the turns to bring us back to the light rows. We literally flew from light to light, pot to pot on a circular course, night and day. Until . . . until we realized that one of these times we would have a flameout and have to land . . . at the only spot visible, the fire pot! With an impending crash and spilled fuel . . . we immediately changed to battery-powered lanterns. God was gracious; we survived a handful of low-level snow flameouts to the ground.

During these trips we'd cut through 51 inches of blue steel ice with a 52" auger to fish for Walleye and Pike, to see them flip only once or twice before becoming frozen rigid at 30 degrees below zero on the surface. We chased mother bears and their cubs; flew formation with migrating geese and ducks; and survived an overnighter in a stagnant trappers cabin that lacked bathing privileges for the winter . . . eventually sleeping in our ship and sleeping bags on the center of a frozen lake, willing to trade warmth for fresh air. By chance, our son Mark would have one of his first job opportunities running a night freight flight company with a man who would marry one of the Scandinavian girls whose father ran the Falls airport. We thought snow flameouts would be a problem, but they only expanded our horizons . . . and trust in Him.

World's Largest Ice Machine

As one of the two largest ice test rigs in the world, this one is located in Ottawa, Canada, the other is in Russia. This was the scene of our most demanding ice/snow test. Water is sprayed from several thousand nozzles on this giant bed spring assembly capable of accommodating over half a 747 aircraft. As water droplets are dispersed into ambient air at -5 degrees F or lower into a light wind of 3 to 8 knots, the trailing super-cooled cloud produced here duplicates the heaviest moisture found in our atmosphere. By air-taxing beneath the cloud we pulled the moisture over the engine inlets, in 30 seconds, power required to hover doubled. When blade angle was reduced to land, one blade shed its ice and so unbalanced the main rotor it was going to self-destruct in 3-4 revolutions . . . when the other blade shed its load and the system regained balance just before touchdown! God's timing is always perfect!

18

The Family Matters

Building our Hot Tub

The kids were growing like bean sprouts; Scott was 8, Mark 6 and Brad 3. We built an in-ground swimming pool . . . by hand . . . behind our tri-level in Speedway, Indiana. By hand, I mean our crew mixed and poured every scoop of sand, stone and concrete. Sharon spent more than her share of time behind the shovel. The real test came when we hit water at four feet; it became a mosquito infested mud hole the rest of the way. We did hire the backhoe man to dig it out and haul the dirt away but we were left to hand dig the bottom pad and concrete footings for sidewalls, underwater. By the time it was finished we were all ready to pass the swimming test . . . two lengths of the pool to qualify for deep end privileges. Even Brad passed. Everyone became excellent swimmers.

Right after the pool was finished, we erected a 6' privacy fence on the tight, 125' deep lot. This helped keep out the wandering basketballs from the hoop fanatics living behind us. We could still see a new barrage of construction trucks that roamed the neighborhood. Two weeks after the last gate was hung on the fence; one of the  trucks stopped at our house and asked if we'd had any recent digging on the property. "Well, we did sink an 8 ½' deep pool and privacy fence", I responded.

Their inspection of the fence line proved we had severed the neighborhood telephone trunk line. Later we received a bill for half the cost of the pool, $4,500, the amount lost by the phone company for the lines being down two and a half weeks. It didn't even include time lost in search and repair by their men. Fortunately, our homeowner's liability policy paid off like a liberal slot machine. Verbal gibes from the family, reminding me they had pointed to the "Call Before Digging" sign on the telephone pole . . . eventually faded to a whisper.

Owning the first pool on the block was a neighborhood novelty. In the first week, we had dozens of kids show up, towel and float toys in hand. If the boys wanted them in, we welcomed them until . . . one family of six, including mother and father knocked on the door, all dressed for a pool day. They were from a block away, no one knew them . . . and we still don't! New rules were established. The most cost effective was, "Bring your own food and drinks".

Time to Change Churches - Again

After a day of fishing, the old girl was blasting across Lake Erie from Put-In-Bay to Toledo in a 19-foot fishing boat one dark night. Mom Cordrey was sitting in the center seat with her friend Bud at the motor in the back and another man in the front bow seat. For some unknown reason . . . something you don't pry into with your mom . . . they torpedoed a 36' cruiser; a direct hit amid ship! Thrown into the hull of the cruiser headfirst, Mom was knocked unconscious. Bud, swimming for survival, passed through her hair, grabbed a big handful and pulled her to the listing cruiser. With the smaller boat penetrating below the waterline, the man in front was pinned and died before the coastguard arrived.

Mom was already in a pickle. A few years earlier, she had divorced my stepfather and her shoe stores were nearing bankruptcy. With acute sympathy setting in, accented by his love . . . Bud married her. They moved 40 miles east to Freemont and rented a nice old house near the center of town. Shortly following this period, she had a damaging stroke, leaving her weak and slow of speech. Earlier she had severed her Achilles tendon in a freak accident, a bottle fell off a store shelf, shattered and cut that dude right in two. The stroke further accented her limp; all totaled, she was a basket case. Knowing she needed God, I asked our Pastor in a little Baptist Church in Indianapolis just what in the Bible would be appropriate for her. I should have known, after all I was a deacon . . . it was my turn. "Stick to the New Testament," he replied and walked off. I knew I was in trouble.

The next week I hit him again, "Which verses?"

"Try the book of John." he shakily said. Now I knew we were ALL in trouble. I went home and packed up my family to look for a Bible preaching church . . . we found one 10 miles west in Brownsburg, Indiana. Two miles out of the "Berg" was a young pastor preaching the Word of God at Bethesda Baptist Church.

A short time later, doctors diagnosed Bud with Pancreatic Cancer. They both needed help; they were losing patience with each other. Bud escaped to our house for a short time, where he heard and accepted the Gospel. He died within a couple months. The Freemont house burned to the ground a month later and mom moved in with us. Everything went well for three months. Her health improved a little to where she HAD to get out and was able to live near us on her own 12 years. She eventually improved to where she could sell houses in our building business, she always said, "A Schweibold is a born salesman!"

This permitted her to replenish her savings and return to Toledo where she died at 67. Her last few days were again enjoyed on the water, fishing with my brother Robert at his cabin in Canada. Did it pay to change churches? You bet! In the first year, Pastor Don Tyler showed up on our doorstep with a record by Jack Hyles, *"How to Lead a Person to the Lord"* and weekly preached a similar message from the pulpit. Both Bud and Mom said, "Yes" to Jesus Christ. If the Word's not preached, it's time to change churches.

Rom10: 13 "Everyone who calls on the name of the Lord will be saved. 14 How, then, can they call on the one they have not believed in? And how can they believe in the one of whom they have not heard? And how can they hear without someone preaching to them?"

Green Acres

It was time to move. Living in town with three active "all boy" boys, led to occasional flare-ups: such as, when a back lot caught fire when one of them experimented with matches. They all enjoyed the fire trucks. That night the guilty one fell asleep, exhausted from his punishment; lighting a whole carton of book matches at my feet. We never burned down another field.

Our young men would be bullied and then accused of brotherly gang action while defending each other. We did the "good parent" routines.

Sharon participated in coop pre-school and I was Big Chief in an "Indian Guides" YMCA group. We kept them active in Peanut League Football and Baseball, where most abuse came from parents directed at their own children.

Mischief soon drew the boys to the local stores and shopping malls . . . where they were bound to get into the same kind of problems I almost didn't survive. It was time to move but I found it wasn't going to be easy. Sharon was tickled pink to have a bunch of friends close at hand. She'd had some lonely years in Chicago and she wasn't biting on my idea of moving to the country! There wasn't much support for my interest until we endured looting. We were robbed twice.

Flying slowed down at Allison. I decided to augment our income potential by going into real estate sales, that would get me closer to country properties. After passing the State Licensing Test, I secured a moonlight position as sales agent with our local bank in Speedway. Traipsing through farms would become our way of life for the next five years. The *Green Acres* TV Sitcom was currently on tube with Eddie Albert playing the part of the dumb city slicker, "Jack", and socialite, Zaza Gabor, carrying the roll of "Sharon". Sharon didn't deserve the moniker … but Jack fit the dumb part well. This show was not well received in our home. Each day as we drove Westward to look at another piece of acreage, the rest of the family learned to echo in unison, "Oh, no-o, not again!"

Sharon would start evaluating the property before seeing it, "Too far out, no neighbors, no church, NO!" The boys became more discriminating, "No trees to climb, no hills, no room for horses, no creek or pond, LET'S GO HOME!" My comments revolved around the potential for profit, "Not enough road frontage, too deep to build a road, no opportunity to develop." Sharon hated the old farm houses. She couldn't get me to fix what we already had. A couple "oldies" we visited were so weathered, we could have popped the lid off a 55-gallon drum of paint and the house would have sucked the paint out of the drum! The boys wanted a few playmates; they were already trying to murder each other while locked in the back seat, three abreast looking for property every day. For five years we all said, "NO!"

Then one day Sharon and I stumbled on a bowling alley lot, a strip of unrefined farm ground 1330 feet long and 165 feet wide . . . of absolutely no value to develop. We set out on the quarter mile hike to the back. First, we crossed a few hundred feet of open ground, "Ideal for a large garden", was about the best I could come up with.

Crossing a small ravine, "Can't get a road over this gully," Sharon quickly pointed out".

Halfway back we came to a 100' near vertical cliff, "Never get a path down this baby!" I conceded. Stumbling and scratching for a foothold we careened to the bottom of a valley, "Useless 300' of flood plain," I added.

"We can't cross this creek, we'll get soaked," Sharon concluded when reaching the water.

It took us ten minutes to scale back up to the top of the hill. Winded, we sat in the grassy meadow under a huge native Sugar Maple tree to get our breath. "Well, if you are going to move me . . . this is it!" Sharon said. Thank goodness I was sitting down; otherwise I would have fallen down faint! "Four strips have already sold; I'll have some neighbors. Only two miles from shopping in Brownsburg, we'll have food. The schools are good for the boys . . . and the lot is so narrow you can't develop it and move us next month."

"No one will ever build behind or in front of us; we can place the house on the cliff, no more bouncing basketballs at midnight." I added, "All we have to do is buy an extra acre or so. Then we can get beyond the front ravine to build a driveway."

Laying there on our backs, looking up through the maple boughs, we jointly decided . . . "We'll buy it!" Once the boys were turned loose, they found almost 400 acres of varied wilderness to explore; they heartily agreed with the decision, knowing the daily search would end. Never did we dream that Green Acres would become Happy Acres for so many years. If God can prepare something so special, how easy it is to understand Christ's words:

Jn 14: 2 In my Father's house are many rooms; if it were not so, I would have told you. I am going there to prepare a place for you. [3] And if I go and prepare a place for you, I will come back and take you to be with me that you also may be where I am.

19

Airstarts - -
My Way of Life

Engineering set out to design an automatic re-ignition system. This devise would automatically relight the engine should the fire be snuffed out by momentary interruption of airflow or fuel. I had become extremely proficient in getting through a normal pilot activated restart sequence; most pilots didn't even consider this option. The Army, in fact, taught their pilots to forget this lifesaving maneuver when below 500 feet. They were to concentrate on the impending landing . . . or crash if over water, trees or rough terrain.

The pilot's response to engine failure in most installations was generally:

- Reduce collective pitch to enter autorotation
- Control the aircraft descent
- Turn the throttle off
- Allow the engine to decelerate below 20% compressor speed
- Turn off the generator switch (a difficult task, on some models it was located above the pilots head. I defy you to take your eyes off the up-coming ground to find that switch ... while trying to find a landing area)
- Hit and hold the starter switch
- Check the engine compressor speed to be above 12-15% speed
- Open the throttle to idle
- If the engine recovers, increase the throttle and make a normal landing when able OR
- Make the emergency landing without power

When initially training our own test pilots or other professional pilots, I would have them study the procedures in the handbook, review it hands-on in the cockpit, demonstrate the maneuver to them in flight, and then take them to a mile above the ground. There, I'd shut the engine down while they were flying. In almost EVERY case they still ended up without the engine reengaged ON THE GROUND. Maybe the Army was right; forget restarting below 500'!

Restarts could not cover all contingencies, such as broken starter shafts, dead batteries, blown compressors, turbine rupture or other catastrophic hardware failures. An automatic re-ignition system, however, could save a high percentage of the engine-out conditions the fleet was then encountering.

When this little engine quit on its own merit, it decelerated faster than a normal power reduction; therefore, it was easy for the engineers to develop a set of algorithms and a little black box to turn the igniters on to relight the engine. We set out to test such a system. The big danger was that if the engine indiscreetly ignited, it might have a power surge, producing an over torque in the engine and aircraft rotor drives. In lay terms, it may rip the rotors off!

Held Together By ...

While the Instrumentation Laboratory installed strain gages on critical compressor, turbine, main rotor and tail rotor drive shafts to record torque

stress during auto-relights, we set to develop a method of flaming the engine out without cutting the fuel supply. We'd already determined the amount of water that would choke the flame almost every time. All we had to do was shoot that slug into the inlet and we'd quiet the little rascal. We installed a "U" shaped clear plastic hose on a plywood board with graduated markings for measuring the H_2O. It was placed between the pilot and flight engineer's front seat position. We hooked up a portable water bottle for ammunition with a regulated pressure nitrogen bottle for propellant. After measuring a water charge into the tube, a switch on the pilot's controls fired it into the compressor inlet. Nursery school "Quiet Time" followed.

Seems like a simple test. What could go wrong? Well, if the compressor shaft snapped, the turbine might instantly run over speed, exploding and potentially taking out the fuel tanks. This was reminiscent

156

of my first day at Allison when the engine blew up . . . ala "There She Blows!" Severing the main rotor drive shaft might drop the blades through the cockpit, guillotine style; giving us a new free fall drop record exceeding any amusement park thrill ride. A tail rotor loss in flight would generate a dicey landing or if actually separated from the ship, shift the center of gravity so far forward we might tumble helplessly through the air.

Prayer was in order. I believe He gave us a set of crack engineers at all levels. To better the odds of personal survival, this test began on tie-down. Everything progressed well. We started the relights at low power, and examined data recorded on a high speed ossillograph before proceeding higher. We looked like a set of doctors examining an electrocardiogram printout from a heart stricken elephant.

All power points were passed within the appropriate manufacturers allowable limits. It was time for flight. We hadn't really considered the advantage of stiffness that being tied to of the ENTIRE EARTH had given. On our very first set of flight power points called back to one airframe manufacturer . . . they yelled STOP!!!!!!!!!

As power was disrupted in flameout, the drive train which had been under oscillatory loads was instantly unloaded . . . producing a backlash torsional cycling on some critical components. The tail rotor drive shaft, being some 18' long was the most severely affected. Much like twanging a thick rubber band under tension . . . you can even see the vibration of the rubber band. The problem was that a relight on the torsional stress upswing reinforced the stress on the rotor beyond desired limits.

This important finding permitted us to install a millisecond time delay in the black box, tailored for each model helicopter. This delay gave us a system that was so efficient the pilot might not even recognize the flameout; therefore, we installed a pilot cancelable warning light, alerting him to the possibility he may be flying in snow or other hazardous situations producing a flameout.

We completed hundreds and thousands of relights each on several different models of helicopters; in all, over 5,000 restarts . . . God did hold all pieces together.

One of His most precious axioms is found in Col 1:17, "All things are held together through Jesus Christ".

NEXT – Envision God's Power

Envision Power

When we see God answer prayer, we have the opportunity to witness His raw power. For instance, seeing Christ's ability to hold all things together gave me the privilege of considering the reverse side. Being ten as the nuclear age was born, I had an early life in the shadow of an atomic cloud. My Uncle Chuck was aboard the ill-fated USS Indianapolis which had delivered the second A-bomb destined for Japan. He spent five days in the water fighting sharks after the ship was torpedoed by the Japanese . . . as the mushroom cloud rose above Nagasaki, only 300 or so of his 1200 man crew survived.

While in service I left Sharon and the boys a couple of times when scrambled into action on Red Alert, assuming Russia had already launched their intercontinental missiles. It's disquieting . . . heading out into the Pacific with blast curtains up to protect your eyes from atomic explosions . . . knowing your family has been left home defenseless.

The plutonium in those WWII Atomic weapons only weighed about eight pounds, the weight of a man's arm. If we consider Christ holding all electrons & protons together in that eight pounds of plutonium *(Colossians 1:17b)*, we can examine the antonym (opposite) and see His power as he allows them to separate, resulting in an atomic explosion. One of the first Russian cosmonauts into space said, "I looked around but couldn't see God." There must have been a pretty liberal eye test in the Soviet Union. It's hard to look anywhere with an open mind and NOT see God. Check out Psalm 8 and Psalm 19.

PS 19:1 The heavens declare the glory of God; the skies proclaim the work of his hands.

False Prophets

As the Army continued to develop their new T63 model engine, the rigors of Vietnamese combat dictated we look at removing much of the air chamber circuitry in the fuel control system and use fuel as a "cleaner" metering media. This new concept Fuel Control System was designed and built in Connecticut. One of their engineers would spend weekly periods with us at Flight test while we balanced critical parameters.

This engineer became an intellectual element our program had never before encountered. He was a mathematical genius but seemed to miss the common sense approach of flight test . . . "seeing is believing!" Strapping him in the ship, then running him down the White River combat course below treetop level, quickly convinced him that rapid control response was necessary . . . bringing reason to an otherwise naive analytical approach.

The next couple of weeks he seemed to lessen his criticism of our evaluations as he withdrew into a reclusive attitude. Subsequently, one Monday he came in, announced dramatically with effusive emphasis, "I won't be with you much longer; my wife and I are selling our home and all belongings to help maintain those going to the mountain with Julius. We will be raptured together with him to Heaven in thirty days!" Wow, you could have bowled us over with a whisper. This intellectual giant had never before acknowledged God . . . suddenly next month, he's riding an ejection seat to glory!

Everybody turned to look at me. That's the trouble with tucking a Bible under your arm or laying it on your desk, some day someone is going to expect you to know what's in it or how to use it! About all I could come up with was, "Well, how about that. Can you tell us about this Julius?"

In all sincerity he excitedly continued, "Brother Julius is Jesus Christ resurrected and He has come to take all His believers in our area from the top of a mountain in Connecticut next month . . . on a specific date. We will be selling our house and all of our assets this week to provide for the gathering multitude."

Dumbfounded, I chimed back, "Well, I feel left out because I always thought I'd be going at the same time!" I proceeded to show him from the Bible that as believers we, ". . . Will not know the time or the hour" of Christ's coming for His church; that "Others will come in my (Christ's) name" and "there will be false prophets". He couldn't be dissuaded he was being hoodwinked. Finally, I asked him, "If I can show you that I can control your mind before the end of the week, will you agree to sit down with me and this Bible to show you why Julius is not Christ?"

"Absolutely", he confidently replied, "Because YOU can't control MY mind!" He had taken the bait, now all I could do was pray.

For the next three days, Sharon and I prayed that God would reveal the truth of His Word to Mr. Fuel Control. I'd always had an interest in simple magic tricks and in Harry Houdini's efforts to debunk mentalists and spiritualists. Their routine was to convince people they could foretell the future or fake someone into a phony encounter with the dead . . . Old Harry defrocked them all.

I simply employed a couple "one-ahead" tricks. The easiest is to take three 8" x 10" cardstock sheets from a manila envelope, place them on a blackboard tray and number them 1, 2 and 3 respectfully. Then tell the individual you will control their mind regarding their selection. Ask them to announce their selection. They will initially remonstrate because *you'll* know. Just tell him to do this so that the *audience* will know you have controlled their mind. They will follow your instructions.

Then, you prove you are in control and will predestine their selection. If they select #2, ask them to turn the sheet over, it says, "Thanks for giving me control of your mind and selecting Number Two." That stymies them in their tracks . . . and they immediately pick up 1 & 2 and reveal their BLANK backs. They are speechless and say it was just a lucky 33% chance . . . but they have taken the bait and the hook is SET. Had they selected # 1, I would have directed them to look in the envelope from which I pulled the card, for a similar prediction. Had he called for #3, he would be directed to look at a like prophesy previously placed under their seat . . . I couldn't lose!

Next, I utilized a little ditty employed by a seer with Prime Minister Churchill during WWII; an ESP, extra sensory perception, "come-on" that employed a deck of cards. The pigeon, "subject", lays them down one at a time . . . sight unseen, in piles of RED and BLACK . . . per my mind "CONTROLING" their "DECISIONS". Obviously, I don't really control their mind ... just tell them I do. By pre-stacking the deck in RED and BLACK, laying out a red and black card to have the subject play on, then changing sides of RED and BLACK half way through, I can mechanically determine how many correct selections they make. It is so simple that it is endlessly repeatable with someone who is trusting in ESP. Of course, if everything is left to chance, you'd have 25 right and 25 wrong . . . anything greater than that after time becomes exponentially awesome. As a mathematician, he figured the odds around a trillion-to-one chance for a perfect score,

I enticed him with 55% right on the first try, in the 60's on the second and then sent him to the motel to "think" RED and BLACK. The second day he made 70 & 80%, the third day the 90's and then a PERFECT score. We beat the trillion-to-one odds.

Surrendering in awe, he agreed to study the Bible with me on Friday but first I showed him how I'd tricked him . . . didn't want to leave the impression I had any "unusual power". He saw the error of the false teacher, Julius, and recommitted his life to Christ. Our friendship moved to a new level.

MT 24:4 "Jesus answered: "Watch out that no one deceives you. 5 For many will come in my name, claiming, `I am the Christ, ' and will deceive many." MT 24:36 "No one knows about that day or hour, not even the angels in heaven, nor the Son, but only the Father.

20

End of an Era

My original eighteen month contract had run for twelve years, I never did expect it to play much longer than three. We'd long ago closed the original hangar, Plant 10. When it was built in 1945 by the Air Force, it was completed in two months on a piece of ground leased for a dollar per year from the City of Indianapolis. The lease was for twenty years and in 1965 the city slipped GM a bill for $70,000/year . . . with the potential of escalating in multiples. Airport authorities around the nation are notorious for plundering tenants, from airlines to auto rentals and pretzel stands. They thought General Motors had bottomless pockets; not so. We no longer needed to hangar large aircraft. Before the end of the year, Allison moved next door to share a new hangar owned by Inland Container Corporation at a fraction of the city rent. We would conveniently and conservatively operate without the headaches of dealing with the airport; we left that chore with Inland's box makers.

Most of the critical flight problems had been worked out of the current engine lines. Our little 275 hp engine had even grown to a healthy 420 hp as a turboshaft for helicopters and a turboprop for light airplanes. It didn't take a mind reader to forecast the next step . . . close Flight Test Operations. Back in the "Big Major" days I had prepared a Letter of Resignation. Sharon and I prayed and weighed the gamble we were taking. If we quit, we saw no immediate income in sight since it takes months to close out your first sale in Real Estate . . . and we still had three young boys to raise. I submitted the letter to the Chief Engineer, Gordon Holbrook to preempt my dismissal.

He immediately called me into his office. "What's this all about?" he asked, waving my letter in his hand.

"You are ready to close Flight Test, aren't you, Sir?" I answered.

"Well . . . yes." he replied hesitantly, "We have been considering such a move but we have always had plans to keep you in the Engineering Department."

"I've never heard that discussed and have always figured that when flying ended around here, so would I," I added as a statement . . . that he interpreted more as a question.

"No, we've never planned that you would leave!" as he inserted his own answer.

"No one ever told me I would be retained and I'm not a pure engineer at heart. I'm heading to form a Real Estate Partnership in two weeks. Next to flying . . . I enjoy sales and want to try my hand at my own business." I firmly countered.

Pondering my thanklessness, he finally added, "Well, a couple of our ex-pilots have gravitated to the Sales Department; one has even managed it for a number of years." Sales was the most competitive field in the company. I couldn't see clamoring over the backs of five or ten others in an attempt to move up a rung or two on the ladder.

"No, thank you, Gordon. I don't think I can handle their heavier travel and drinking environment . . . my mind is pretty well made up," I said, slamming the door on his kind offers.

"Well, Jack," he continued in closing. "I see you are serious and I appreciate your candidness but I'm tearing up your Letter of Resignation. Instead, we are going to lay you off. We have valued your work and with your seniority you will receive a half year separation pay. How does that sound?"

"Sounds great!" He could have blown me over; I never considered this an option. Gordon had saved me from a bloody act of political Hari Kari and was God's answer to the long wait for those first commissions . . . if there would ever be any!

Even happy with the extra greenbacks, it was pretty hard walking out of Allison that day, knowing I might never fly again. I was walking into emptiness, the end of an era. I'd recently learned about <u>flying</u> "In the Safety of His Wings", now I was going to learn to <u>walk</u> in it!

First House Sale

Finally, the first house sale! A lot was learned during the sale but an immense more was to be learned from experience. Someone once said, "The young believe that knowledge comes from **intelligence,** while the old believe that knowledge comes from **experience**; reality lies somewhere in between.

The whole family was excited about this first sale. They had all sacrificed while hubby and daddy invested hours and days away from the family while he still held his 8-5 job at Allison. Now it was nearing time for that first deal to come together, a sale to two brothers who had moved from Europe. This was a coup during a period of high interest rates and tight mortgage money. We found a friendly banker and the deal was set for closing. I was to learn that the closing table only gave opportunity for the biggest bombs to fall.

Come to find out, the brothers weren't brothers, just friends. The closing agent seemed sympathetic and stated that their credit checks were fine. With the new Equal Opportunity Act in force, there were no grounds to deny the loan as they had disclosed their situation to him several days prior. Joy, everything consummated and I returned to my office with commission check in hand.

That evening I was invited over for a preliminary celebration at the new house, kind of a christening by friends. Larry Summers, my broker, suggested a small gift, such as a plant or flowers might be appropriate. Sharon and I drove up just a few minutes after the stated hour; cars already packed the drive and street. Leaving Sharon in the car, I walked to the door and rang the bell. One of the "brothers" met me with a warm embrace. I handed him the plant and he welcomed me in. I could see over his shoulder it was not my kind of crowd. All of his other "brothers" seemed to be hugging each other, including the banker and closing agent. "I've got my wife in the car and we are heading . . . somewhere, ANYWHERE!" I responded; they frowned.

As Sharon and I sped off, I saw disappointment and tears in their eyes as they all waved goodbye in unison. Discussions with our boys at supper that night allowed us ample platform to reflect on the rise and fall of Sodom and Gomorrah. Not all dangers occurred in flying.

Partnerships are Tough

Entering your own business is scary; many of us do it in steps, like a partnership. I've had three official partnerships in life, the best one, of course, was with Sharon. Another successful one was with Frank Wiles, a close friend from church and Allison. A third was with a leader in our church that was to be short lived . . . ending in divorce. In a partnership,

165

hopefully, each brings something of equal value but of a different nature to form a balanced unit.

John and I weren't all that different: same stature, same faith and both salesmen. His asset was several years of a small but growing Real Estate business and mine was fresh enthusiasm. He was burned out and building a new home as the contractor. I needed his experience in a new field and he needed someone managing the office while he was building. It was successful and working well. John built a wonderful home, the business grew and I learned a lot about listing, selling, financing, developing land and contracting new home construction.

The most significant thing I learned was how important names are to people. To me, even my own name isn't significant, couldn't spell Frederick until I enlisted in the Navy. My birth certificate didn't match my application. John, on the other hand, must have felt differently about "John". We had agreed when incorporating the company that we would change the business name from John's Company to one that would include mine . . . if I out sold him. You guessed it, I out sold him the first year. We made an appointment the next week to make it "John & Jack". When we were at the lawyer's office, he couldn't choke it down. We mutually agreed to dissolve on the spot. Unfortunately, he couldn't or wouldn't come up with the sum of money he yet owed. It was heartburn for both of us but it became a growth point for me. I forgave him and told him to give the money he owed to the Lord. I had total freedom; unfortunately, I believe John continued to be bitter.

What does all of this have to do with life? Twenty-five years later, one of our boys was likewise wronged but over one-hundred-fold the amount. We saw him wrestle, as I did, until one day he came in total joy. He said, "Dad, it was settled by giving it to our church and to their charity . . . just like you did!" He was free and I've never heard remorse since. Our children are always watching. When we put God in the solution, everyone wins.

Sell My Commune!

Divorce from the first business partnership had not been anticipated. A livelihood to provide for the family was needed. Sharon and I formed a Sub Chapter S Corporation to operate a solely owned real estate company known as Western Estates, Inc. The advantage of the "S" corporation is that you effectively function and are taxed as an individual. I don't particularly think that it protects you better in liability matters. It does give you an illusion of third party separation and stature . . . shielding the reality of working out of the guest bedroom.

To move up one level from a boudoir operation, we rented a small structure, a converted two car garage behind the local Diary Queen in Brownsburg, Indiana. After sweeping the remaining hair from the unit (it had been a two-operator hair salon) we moved in with a desk, file cabinet and three chairs. Doesn't sound like much but with the phone installed, it was FULL! In the next six months this little business flourished to the point of sustaining our family of five. We were able to continue our lifestyle and run a used 19' ski boat with the boys on various Indiana waters, never missing the ventures of aviation.

The very first business out of this humble operation was to fully develop a forty-acre tract of remote farm ground. "Bridlewood Estates" sounded like an exclusive sounding subdivision . . . forty flat barren lots cornerstoned by a 5 acre stable and tack shop. The original farm house and stable at Bridlewood would accommodate horses from the rear of 37 other lots via a bridle trail. We eventually had the privilege of contracting modest homes on over half of these parcels.

The buyer and operator of the stable would come from a gentile kibbutz located on the west side of Indianapolis. I had never before been in a commune. When I walked in to appraise the property, it had at least four to six mattresses or sleeping bags on the floor in each room. Incense

and candles were burning everywhere. I could have imagined they were to heat the house but it was mid-July. There didn't seem to be any formal relationship between any of the men, women and children laying or sitting about. In reality, it was his Floridian parent's home, a small-prefabricated residence on a slab. Built right after WWII, it was worth all of $12,000. He had the responsibility of maintaining it in their absence, now the parents WANTED to sell. My one and only conversation with the parents left me with the impression they perceived I might be the only sane person remaining in Indianapolis.

During the sale of the parents' "group home", we invited this couple to our home where we able to share Scripture and model the attributes of God's plan for couples living together; i.e. salvation and marriage. They and another couple left the commune life and accepted His plan for their life.

167

Western Estates sold and contracted over 150 other new houses, helping many clients get into starter homes with very little or no money down; hopefully, they were excellent investments for all. At this point, another friend and I formed a partnership to build a few rental units. I pulled out our tenured Allison retirement savings of $4,000 for this project. This partnership would eventually permit us to retire early. Frank, an engineer with diligence to detail and accounting, was an excellent balance to my sales and sanguine nature.

Oh, we had a few problems over these entrepreneurial years:

* Murder (?) on Route 66 – Husband shot his wife in a rental unit, she "accidentally" fell on his loaded shot gun, chest first . . . and it happened to fire. She lay overnight, after which the sheriff quarantined the house without cleanup for 30 days. Maggots from the fly eggs ate their way through the carpet and blood, blood that also dripped into the crawl space. The only renter we could attract for the next few years was an ex-Vietnam helicopter combat pilot. He could expel the ghost stories told his children by neighbors and overlook odor still rising from the crawl space.

* One subdivision of nine homes was at the bottom of a several-acre hill. The excavating contractors never confessed to cutting the field tiles which ran through three homes' foundations. Their sump pumps never quit running . . . until they burned out. We named each by the owner's names, Lake Roberts, Lake James, etc. Ultimately, we ran new tile, added septic footage and installed giant sump pumps . . . the entire project at least broke even.

* A fire started by two small boys in their bed broke out in a remote new four-unit apartment complex. They had been amusing themselves while their mother was next door with a guy . . . whose wife was at work; or did I just misplace "amusing"? The Lord is even in things such as this: the children were uninjured, the insurance company settled our $30,000 cost in gutting two units and He prompted us to sell early this distant project that could have generated even greater problems . . . teaching us to keep rentals within surveillance range.

Business seemed to be going well, until a man stumbled over our legs at the Indianapolis Symphony. . . .

Ops . . . I'm scratching on the Window

"Pardon me," the man said, as he and his wife stumbled over our legs. We were sitting in the center floor section of the newly remolded Circle Center Theater, home of the Indianapolis Symphonic Orchestra. I looked up, couldn't miss that voice, towering above was "High Pockets." "Hello, Gordon!" I responded in surprise. It was Gordon Holbrook, Allison's Chief Engineer nicknamed "High Pockets" for his stature . . . the man who graciously laid me off with severance pay rather than let me quit empty handed.

"Jack!" he continued, pausing a moment, "This is a coincidence, I was just going to call and ask you to come back to reopen Flight Test. We are building a new engine."

"Oh, thanks Gordon, but we're really happy in real estate," I nonchalantly replied as they both continued to their seats.

Dropping to his chair a quarter row down, he added over the other occupants, "We'll still be calling you soon." It was a great concert. Gordon knew we really <u>were</u> doing fine; we were sitting in his same high dollar seats. He was a man of his word. Bill Stiefel, Supervisor of Engine Test called and set an appointment to visit and tell about the new 650-800 hp engine in design stages. He said Gordon directed him to invite me back as Supervisor and Chief Pilot of Flight Test.

Meeting at a local restaurant, Bill painted the picture of a new up-rated version of the small 250 engine, almost double the horsepower . . . but I was happy selling. It was easy to immediately respond on that winter day, "No thanks, Bill. I really am content."

Sitting in amazement, Bill closed the luncheon saying, "If you change your mind, give us a call. This new C28 is still a year away from flying!"

The winter took a turn toward cold, not just climatically but also business wise. An Arab oil embargo was cutting into the economy. People were moving out of the suburbs, returning to the city to conserve fuel and personal resources; our rural properties weren't moving as well. Interests rates were approaching 20% and all but government subsidized loans on real estate came to an end.

Three months later, I was on the way home at midnight. I had just weathered a long, hectic contract negotiation that seemed to be fruitless. Making the turn at the only traffic light in beautiful downtown Brownsburg, my heart and head were pounding . . . pounding . . . pounding. Was I even going to make it home, I'm only 38 . . . is this all worth it?

169

The next day in my office, I was contemplating the situation and gazing out my window. A crystal blue sky back dropped a moderating spring day, I could picture an airplane climbing above the lone cloud . . . and I was piloting it! I had said, "I'll quit flying the day I don't claw at the canopy to get in!" Now I was scratching at the window  in my office to get aboard that imaginary plane! I picked up the phone, "Is your offer still open, Gordon?" I asked excitedly.

"Well, component build is running a little behind schedule. It's still a year away but you can come in anytime and follow the engine as its assembly engineer. Are you interested?" Mr. Holbrook offered.

"Gordon, I'm at the point in my career, if I come back I'd like to plan to stay until retirement" I said matter of factually.

"Jack, we can't ever guarantee retirement but we'll do our best to plan for it. We hope you will come back and run Flight Test. Your seniority date will be as if you never left two years ago." he countered. "Call Bill and set up a reporting date. You can work for him until you get your aircraft." I started the next Monday. Onlookers might say this was all chance but I believe that from the night at the symphony until this moment . . . God was conducting.

21

Blizzard of the Century

Lean and Mean

Coming back to GM out of our own business gave me the edge of running lean and mean. The sales and building business wasn't overly flush. We had learned how to squeeze costs and labor while keeping the family fed, without the cushion of corporate or government funds. Setting that lesson into practice, I negotiated a small slot for our sole Bell Long Ranger Helicopter in what was the largest hangar on Indianapolis International Airport. It was a large Quonset building, capable of housing all but jumbo jets. Built for Roscoe Turner in the WWII era, one could envision Roscoe taxiing in his open cockpit plane with his lion perched in the rear seat. The two of them were a hit flying around the nation . . . upside-down. The hangar attracted a variety of fly-by-nighters from travel clubs, night freighters and now our reemerging Flight Test Operations.

Included in the deal was a small office in the front of the building as well as an unheated storage area between two of the Quonset girders. Comb/Gates Aviation provided fuel and tow service as needed. Installing a couple of wheels on the skids allowed me to move the ship around. I acted as Engineer and Test Pilot, requesting instrumentation and special engine maintenance from the other plants as needed. The men were always anxious to enjoy the airport environment. We contracted aircraft maintenance from Bell's closest maintenance center, at Bedford, about an hour drive or a quick twenty-five minute flight. These arrangements permitted us to expand on short notice as additional space could be secured on an overflow basis, just by tucking a plane under our closest neighbor, Ambassadair Travel Club's Convair 990.

A new asset available was pilot/mechanic, Harry Sutton, a good natured ex-Army Warrant Officer the company hired during my sabbatical. Harry lacked a number of flight skills but was great with hands-on maintenance when operating offsite. During slow periods, he could gravitate back to the test stands at another plant . . . and be happy. This wouldn't ever be mistaken for the old country club atmosphere; it

171

was more like operating out a MASH field hospital! The humble environment would soon expand to encompass the world.

The Blizzard of 78' ...In Paradise!

In the winter of '78 we headed west out of Indianapolis in the Long Ranger Helicopter. The Colorado Rockies was our destination to accomplish High Altitude/Cold Weather snow Tests. We departed as the last snow cloud was dumping one of heaviest snowfalls ever to hit the mid-West. It's still in the record books! In typical fashion we picked up Interstate 70 immediately after lift off and felt toasty in the cockpit as we viewed the motorists digging their way out of driveways and roadways. Actually, we had already gone through the same process, slipping and sliding to the airfield for this early exodus.

The ship was moving along nicely as we broke out of the backside of a strong, passing cold front. With a 30-45 knot quartering headwind, we were still enjoying a comfortable ground speed of 100 knots plus, not bad for having the extra drag of snow skies, the weight of extended range fuel tanks and a cabin full of test gear. Cruising at 500-feet, we were gifted with a pristine view of the winter wonderland passing below. Four-lane I-70 was down to one lane as it departed Indy. The eighteen wheelers were starting to get stranded as they made for the exit ramps. Soon . . . not even a car was making it up the cloverleaf grades. Just forty miles enroute, this super highway became fully strangled by one to three feet of smothering snow. Even though it was 10 a.m., in full daylight and with an emerging sun, nothing moved. Over the ever present engine whine and throbbing rotor passage . . . the world appeared mystically silent.

As we continued West beyond the Indiana/Illinois line we dropped down to a hundred feet to look for people in need of help; it looked like everyone had vaporized or been raptured. Most all vehicles had long been abandoned as occupants were rescued or sought shelter at roadside farms to survive the bitter cold. High winds were now drifting sheets of snow over hoods of the semis and tops of cars. At our altitude, it was crystal blue but the earth below was still being ravaged by a horizontal storm.

Winds increasing out of the west dictated that we land at a small airfield just East of St. Louis for fuel. We were able to raise a response from the airport operator who had spent the night in his office and was ready for someone with whom to share a pot of coffee. Fortunately we had taken the extra time to secure the skis for this trip as it is impossible to set most helicopters in deep snow. When the landing gear punches though the

172

snow's soft surface, it dangerously drops the tail rotor for potential impact. Harry, flying in the co-pilot seat, set the helicopter down smoothly . . . right next to the pumps but about 2 ½ feet higher than normal.

After refueling and trudging to the office . . . Harry, not being a coffee hound, signed for the fuel and I filled the thermos. Lifting off Vandalia and skimming over an immobilized St. Louis, we veered slightly southwest along Route 66 and didn't see motorized movement again until reaching Central Missouri!

By mid-day we thought we would have no trouble making Denver by nightfall. This would permit scaling the Rockies in daylight, late the next day. Our destination was Leadville, the highest paved runway in the lower US; not that a helicopter needed a runway. Its local FBO (Fixed Base Operator) was "manned" all year long by two sisters. They catered to occasional Artic crews testing equipment ranging from aircraft to Die-hard batteries. Normally these frozen periods would mean "no business" at any other airport. Reaching Central Kansas, the topography was beginning to change from endless fields of sheared crop stubble to rangeland broken by winding cap rock which would cascade back into the valleys. Only an occasional crop of milo spotted the land, sharing what little moisture falls in this remains of the dust bowl.

On my watch at the controls, we crested a ridge of cap rock. In the open draw on the left, I spotted a beautiful group of five or six coyotes a few hundred feet below. I banked sharply left to show Harry, perfectly targeted in full sight below my left shoulder. They stood stealthy, watching this intruder to their domain, when suddenly . . . THE ENGINE BLEW!

POW - - RRRRRrrrrrrrrr, When a compressor traveling at 51,000 rpm lets loose, it's a SCREAMER!!! A lot of noise but NO power, so-o-o down went the ship. Now, you talk about a God thing. He had those coyotes there just to focus our attention on that special spot. Why special? They were standing in the only clear, level area for miles. The wind had been screaming off the cap rock into this wide valley; on reaching the bottom, it swept the floor clean leaving only a couple inches of snow … a perfect emergency touchdown zone! In fact, I was able to hold the already established left bank, execute a 360 degree spiral drop 600'. . . . right to this "port-in-a-storm". Completing the turn permitted alignment into the wind, giving better autorotation lift to the rotor. With a slight flare aft at touchdown, we were able to come to a perfect stop . . . right over the heads of the coyotes . . . before increasing momentary lift on the rotor blades and gently settling the final three feet to the ground.

The bitter cold front that produced the blizzard left Kansas in the freezer. Even though the sky shown brilliant sun, the outside air temperature gage was reading -10 degrees Fahrenheit at noon. One rule we always followed was to dress in, or have aboard, adequate survival gear for the terrain we were flying over. It looked like we were going to need it today. The good thing about the 360 degree turn on the way down was that we had an opportunity to survey the horizon for signs of human life. The bad thing, other than an old abandoned house about a mile away, we didn't see a homestead within 3-4 miles in any direction! There was no rush to get out. We secured fuel and electrical shutoffs before landing and with no smell of smoke there hadn't been a fire. We were both probably waiting for the coyotes to get a good distance away. They had each scattered in different directions.

After about ten minutes, donning coats and confirming that neither saw anything worth walking toward, I stepped out of the cockpit and turned rearward to survey the damage. Lo, there on top of the ridge about a half mile away was verse 15 out of Psalm 132 . . . "God's provisioning". There were two men standing gaping at us. Exuberantly I took off running toward them waving my arms in hope they saw us. Yelling while I ran was useless and only winded me as I struggled out of one drift after another, sometimes in over my head. My mind kept flashing back to high school, where I was the slowest boy in my Senior Class of 800. In Flight School, I labored to finally rise above the bottom five . . . who had to repeat the morning daily run. If I hadn't prayed up to this time, I was now, that they wouldn't leave before reaching them!

Collapsing in the snow, I lay soaked from sweat in my insulated flight suit. Lying on my back, I looked up the 100 foot cliff and found them laughing at me, I gasped,

"What's so funny?"

"Why the hurry?" they casually replied.

"Was afraid you'd leave!" I wheezed back.

"Why, we wouldn't have missed this, no how. It's the most exciting thing that's happened out here since winter set in." Their laughter continued for what seemed hours as I spent all remaining energy climbing the hill . . . again and again . . .

Baptized "Cow Hands"

While I struggled up the hill, Harry determined that we'd sustained a major failure in the compressor, secured the aircraft and began his trek up the hill . . . at a more relaxed pace. Jake and his ranch hand offered us a ride in their pickup to a phone at their ranch several miles away. But first things first!

They were on their way to the back 400-acres to water their cattle herd. The severe cold snap had frozen all the water holes. Jake plowed through drifts atop the ridge and navigated our way to a lower valley, actually the upper end of the draw where we landed. The ranch hand removed an ax and a cut-down oil drum from the rear of the pickup. Chopping through the pond ice with the ax, he floated the oil drum in the water. Then he lit a wick floating in about a foot of oil at the bottom of the drum. This acted as a heater to keep the cattle watered for the next few days. Jake added as we watched from the warmth of the cab, "Of course, this might help protect your copter, too", he mused. "These o'l buggers are pretty nosey . . . and if they see something strange in their stomping grounds, they are liable to investigate. Cauz' if they see their reflection in the windows, hard tell'en what they might do to your machine! If they have water, maybe they'll stay here for a while"

With that comforting thought, we back-tracked across the previously plowed trail. Coming upon a small feed pen, a lone cow stood mournfully looking at us. "She's in trouble", Jake mumbled. Without further words, the truck stopped, both ranchers jumped out, took some gear from a box in the back and headed for the heifer. They walked around her a couple times and then waved for us. What we saw was a cow with two frozen forepaws of an unborn calf sticking out it's rear-end. What now?

"The calf's breach", the ranch hand stated mater-of-factly. "It'z gon'ta hef'ta come out!" They led the cow over to a lean-to, three sided shelter. Without hesitation, Jake stripped to the waist in the −10 temperature, grabbed a chain, wrapped it around the calf's frozen legs and attached it to a 'come-a-long' pulley set. Again signaling us into the act, we were told

175

to hold a rope on the head and the 'come-a-along' at the rear. Being senior man on our half of the team, I elected the front-end. I couldn't handle seeing our sons being born, yet alone getting a ringside seat seeing this master obstetrician at work . . . that was Harry's view.

I did see Jake plunge both arms up to his chest into the heifer, just before she ran over me! "Hold on to her, Harry", I yelled, but that was unneeded. Because as Jake and the hand started turning and pulling, o'l Betsey backed right over Harry, then over me AGAIN, then Harry, then FINALLY . . . a new calf was born!

Carrying the calf over to the truck, Jake asked, "Where you boys gon'na ride?"

"What do you mean?" we naively replied. "Well, the calf's go'n up front with us. You can squeeze in with us or enjoy the open air in the back, your choice". Needless to say, we didn't need much time to reexamine ambient conditions and immediately climb inside the cab where we, too, could fall in love with one of God's special creatures . . . dripping afterbirth over us all.

After reaching Jake's ranch house, we made the necessary calls to FAA and Allison . . . setting a weeklong recovery in process. I was able to check in with Sharon at home. "Where are you?" she asked, always curious how far we were along the trip.

"I'm in PARADISE!" I replied happily . . . a little town named Paradise, Kansas, USA".

Epilogue: We re-engined the helicopter under some pretty adverse conditions and for one week effectively lived with a very loving family.

We shared our relationship with Christ, saw the calf walking and eventually completed our mission in Leadville. Our son, Mark, traveled to Paradise two years later on invitation to hunt the hundreds of pheasants we had seen huddled around the food pens . . . only to find they don't flock there during hunting season. The next year Jake died . . . but after accepting Christ. God provided many miracles on this trip!

22

How Big is Your Gun?

When Dick Cordrey, my stepfather was 87, we planned a special trip west to LA to visit him. His age was not an eminent factor in seeing him. He was in good health, playing golf, shooting pistols at the LA Police Department range, physically an outstanding example to all of us . . . Grandma Marion lived to at least a rousing 106. While corresponding regarding schedules, we established a regular e-mail exchange during the period. He told me about his .44 cal. Magnum Super Redhawk revolver, a pretty impressive weapon in anybody's hand. We began discussing our different armament. I reminded him that he had primed my interest in guns at eight years of age.

He championed a Crossman pump pistol. One day he was firing it at a tree in front of our Cleveland home, when it ricocheted and struck me just below the eye. I'm certain I feigned near death, by doubling up on the front sidewalk, to milk a moment of compassion. That gave me a reasonable respect for guns . . . but not enough to dampen my curiosity. He and my mother extended unwarranted trust as they elected to leave me home alone at this early age. In fact, I was shuttled alone between Cleveland and Toledo several times by train during the height of WWII.

One night I decided to further examine the mighty Crossman. Its 12" or so length was like holding a shotgun in those eight-year-old hands. After loading it with a pellet and pumping several times, I was overcome by a sudden need to discharge this potent device. Looking around the room, the bottom of a seat cushion appeared to be a solution to defuse its energy . . . but a pillow lacked any challenge to my racing mind. Then I spotted it, across the long living room and the far side of the dining room, hung the cuckoo clock! The hands read twenty-six minutes after the hour, only four minutes before the bird would sound off. It was a long wait. As I held the gun level those last seconds, it got heavy. The long barrel was waving in the air . . . the cuckoo squawked once and retreated, then jumped out to squawk again, I fired . . . the pellet missed by a foot and pounded into the plaster wall. Climbing a chair to evaluate the damage, I was chagrined to learn that when plaster is hit at high velocity, it also shatters. There was a moment of remorse; oh, not for the damage, but that I had missed.

I quickly determined the trouble, the wait. This was easily remedied by advancing the big hand to one minute before the hour, deleting the delay and giving the cuckoo four full squawks! Even as a boy, I could remember newspaper recon pictures showing high altitude bombing results. The wall looked much the same; bomb craters scattered about a munitions factory with a couple of strategic hits within the plant. The cuckoo likewise hung dead, restrained only by a strand of coiled spinal wire spewing from its inner body . . . surrounded by rings of pock-like misses on the wall. I can no longer remember the outcome of that raid but have since read that psychologists say children forget much of the pain and suffering they bring on themselves. I wondered why father/son communication sometimes seemed difficult.

"Bring Out the Big Ones"

When Dad mentioned his .44 caliber, I reflected that when qualifying in the Navy with a 45mm pistol . . . it was pretty awesome. His return e-mail agreed that *45mm* (2 inches in diameter) WOULD be pretty awesome! It should have been .45 caliber. Such 2" guns are found on substantial installations like U.S. Naval cruisers. In dunce like fashion, I was only able to recover from my mistake by relating an experience with a really big gun, a 105mm (5") German Automatic, gyro stabilized cannon mounted on a new General Motors experimental X-1 Tank. In the mid 80's, I flew Allison's Long Ranger Helicopter to the Aberdeen Proving Ground, near Washington DC to transport the GM cameraman to film the tank firing this weapon. As custom, we removed the right rear door, strapped in the photographer, and let his feet dangle on the skids.

We had practiced a beautiful dash sequence. The helicopter sat on the brim of a small hill, parked 90 degrees to the roadway, rotor running, poised for jump takeoff. The tank charged up the hill, with only the turret in view. Just a few feet before the tank hit the rotor, we shot upward with the tank passing a few feet below while we made a 270 degree tail rotor turn to the right, climbing and panning forward to show the oncoming zigzag course cut through the woods and continuing out through open ground. As the tank cleared the trees I dropped the copter level with and just clear of the cannon. It was amazing. While the tank zigzagged and bumped along, the gyro stabilized gun turret held its 5" cannon precisely on target . . . 1 ½ miles down range. Then, just as we were coming through a tight turn, BOOM!!!

I thought we were dead meat! The concussion of the 105mm shell firing . . . instantly displaced the helicopter a couple feet sideward. My head struck the door frame HARD. The FLASH, even in daylight, grayed my vision.

All doors popped open . . . even the nose battery compartment door flipped up, blowing over the windscreen. Once senses started to return, we made an immediate landing. While the mechanics were going over the aircraft, the tank crew taxied back, lifted the hatches and roared with laughter. The ship was found OK, the cameraman was ecstatic and said it was the most fantastic footage he ever shot, no retake needed . . . he WASN'T going to get one!

After the tank crew finished with their private joke, we agreed to exchange rides. I popped into their cockpit, my first time ever in a tank. It was confining, I'd nursed a desire to be a submariner when seventeen, but this was really tight. The pilot seat, placed in center, was spacious. I sunk comfortably into a generously padded seat. Once belts were secured, I donned their helmet. Mine was still recovering from the window jam impact. This headgear was equipped with a video screen overlay for laser targeting. I'd run similar gear when firing airborne missiles but this system was improved by several generations. Fortunately, I had some Hughey Cobra experience with similar side arm controls located on the forward portion of the armrests. This layout permits a disabled body to slump forward into a neutral area while permitting the copilot to take command without weight on controls or steering wheels. In a few seconds I was able to keep the tank treads on the zigzag road and barely felt the alternating three-foot bumps pass. Speed was increased toward 45mph – wow! In a few zigs and zags, I was persuaded to pinpoint the laser on a 4 x 8-foot target over a mile downrange. "FIRE", the copilot shouted.

"You mean we're running LIVE", I replied panicky.

"Yeah, pull the trigger!" He laughed in the same manner as before. BOOM, just as loud, but without the jolt. It helped to have the weight of the massive tank with its recoil capability. Through the sights I saw the impact, not a bull's-eye but a KILL, within the four-foot circle. Amazing, fantastic, awesome . . . what a weapon! Previously, I always considered a

181

fleeting helicopter to be an elusive target. A new frightening respect for the tank boys was engraved in the gray stuff!

Now it was their turn in my machine. They found it much less stable then their multi-million dollar, multi-ton vehicle. They were unable to keep it level even a few seconds, yet alone command direction. Once they cried "Uncle", I picked the porpoising ship out of their trembling hands, slipped below the treetops a couple of feet off the roadbed, rolled left and right through the trees . . . lifting only to clear the confining pines. Just before breaking into the clear, I accomplished a high speed popup maneuver with a pedal turn on top . . . heading almost vertically down on TOP of *their* tank, with our imaginary missile sights steely set for our own KILL! Talk about mutual respect. I didn't return their laugh as we landed to permit one of their crew to relieve breakfast. Later, as we exchanged war stories over lunch, it became apparent that I worked harder; I had the bigger appetite!

Thanks, Dad, for introducing me to guns.

23

The Rest of the Story

Our Children Defend Us

Sharon and I learned too late that our children tend to take up our position on matters of all sorts. One of the first instances that we noted was when we moved into our current residence, Scott was about eleven, Mark, nine and Brad, six. The first night in the center of four hundred undeveloped acres was unsettling, a wilderness to city dwellers. Our home sat one-eighth mile off a dusty stone road behind a blind of trees, pretty spooky sleeping on bare concrete floors. Teaching the boys the art of small arms was not a problem. One could shoot out the back door and not hit anything but trees and hills for two miles.

While our tri-level was being built, I would visit almost daily by helicopter. One day our *very* German contractor, Siegfried Straube . . . hollered out in frustration, "Mr. Schvibolt, dez ariel inspection eez naut in zee contract!" Ziggy was precise and reasonable. Another time when walking from the ship, a receipt for some lumber blew across my feet, it was for $37.83. Slipping it into my pocket, I walked into the recently framed garage and was met by Ziggy. He jumped my frame and spouted, "We can't have anymore *free* additions; do you know how expensive that wood for your *free* shelves was?"

Casually taking a pencil from my flight suit shoulder pocket, I picked up a piece of scrap lumber (as he always did) thought intently and scribbled a few numbers. "Oh, I say it is roughly . . . somewhere between $37.82 and $37.84, Ziggy. Just keep accurate figures and we'll trust you for the cost!" I matter-of-factly told him as I handed him the board and strolled into the house. At closing, Mrs. Ziggy presented a well documented folder listing every extra we requested . . . to their dismay, we never looked at it. The final price came 10% under what we would have been willing to pay! Diligence is important.

PR 21:5 The plans of the diligent lead to profit as surely as haste leads to poverty.

As the years went by we became aware that our boys were diligently and unknowingly taking up our defense. The first case came about a year after moving into the new home. The neighbor on an adjoining lot was having his home built by a different contractor who erected a floodlight at the building site. While our lot was 1330 feet long, it was only 220' wide. The light was obtrusively filtering through the trees, shining on our curtainless walls at night. Our privacy had been VIOLATED! When Sharon and I mumbled and grumbled about, "that darn light," we noticed it would occasionally be off for a few nights.

One day our new neighbor crossed a small ravine and asked to talk to us in private. He had a request, "We know you moved out here to have privacy but our contractor's insurance company demands he have a nighttime security light. If you would have your boys stop shooting out the light, we will have it removed as soon as we move in!" Scott had negotiated a standing contract with his brothers to take out Mom & Dad's offending light!

Years later when Mark was working at Combs/Gates Aircraft in a hangar we were co-using at the time, I noticed him standing at the hangar door, arms folded and glaring at me. This was to be my first flight with the daughter of one our company engineers; she, too, was now an engineer working for Allison. With the advent of the Equal Opportunity Movement, she gained approval to be trained for a helicopter rating . . . taught by no other than, yours truly. After our son watched us take-off and land, he sauntered forward, opened my door and said . . . "I just wanted to make sure Mom didn't have anything to worry about . . . and she doesn't!"

Our boys remain thoughtful in their protecting attention . . . one of Brad's gifts, a chimney screen, still keeps the Chimney Swifts out of our fireplace; he even installed it. He and Nancy also invited us to build a home on their adjacent lot; as did Mark and Mindy. They all still keep an eye on us, Brad and Nancy at church activities . . . Brad took over my Eldership responsibilities, and Mark around the yard . . . he, David and Steven mow our acreage. Other grandkids help too, Kelsey with the house, Daniel and Derek prepare the pool in the spring. The rest come and call . . . and love. Our children have done their job well. I've got to keep stepping up to my part.

PR 17:6 Children's children are a crown to the aged, and parents are the pride of their children

The Rest of the Story

Paul Harvey is still on syndicated radio with his daily "This Is . . . The Rest of the Story". Some fifteen years ago, I had the opportunity to fly Paul from the Oshkosh Air Show into the University Of Wisconsin for one of his speaking engagements. An avid pilot, he eagerly accepted my invitation to try his hand at the controls of the Long Ranger Helicopter. Enroute south, we made a few approaches into various farm fields. He quickly became adept at maintaining some semblance of a hover, quite a feat for being the near 70 I guessed him to be. As he disembarked in the center of the campus, he shouted back his final comment, "The rest of the story is . . . helicopters are more difficult to fly than airplanes!"

This year as we prepared for our annual Christmas Eve family time, I began considering my job of putting all the grandchildren to work reading or acting out the Luke 2 Christmas story. Sharon always had the family Bible open to this chapter, dressed with a big red velvet bookmark. As I assembled the handful of NIV Bibles in the house, I quickly realized they all had been heavily marked with inserts of children's names for verses to be read with accompanying titles of songs we had sung past years; however, the text was vividly untouched after verse 20, where, "... The shepherds returned glorifying and praising God. ..." The next Sunday in church, Reverend Shane Fuller preached the same Luke 2:1 - 20 passages. So, for a change, I decided to read "The Rest of The Story", Verses 21-52.

These passages are rich. After Jesus was presented to the temple for circumcision, he was seen by a godly man named Simeon and a faithful widow named Anna. They both recognized Him and many of His attributes, but most importantly, they extended the baby their blessings. Later at twelve, Jesus was accidentally left in Jerusalem after the Passover feast and not recognized as missing for a day. He was found three days later doing His Father's work in the temple, debating scripture.

I shared this with Sharon. She agreed we would set out to **bless** each of our children and grandchildren this particular Christmas, similar to Simeon's and Anna's blessings. We individually assigned our children and grandchildren two positive traits we saw in each of them. After the children read the "Rest of the Christmas Story", Kristin, age eight,

185

personalized the scripture by telling about being forgotten at our house for a couple hours when she was four. Steven told about just winning a debating contest at fourteen, both paralleled the story to a "T". Then we impressed upon them that the average age of our grandchildren was now 12-14 and this seemed to be a crucial age when our son's interests turned into their vocations. This pricked their attention and even the parents nodded in agreement. We presented each of them simple scrolls that included the definition and supportive Bible verse for two attributes we saw in them as a Christmas blessing. It seemed to go very well.

The rest of this story is to add an epilogue of what we again learned; sibling rivalry exists even in the best families. Today we would repeat "The Rest of the Christmas Story", but with each individual family privately. Yes, we are still learning as parents and grandparents.

Fishing and Boating with Jonah

As a small boy our son, Mark, had a pattern of wanting to be punished after being caught in or confessing a devilish deed. At first we thought these were acts of machismo when he seemed to seek out a good paddling. We soon learned that his desire was to be restored into fellowship and LOVE of the family, most specifically with Mom and Dad. The same thing works with God's children. He doesn't want us to get away with anything so that we may restore our relationship with Him . . . rather than become an agent of Satan.

Jas 5:16 Therefore confess your sins to each other and pray for each other so that you may be healed.

It would be easy to relate many of *my* getting caught stories here, but one of the Schweibold's most famous was related in our Adult Sunday School Class. Our teacher used it as an example in his lesson. It seems I had related the occasion the previous evening at a Christmas dinner party.

Our teacher's story of a "Very Godly Woman" follows: "While this certain family was fishing on the banks of Raccoon Lake in central Indiana, a Conservation Patrol Boat pulled up quickly to shore, probably to check fishing licenses. This *"very godly woman"* threw her pole down, ran up a very steep bank and disappeared over the top of the hill. When the officers called after her . . . she was dumb enough to come back!

They signed her up for a significant ticket. As the boat roared off, the laughter of her children and husband still sitting on the bank grew louder

186

while they continued to fish . . . they didn't have licenses either!" Mom had willingly come back under her authorities, accepted her punishment to be restored to the community. A pretty good laugh, yes! In the long run it was also a pretty good example; looks like the fish weren't the only things getting caught!

Years later, well after the children were off on their own, Sharon and I had the opportunity to fly a Cessna turboprop amphibian to our new dealer in North Carolina. He had a summer home on a private 200-acre island in the middle of a long lake. When we circled the airport for landing we found the runway in process of being resurfaced, with equipment parked at both ends to prevent traffic and damage to the new blacktop. Being amphibian, we sucked the wheels up, landed as a seaplane and taxied right up to his island cottage. Nestled in a small cove, it was an ideal place to beach the plane overnight.

Early the next morning we assisted Robin in his dawn departure to Raleigh for a demonstration flight with his client. He left us a beautiful new cedar canoe to enjoy for the day. After breakfast we donned swimming suits and pushed off in the boat, letting it drift leisurely out from shore. Since the sales demonstration schedule had kept us apart the previous few days, we enjoyed this opportunity to just kick back and enjoy the sun and conversation. In a half hour or so we found we had drifted out to the center of the lake and would have a long paddle back against the light breeze. Robin had pointed out a small trolling motor with a battery which could be hooked up if needed. I decided we now "needed" and set out to see if there was any juice left before I had a tryout for the Olympic paddling team.

As soon as the propeller silently started to turn, we had another of Sharon's Conservation Department boats and officer right along side . . . out of nowhere!

"We weren't fishing. What's wrong officer?" we offered as unsolicited defense.

"Oh, we've been watching you through binoculars," he responded. What's this WE stuff? He was alone in the boat. Boy, we weren't even necking; this guy must be weird!

"You were okay until you hooked up the battery," he continued; "then you became a Power Boat, a new classification. Since this new boat doesn't have registration numbers, you are operating illegally!"

For the next 45-minutes he grilled us about ourselves, this mysterious island, where we were from and the dusk-to-dawn operation of our sea plane. Finally at the end of this fatiguing questioning, we realized he was

187

interested in drug runners more than escapees from the drudgery of aircraft sales. Agreeing we didn't fit his suspicions he issued us a ticket for operating a watercraft illegally. This time it was my turn to sign for the ticket and we paddled back to the island. His suspicions about the island and plane were obviously without foundation as Robin has since served several years in our United States Congress.

24

The Family Sprouts Wings

Moving from big engine test to small engine test . . . with sales activities, we moved Flight Test Operations off Indianapolis International Airport. The larger airports were becoming less friendly to general aviation. Lighter aircraft not flying under air carrier banners like TWA, Pan Am and Eastern . . . even though these companies would soon be out of business. Flight training, a necessity in sales and training activities for new product lines and the backbone of most general aviation companies, was outlawed at Indianapolis International. So we packed up our aircraft

which now numbered two Propjet Bonanzas, a Cessna 210 Turboprop Amphibian, a twin-engine Australian Nomad (shown here) and a Bell Long Ranger Helicopter and moved five miles north into private hangar facilities at Eagle Creek Airport. This location brought a lot of amenities: relaxed airspace, no control tower, privacy for test operations, six miles closer to home plus the ability to contract our own labor force for specific talents and disciplines necessary to run a mixed aircraft fleet. It was to become satellite home for Allison's own "Skunk Works".

We received the go ahead from management to challenge the World Aviation Record on all fronts. Our giant flight planning map in the hangar became a

posting board, showing specific missions to make Indianapolis not only the automotive speed capitol but also the aviation speed capitol of the

189

world. I was specifically proud of the flights where I was accompanied by my sons and wife at various times. Oh, yes, each of the boys were licensed to fly and Sharon was even granted an official position as company copilot . . . to cover requirements to be an official flight crew member in certain experimental aircraft license categories. I always appreciated the company respecting the importance of Sharon in our sales activities; whether as a hostess with clients or attending conventions, they always considered her a valuable asset.

At first, I thought I'd drafted Sharon into the program . . . until she confided later that she had prayed the "Prayer of Jabez" long before the same named book was written, *1 CH 4:10 "Oh, that you would bless me and enlarge my territory!"*. Little did she know that once strapped in her copilot's seat, those boundaries would expand to the Alps and Australia! We still share memories of remote beach, desert and mountain top landings; skirting canyons searching for Indian cliff dwellings and coming off the top of a loop.

Scott, Mark, Brad and Sharon all took to the air on their own, here one of the boys climb aboard to fly with dad, typically more pressure then when flying alone or with their instructor!

Scott gave up flying fun to raise two beautiful girls and own a gas station where he could enjoy utilizing his mechanical talents. Mark went on to secure all of his FAA pilot and maintenance inspectors licenses and was eventually hired by Allison thru his own merit. While raising two great boys he fathered future test programs for us with Sikorsky Aircraft, Aerospatiale, Bell Helicopters and then went on to became a master salesman in corporate Jets for Cessna and with his own company. Brad continued his private flying as he entered computer software sales, eventually managing dozens of salesmen, but having better sense than his dad, realized that being father to six wonderful children left little time to toy with the cockpit. He flies the world in the cabin. Somehow, out of all this buzzing around we have enjoyed a delightful complement of sons, daughters-in-law and grandchildren who feel as comfortable in the air as birds. You see, they too, have learned to fly in the safety of His wings.

Killer Clouds . . . Cumulus Granite

A job that quickly gravitates to a Test Pilot is assisting with accident investigations when flight operations are in question. "Jack, grab your gear and jump an airline west. We just lost a 250 powered twin turboprop into the side of a mountain," were the words crackling through the phone. "NTSB and FAA have dispatched an investigation team and you have been invited to join them."

Ironically, we landed in a Convair 580, powered by two 3000 HP Allison's. I'd probably flown this very ship. Only a handful of passengers deplaned from its 50 seat cabin. It was not difficult to pick out one of my co-investigators. His flight case had "NTSB" (National Transportation Safety Board) stenciled in big white letters, it nearly matched the "FAA" bag carried by the other team member waiting for us in front of the terminal. Clear, crystal blue skies framed a range of snow capped mountains that the FAA investigator was pointing toward. He was describing where the crash site was located. It was some 30 miles away and I'm sure we could have seen it except it was on the backside of the range. "I've got a helicopter standing by to take us up there now," the NTSB man interjected. "Is everybody ready?"

"You bet!" I replied. My bag was always packed with camera, measuring equipment, fluid sampling bottles, plastic baggies, manuals, etc., "Glad you have the helicopter. It looks like a long hike from a road." Just then the Jet Ranger hovered around the corner of the hangar and we boarded for departure.

"About the best I can do is to get you to 6,500-foot in the foothills", the pilot advised. "I've already flown over the pinnacle they are pinned on . . . it's above 11,000-feet and surrounded by jagged rocks."

He was right, as we dropped over the peaks, the wreckage was right THERE . . . less than a hundred feet lower than the higher ridge that jutted up as if to say . . . "Gotcha!" After a couple of passes for our photos, the

191

pilot dropped down toward his lower landing area, which meant we were going to have a good mile climb . . . UP!

"Hey, how about landing on this ridge, right here?" I suggested.

"Naw, too high and rough!" he retorted, asserting his command. I pulled the flight manual from the door pocket and paged through the performance tables and showed him we had a few hundred foot margin at our weight and pressure altitude for the "average pilot". "Certainly a good mountain pilot can set us there?" I challenged. That was all the prodding he needed. We made a nice shallow approach crosswind on the upwind side of the cliff . . . and deftly placed the ships skids on the smooth saddle between two peaks. "Thanks, you just saved us two hours of extra hiking," I heartily added.

"It's 2 o'clock. Pick us up by dark, we'll be back by then," the NTSB investigator instructed as he led us uphill. It was a still, crisp cold day. Only the bright sun blazing through the lesser atmosphere made it a comfortable climb as we picked our way up the snowy out croppings. It was going to be a cold night if that ship didn't return. The FAA man was slowing down as we completed our first 1,000-feet; he had already turned 60 a couple years earlier. At 10,000-foot elevation he pooped out and said he couldn't go further. We were glad to see him call it quits; he looked like a blue faced heart attack candidate gasping his final breath.

The remaining NTSB man and I left our flight cases with him, filling our pockets with cameras and note pads for the remaining climb. I was now coughing blood . . . "Should have brought water. We were dehydrating. Ah, snow should do just as well," I thought. Sitting for a rest, I ate a good snowball worth and stopped vomiting. Suddenly the familiar roar of thundering rotor blades came from the far side of the ridge. A Jolly Green Giant swept over the peak, just a few hundred feet above us. The big Sikorsky surveyed the scene and then gingerly air taxied above the site, hovered out of ground effect . . . flexing its muscle. In moments, several paramedics rappelled, disappearing into an area we couldn't see.

It took us an hour to scale the remaining 500 feet. We were almost resentful that the Jolly Green was hoisting body bags aboard when we arrived at the wreckage. As the first paramedics were being lifted aboard, the remaining two were untying the ropes they had secured to the aircraft fuselage and upper rock structure. We asked if they would be kind enough to leave them in place for our investigation. They agreed.

By now we had lost all ill feelings of the Army removing the casualties. I'd long ago peeled enough carnage from instrument panels and wreckage. I sighed in relief when my leader said, "We don't have much daylight left . . . you check the engines and exterior and I'll map the cockpit and interior."

The aircraft had impacted almost level on the near vertical rock face, just a few feet from the peak. Even though the propellers were smashed into the face of the cliff, it was easy to see the engine compressors and turbine were folded by rotational damage, indicating they had been running at stoppage. After completing exterior inspection and photos, I was summoned to photograph the interior.

As I stepped aboard the rear door well, I hesitated with my back against the rear baggage door to take a picture forward. **"Scre-e-ch"** was the sound emanating from the rocks as the ship shuddered violently, lurched aft and dropped . . . into the Army's abandoned rope harness. I stood breathless, now looking out the door . . . straight down into the 3,000-foot chasm below. Mr. NTSB was also looking aft, mirroring my blank motionless, expression. We didn't move. Then we slowly inched forward, taking final snapshots and notes as we exited through the broken windows. Carefully deplaning, we met the FAA man . . . reaching the last rock at the wreckage's edge. "We're heading down", we stated. I think he would have rather died and been evacuated in a black bag.

Our findings indicated the pilot was probably blown off course during the first snowstorm of the year. Had he been on course at that distance from the airport, the ship would have been well clear of the impact point. Had the military not left their gear, our impact point would have been 3,000' below. Resting "In the Safety of His Wings", those feathery wings sometimes feel like ROPES!

Artic Hot Tub

One benefit of being Chief Instructor for the HAI (Helicopter Association International) instructor pilots is exposure to a number of fabulously talented pilots and instructors. Al, Chief Instructor for a Canadian School attended our classes a couple of times, then invited me up to see their facility. He didn't directly call us "Woosies" but indicated they had a unique operation I needed to see. They were operating a small fleet of Bell 47 reciprocating engine'd machines. He baited me by suggesting they might be picking up a turbine ship or two, "How about coming up to teach turbine engines, to help get the new program started?"

Always looking to expand the turbine concept and sell engines, I finally gave in. "OK," I said, "When is a good time?"

"Let's plan for next February." He already knew the date, "Near the end of the month will be just right. I think you will be surprised by the experience."

"Was thinking more like opening day of Small Mouth Bass season", I choked back. It was settled, he'd teach a period for our Certified Flight Instructors Course on Canadian regulations and, in exchange, I'd travel to North Bay, Ontario next winter to teach a Turbine Engine Course. I actually forgot about the commitment until he called in January to confirm dates. He said the classroom would be ready by the end of the month; I'd always pictured his college to be a series of existing buildings. I agreed to show up on his schedule.

North Bay sits on Lake Nipissing, 200 miles north of Toronto in Central Ontario. Getting an airline seat in February was no problem, not many people were headed in that direction during the middle of the winter. On landing, he picked me up, then had a delightful tour of what we in the U.S. would call a small technical Junior College. The province had a great idea, providing courses geared to segments of commerce *needing* workers; i.e. subsidize and teach youth a skill for waiting jobs, rather than provide welfare for a bunch of flower children who took basket weaving and poetry on scholarships. But, where were the helicopter students?

They did have an adjacent hangar, but no bodies . . . "We will have to fly by helicopter to meet the students," Al said. Then he began to tell me the whole process. "The student pilots begin their training in August; by December they have soloed and obtain a modest proficiency by February. We don't believe in training in the sterile environment of a flat, concrete airport," he stated. "We teach around the real environment they'll be operating in at work. Who wants to hire a raw student? Here at OTC we train pilots who are proficient to start working in the bush the day they are licensed. So, on the first of February they pack their ditty bags for 30 days of survival in the wilderness. They fly three place ships, transporting 25-30 students, tents, supplies and a small lumber mill to the lake. They normally get the trees cut, cleared and cabins built on the edge of the ice within the first 7-10 days. They are pretty motivated to get inside and

194

warm with these -20 to -40 degree temperatures. The only flights permitted back to school are for periodic food supplies or medical emergencies. Final flight training continues from a camp built with their hands and flying skills."

A 25 minute flight took us about 50 miles out in the bush, over solid trees interrupted occasionally by a frozen lake. Not even a vacant cabin broke the emptiness. Finally, we came upon a small lake with a long row of 6-10' pine trees poking out of the ice every 50 to 100' leading up to three parking spots on the ice. My thought was we must be making an approach into Santa's North Pole; they had even erected Christmas trees.

Walking up to the cabins we found a group of sober men dedicated to completing chores and training flights. I was a welcome visitor to break their monotony and isolation. My time with the men passed quickly. I think I learned far more than they received from me; for instance, the row of pine trees were planted to provide depth perception hovering under whiteout conditions on open ice and snow. The smallest building at the edge of the lake was a sauna with a hole cut in the ice, dip in for washing, and sit out for drying. No one was in the sauna. I headed home, challenged to do a better job of real life training.

A year later, I repeated the trip in our own Long Ranger. When I landed at the camp I witnessed new vitality in attitude, a smile on everyone's face as they met the tasks at hand. Instructors must have done an awesome job this season. Our time together passed like lightning, a total involvement period. The key to this new found joy seemed to radiate

 from two students, both women, making it the first coed class. On departure for home at the edge of the lake, I could see the sauna was full for the evening dip.

25

Jewel of the Orient

"We've already started your Japanese visa request in Chicago; you are scheduled to meet with Japan's NTSB officials regarding a couple of reported engine failures". This was one of the few world travel opportunities I truly wanted to turn down. The specific engine and ship I had been brought back to test was suffering problems after it was released to production. Early electrical power to the starter system and marginal temperature indicators potentially exposed the pilot to over-temping the engine, subjecting the turbine wheels to excessive heat and potential distress. It appeared two of these rare occurrences could have happened on the island country of Japan. The cabinet level director of their NTSB was threatening to ground the aircraft. "Jack, your job is to head that off!" This sounded more like a Mission Impossible . . . without the option to accept or reject the assignment!

Given the 14 airline flight hours, I had plenty of time in prayer and in my Japanese phrase book. I had been in Japan two or three times previously and met our local representative, "Haz". Haz was a gracious man who accompanied me while we visited various manufacturers utilizing or interested in our engines. During this period he schooled me on  many of the amenities of his beautiful country: their transportation, factories, castles, tea houses, his home, etc.

Their rail system at that time had the fastest trains, the Bullet Train, traveling at speeds nearing 200mph. One of our stops was to visit the president of a Japanese airline designing a new high-speed train. His company was considering one of our Model 250 engines to power a generator developing an opposing magnetic field to lift each car a fraction of an inch off the track. This would "fly" the train, with larger turbine units providing thrust with pusher propellers. Sitting in his office for the first time, the importance of "courteous control" was demonstrated to me. My associate and I had taken a respectful token gift as required in business.

The president responded with a very generous offer to immediately, before the meeting could start, visit any of their other divisions (car companies, wholesalers, shipbuilders, diamond importers, etc) and select from inventories, a product at a "very special discount". We chose a major pearl company and were immediately shuttled off by the company limo. Pulling up to a modern 10 story building we were ushered into the company's pearl vault and viewing chamber, a long room of significant size and height. Except for two doors, the walls were decked with narrow, shallow drawers . . . hundreds of them, each holding multi-strands of every conceivable variety of pearl. "Where would you like to start in price," their chief curator asked, "Say about one hundred thousand?"

Quietly gagging, I cautiously replied, "That's yen, I assume, about one thousand dollars U.S. dollars?"

"No," he politely replied, "We'll quote in terms of your currency, $100,000 U.S."

Gathering my best composure, I responded, "Well, I was thinking more like $1,000 U.S." A deadly hush fell over their staff of six set to serve us. They stared at each other in amazement as the library type ladder was moved on rollers to the furthermost corner of the room. A white jacketed young lady, whom I had mistaken as a janitor, was tasked to retrieve the drawer at the top. It exchanged hands several times before being laid atop one of several large marble top tables that could have doubled for cadaver benches in the local morgue. Several strands were spread before me by white gloved assistants. I evaluated them intently for a moment, as if I knew what I was looking at. I'd never looked at a piece of jewelry for Sharon worth $500, yet alone $1,000. "I'll take that one," I confidently ordered, "but she wants it three inches shorter".

Again, the staff just gawked, "Fine, Schweiboldson" (Mr. Schweibold in Japanese). "We will have you oversee the restringing process on the way out so you will be assured of the proper length. You will then be taken to the cashier after they meet your approval". Once at the cashier, I paid my bill of $1,000 US discounted to ... $183.00 US! The airline president had gained the upper hand with his gift; this "piker" was not of significant stature to waste his valuable time.

After observing company gymnastics for ten minutes at the ten o'clock bell (with the president jumping as high as the rest), I was removed from his office and assigned to a set of underlings to discuss the project. Aside from the restrooms, the president's had been the only private office in the building. Haz and I now sat in the center of an open office housing hundreds of people involved in their individual work. We were politely positioned in a conference area on three opposing couches. As we presented our proposal for the lift engines, occasionally a consensus was taken among their team . . . and outsiders from the area who had apparently been quietly listening . . . lifted hands and were also tallied and counted in the vote. This was the Japanese team concept we heard about in the states. Haz taught me a lot on that trip.

When I returned home, Sharon was very pleased with her pearls and still wears them today. She was so delighted and amazed at the discount, she promptly said, "Why didn't you ask to see the $10,000 sets? You might have stayed with the president." I wonder if that was her only motive. Actually, I was thinking more along the automotive line.

Favorite Sports Team

TWA touched down at Narita Airport around 4 p.m. I would meet Haz in the Ginza shopping district for supper at 7 pm. I boarded the express train from the airport. On the previous trip I'd taken the bus. It took hours because airport protestors had closed the roads with human shields. Before I left the airport I called Haz to arrange meeting my train in downtown Tokyo, I arrived at the terminal within the hour. I'd never been in the shopping district at 6 pm before . . . it was chaotic! Where was Haz? I was in a sea of people, all pressed together in one flowing amoebic mass moving toward the terminal.

He spotted me. I must have stood a good head above the rest of the crowd and I'm only 5' 9 ½'' tall. "Hello, Schweiboldson", Haz greeted.

"Kanitchiwa, Haz", or good afternoon, I shouted over the roar. "Knock off the formality, I'm JACK, remember?" as I immediately tried to break him of his Japanese business formality. I was lugging two full suitcases and a heavy flight case. "Where do we eat?" I asked as he reached to carry one of the suitcases.

"We will go down one level and catch a local toward your hotel. Stay close so we don't get separated . . . and watch out for the Packers!" he panted over his shoulder as he was having difficulty hauling my big bag and his briefcase.

"Who are the PACKERS?" I shouted ahead as we ran along a long narrow sub alleyway lined with shops, each the size of a 10 x 12 mini-

199

barn, selling everything from silk ties to electrical devices not yet available in America.

"They are those young men standing along the rear wall," he responded as we descended two flights of stairs and entered the subway's northbound loading area. "They are high school and university football players hired by the railroads to pack us into the cars!"

We were already person-to-person on the platform. Even from the back of the solid lines, I could see the trains brushing the clothes of the waiting passengers. "No one better push now or we'll all be mincemeat on the tracks," I thought. Once the train stopped, there was a backward surge as the people struggled to get off the train. Then the living mass slowly moved forward filling minute vacuums opening on each car.

"Hurry, Schweiboldson," Haz called. I could see I wasn't going to make it, and then I heard behind me...."

"HA-ZZ-e-e!" The PACKERS hit us with running blows from their back wall positions. Haz made it aboard in the first squeeze. Then I was swept directly into the car but my flight case was violently stripped from my hand before I was inside . . . several others were literally pounded and pressed behind me as the doors closed. I was pushed up tight against the opposite door window, my face turned sideways . . . with cheeks flat against the glass. Just below my chin was Haz, looking straight up at me with the same ghastly mash to his face.

"Don't people get hurt?" I managed to struggle out while bemoaning the loss of my flight bag.

"Sometimes these windows break and people are spit out into an oncoming train", he said matter-of-fact-like. "Our old people get to ride free between 10 am and 2 pm". The few minutes it took to go our two stops felt like an eternity, each flashing train seemed to have my name splattered on its front end. At our stop Haz grabbed my arm and we struggled to the door. Just as I stepped off, there was my bag . . . neatly stuffed behind the side facing seat. In one easy pull I had it safely off.

The Packers may have been brutal but I bet they were a team that could never be bribed . . . at least not for my flight case!

Sucking Wind

The next morning, Haz met me in the hotel lobby and we took a train to a local airport where the accident investigation team had prepared the engine for examination. Hurrying with our baggage, I was panting a little and Haz asked if I was OK. "Just winded", I responded, not wanting to tell him I was more than a little nervous. Actually, I was starting to "suck

200

wind"; beginning to mimic a custom I previously assigned Haz and his countrymen. I noted on previous trips that whenever they would get into a delicate personal or business situation, like them remembering Hiroshima or me remembering Pearl Harbor, they would clench teeth, redden in the face and start hissing as if "sucking wind".

Reaching the hangar at a politically prompt time, we found the engine displayed in the hangar's repair shop, looking much like a cold cadaver waiting autopsy. Following preliminary introductions at the hangar's maintenance shop, in strode the administrations leader, Dr Ohama. The whole team grew about two inches taller as they seemed to snap to formal attention. He crossed the 50 foot room and stopped close to the engine . . . in an obvious command position. I was immediately introduced in English as Schweiboldson, Chief Test Pilot and Supervisor of Flight Test for Allison Engines. Dr. Ohama immediately spewed a volume of Japanese at his colleagues while occasionally pointing to me and then the engine, stopping with his heated eyes resting on mine.

In the moment of silence, I boldly took one step forward, as we have trained our boys when being introduced, continued to look him straight in those fiery eyes and replied cheerfully, "Ohio Gonzama, Ohamason" (Good morning Mr. Ohama, in Japanese). Then while bowing ninety degrees with arms at my side, I continued, "Haminimaska dozo yaroska. Chachetawa Schweiboldson sandas." After this very polite introductive response, I continued in Japanese to extend "thanks" from our company President, and for my being able to represent him. The ensuing hush resembled that which accompanies new falling snow on a crisp winter night.

Switching to English, I added, "I have heard your English far exceeds my Japanese. Please, may we continue our conversations in English?" He immediately took two steps back and bowed deeper than mine, as he became erect I could see the face tighten. He continued retreating backward with an occasional bow, each one lower. As he turned to depart, I thought I could hear the familiar "sucking wind". The investigation eventually moved forward with courteous attention given my conclusions and recommendations.

On the trip back to my hotel in a private car provided by their team, I quietly asked Haz what had happen to Dr. Ohama. "Oh, he was offended Allison merely sent a dumb, stupid pilot rather than a group of engineers and thermodynamicsists. He called you many degrading names . . . until you correctly responded in almost perfect Japanese. He assumed you understood everything he just called you . . . and figured he committed political Hari Kari!" A couple days later, when checking out of the hotel, the desk clerk had waiting a small "Thank You" package from Dr. Ohama.

Once on the express train heading back to Narita Airport I was able to open the token souvenir and note which read, "Thank you for coming to Japan to add your valuable assistance to our investigation." My part in studying the phrase book obviously helped and I fully appreciated God's answer to my fervent prayers . . . it was the same answer he gave Moses:

You shall speak to him and put words in his mouth; I will help both of you speak and will teach you what to say. Exodus 4:15.

It was a good trip home.

26

The Cold War

A Roman Vineyard

"Da Rosa . . . the red light again!" exclaims Siai Marchitte's Chief Pilot, "I told you, it would only take a couple minutes before the Propeller Gear Box Chip Detector light would come on again!" We had just taken off from their company's side of Malpensa International Airport near the suburbs of Milan, Italy. We were in their copy of a lightweight turboprop model of our army's L19 spotter aircraft. To vividly make his point he pulled the throttle back, rolled abruptly to the left at our mere 300' in the air . . . just off the end of the runway … and plopped us in a vineyard between rows of ripe grapes. With leaves and dust engulfing the airplane he shut the engine off and said, "See, your handbook says to land and check the magnetic oil plug." He made his point! What a place to check the plug. As pilots, we don't always carry the correct wrench in our flight suit. We radioed their operations and a mechanic was sent to check the oil plug for contaminant while we had lunch in the nearby Aero Club.

This was my first visit to Europe and introduction to the Aero Club, a tradition still running strong since WWI. It was a small country type pub located on the airport where *all* the local aviators hung out. Memorabilia of the areas experimental and production aircraft decorated the walls and ceiling. Several shelves held beer mugs belonging to current locals and those left by famous persons from the past. I was introduced to the proprietor and his family and treated as though I had dined there forever. Every member of the household, from the children to the grandparents, served us the meal of the day. Here, there was never a question about your nationality; everyone was an airman . . . that placed all of us in a universal

203

family. It appeared much like my father-in-laws yacht club. Membership in the club made one a transient member of the club at which one docked . . . even on the other side of the continent. In the Aero Club, Aviation World Record holders were immediately elevated to commodore or admiralty status. Problems of the day were not discussed here. It was like being home but able to feel safe even though bombs were dropping and planes were falling from the sky . . . as ours just had.

We were back in the air after lunch and siesta. Their whole factory shut down for several hours while most of the workers returned to their homes for meals and rest. They would return and work until 7 pm. The flight that day was memorable, but not from the forced landing. I believe that episode may have been staged to direct my focus to the problem, a too sensitive magnetic sensor. What was memorable was the winding flight through the Italian valleys. It testified that Europe was laid out by footpath and cow trail, not by the surveyors who platted most of North America. Red clay tiles, capping almost every building, reflected the sun and rain as they had for millennia. My wistful state of mind yearned to have Sharon see this. Hopefully, some day she would.

The Cold War

Just up the road, a few kilometers from Siai Marchettee was another major Italian airframe manufacture, Agusta Aircraft. Following WWII, as the Axis countries were again permitted to build defenses, Count Agusta secured licensing agreements with a number of international helicopter companies to manufacture their ships for use in Europe. Even though war wasn't brewing in the Aero Clubs, the Cold War was at its zenith. The Berlin wall had just been erected by the Soviets and Italy was still torn politically a quarter century after the end of WWII. Most of the country's manufacturing and skilled craftsmen were located in the Northern Provinces and drawn to the party line of the "Workers" Communism while the balance of Italians were lovers, not fighters, with no interest in upsetting their perpetual happy hour.

Agusta's USA affiliates were Sikorsky Aircraft for large helicopters and Bell for smaller ships, most specifically the Jet Ranger Series powered by our small engine line, making us one of Agusta's prime vendors. The major advantage of this consortium was they were able to sell into markets that might otherwise be politically closed to U.S. manufacturers. Agusta was ready to design its first from-scratch helicopter, the Agusta twin engine, A109, presenting an opportunity for me to get my first twin helicopter experience. Allison was liberal in allowing me ample training at airframe companies because all of our first experimental installations were well in advance of any formal Pilot Course. This meant . . . "Go live with the airframe's test team as Liaison Engineering Pilot". Some of my most special friendships were established in this fashion.

Awaiting the first flight with Senior Luchono Fortsoni, Agusta's Chief Test Pilot, our local Service Representative billeted me at La Rocca Hotel. Sitting 30 kilometers further North on Logo (Lake) Maggori in the romantic tourist town of Arona was the La Rocca, translated, "the rock". The hotel was impinged on rock outcroppings above the lake. Here I would experience my initial impression of Italian  lodgings: few parking spots; surrender of passport to proprietor at night (remnant of Mussolini, leaves you feeling like a man without a country); cell like rooms, with one high window above reach or view; cold, carpet-less tile floors . . . but with food you'd die for! Arona abounded with delicious pastries. La Rocca, specialized in miniature, golf ball sized chocolate éclairs.

After a few evenings wandering every inch of narrow winding streets and lake front promenades in town, I decided to head into bustling Milan and its sites. Against the experienced advice of our service representative  (because of the Communist recruiting frenzy with the local unions), I boarded a train the next morning alone for downtown Milano. Being cheap, I intentionally ignored his directions and purchased a second class ticket to get a view . . . and smell . . . of the locals. It was a wonderful escapade; I've always been enamored of trains. My Grandma, Nanny, lived in a trailer adjacent to a switching yard when I was a kid. Now I had a whole antique European train set of my own to view. Being Saturday, the old coach car (these really old ones were assigned second class) was relatively uncrowded, had

205

worn wooded seats and smelled of a century's worth of sweat. Needless to say, in a brown leather trench coat, I was more than overdressed for second class of travel.

Once downtown I headed for the Cathedral Domo, a splendid structure begun in the late 12th century and finished in the 13th. It was a testimony to the craftsmanship, artistry and tenacity of local people, the first Italians to be aware of European technology filtering over the Alps. Rather than signup for pilgrimages faithful Catholics (climbing all the ramparts to view its 135 pinnacles and spires, 150 gargoyles, 96 giant statues, 164 large stained grass windows and thousands of little statutes), I merely walked through the center and climbed to the top of the dome. Here I was awed not by the beauty but by overwhelming wonder . . . that my mere faith in Christ's death for my sins and trust that He will take me to heaven, released me from the meaningless works of man. There were hundreds climbing these thousands of steps (some on knees) . . . only to go on to the next cathedral or relic and repeat the process ... never knowing when  they'd done enough. Jesus Christ already did it once and for all!

Eph 2:8&9 For it is by grace you have been saved, through faith—and this not from yourselves, it is the gift of God-- 9 not by works, so that no one can boast.

Drafted into the Communist Party

Departing the Domo at lunchtime, it was convenient to grab a bite to eat. The cathedrals in Europe are surrounded by a generous line of restaurant and junk shop entrapments, set to profit from the tourists. The great advantage is that they have menus in most languages. While it's fun to try sidewalk Italian, I've learned that just speaking in English immediately shifts them out of their native tongue. They shove you the English menu . . . they don't want to waste their time in repeated pantomime. When in doubt, I always order Spaghetti ala Bolognese, its spaghetti and meat sauce anywhere in the world . . . and you can't beat the Italianio version.

Following lunch, I located a native department store where the locals seemed to be shopping. It had a narrow street front but was six stories high. I went to the top by way of an old wood treaded escalator. It was only wide enough for one person, similar to the first one in Toledo at Tidkee's Department Store. It took me back 50 years! Prices here for the same goods I'd seen in the street market that covered several blocks in Arona once a week were 30-50% less. But at fixed cost, you missed all of the fun, or trauma, of bartering.

The escalator returning to the main floor was packed with bodies and packages as people were heading home for siesta. I was about six stairs from exiting when a big woman at the bottom screamed in terror as she fell. In slow-escalator-motion I could see it had eaten her dress and ... was pulling her INTO the grating. Each person was piling up on her, driving her further into the machine's jaws. I tried leaping in O.J. Simpson style but couldn't clear the growing hurdle. I tripped and fell just beyond her still shrieking body. As I stood, her terrified yells ended. I turned to see the carnage and to my amazement saw her laying, shaking violently,

stripped to bra and underpants . . . with one short sleeve dangling from her shoulder. The monster staircase had ripped the balance of her clothing off and was methodically digesting the dress. She was assisted to her feet and appeared to be without a scratch. I wanted to stay and see what happened next but the lobby quickly filled with dozens of hand-waving

excited shoppers. I headed toward the Swartzcaw Castle.

The old Castle was once headquarters for the ruling family in the 1200's but now served as the city's major museum. I spent several hours roaming its various rooms, treasure troves and ramparts doing my best to decipher inscriptions with a very limited English guide book. I stayed until the 6:00 pm closing, realizing how much richness I missed not knowing the language.

Exiting through the castle's main gate put me onto a major boulevard heading back to the train. A crowd was streaming by and I was picked up by its wake, fortunately they were heading toward the station. Then I realized by the chanting, large red banners being carried, and drums beating . . . I was in the middle of a Communist march heading for a rally in the central palazzo. Now, my trench coat served a good cover. I vowed not to say a word, no matter how hard I was jostled or shoved. They may have lynched this English speaking ex-GI in the plaza.

Eventually, I zigzagged a block to the right and paralleled the mob back to the station boarding my intended 7 o'clock train back to Arona. Getting into the hotel that night I called our local rep, as he had requested, from the only pay phone. Slipping my getone, teletoken, into the payphone, I called Fritz at his home where he was having a party. He couldn't hear me well for all of the commotion going on at his place and in my adjacent bar and dance floor. I told him about being "drafted into the Communist Rally" . . . and then was the cut off because my time expired. It took me several minutes to get to the cashier upstairs for more getones and finish the call. By the time I replied they all thought I had been kidnapped and were wondering where to start searching. I believe that was the last time anyone at Allison ever worried, "Where in the world is ol' Jack?"

27

Who Rescues Rescuers?

"Hey, Dad, here comes one of the boat trailer tires!" reported Brad from the back seat. Sure enough, there it went, racing ahead of us . . . again. I don't know the physics involved but when a trailer wheel comes off, it speeds along AHEAD of the car running at 70 mph. Fortunately, a car wasn't coming in the lane now controlled by the tire. Those little 8 inch wheels just weren't designed for long distance travel with a 19' ski boat loaded to the gunwales with tents, bed rolls, cooking equipment and a week's worth of food. Two blowouts and this second wheel separation got us to Little Current, Canada in the center of the North Channel of Lake Huron. At this point we were to meet Sharon's brother and lead him (in his boat) forty water miles into Frazier Bay. There we were to camp with Dad and Mom Crouse on Blueberry Island. They would meet us to spend a week together; the previous year we had enjoyed a "family blast" in this pristine environment. Everyone in the car was excited, anticipating this year's wilderness experience and tolerated the inconvenience of occasionally shopping for an odd tire. Mark and Scott, 12 and 14, were crewing Dad's boat as he was coming the full 700 miles by water.

Larry, Carol, Danny and Stephany arrived in town around 7 pm; we grabbed a quick supper and checked into the "Sundowner", a shaggy bark special motel about 8 pm. No, this one wasn't the cheapest I could find, it was the best . . . but still smelled of highly seasoned mildew. This fisherman's dream was the beginning of our nightmare. Everyone was so excited we couldn't sleep, so at 9 pm we checked out of the motel, backed the boats into the water and secured our cars in a public lot. By 10 pm we were crossing an open sea that we'd only traveled one season before. The sun had set long before. Larry, an ex-Coast Guard seaman, was fresh off an around-the-world voyage on the Eastwind Icebreaker and this ex Air/Sea Rescue pilot . . . should have known better than to attempt this mission at dusk. We had more than an hour's travel.

The two women were starting to get a little edgy as we headed out of the harbor. I could see no joy on Carol's face in Larry's boat, as she clutched her two children and one of ours. Sharon was already praying aloud by the time we were in open water, hoping I would sense her concern and turn back. By the time we should have see a line of tidal outcroppings to our left it was dark . . . as we continued to run at maximum cruise speed in our little 85 hp runabout. Larry was just idling along behind our wake in his big 200HP+ inboard speedboat. Sharon, recognizing if we hit those rocks at this speed, we'd all be a bloody mass for whoever found us at low tide, became highly concerned. She couldn't see the rocks depicted on the chart she was clutching. Her eyes were tearing as she tried to read through spray and bounce . . . it's the mothers who have true survival and protection instinct. For all Larry's and my rescue experience, there would be no one to rescue us in these waters. Ice had just surrendered the surface a couple weeks before.

We finally came to the inlet and harbor leading into Blueberry Island. Using our searchlights, we found the loan dock leading to a seldom used cabin. We couldn't use the cabin but Dad had docking privileges for his cruiser this week. Unloading, we recognized our next enemy . . . mosquitoes. We decided to sleep in the open, it would be impossible to erect a tent at midnight on the rocky island we were assigned. Our only protection would be to zip up in our sleeping bags and sweat out the hot night. The ensuing battle with airborne pests lasted through daybreak. No one slept and fortunately God provided an early sunup, as He had provided us the late 11 pm twilight, both for our safety and survival. Coffee, hot off the morning campfire . . . never tasted so good.

The Prodigal

Everyone has heard about the prodigal son. Well, Larry, who had spent the night with us fighting mosquitoes, was our family's returning prodigal.

He was on his third marriage and this was his LONG announced introduction of his newest family. Mom and Dad wouldn't arrive with the rest of our boys until noon this second day. Once in position, Dad rightfully welcomed his son and family home. Larry and his family were berthed aboard Dad's 42-foot Hatteras Cruiser to spend the nights. We'd never had that invitation. We were still out on the island in our tent . . . with the bears and bugs. Our kids got on Dads nerves (Scott caught the biggest fish); Larry's kids could do no

210

wrong. Then, Dad broke out the fatted lamb and the feast was on . . . a case of beer for him and Larry. We rowed over to our island to sulk.

I believe the whole point of the Prodigal Son parable was not about the son or dad but about the older brother's stinking attitude . . . in this case the brother-in-law's, MINE! The more I brooded, the more I failed to see we had always been Dad's favorites. Maybe we'd not been told so, but we knew we faired better than Larry. Blinded by anger, I couldn't understand the joy Mom and Dad were experiencing in being reunited with their lost son and his ready made family . . . with older children who wouldn't get their jelly fingerprints on his boat.

So, the next morning without any further ado, I loaded our boat to the brim and proceeded to run the forty miles of rough water back to our car at Little Current. Fortunately, Larry, only feeling joy at being welcomed back into the fold, was sober enough to intervene. He took some of our load and broke waves with his bigger boat as we headed back to the mainland. Mark and Scott were abandoned to crew Dad's boat return to Toledo at the end of the week. It was a bleak 1000-mile, non-stop drive back home.

After a non-communicative summer and fall, Mom and Dad did come for Christmas and Romans 8:27-28 was proven to be true; God works all things for good for those who are called according to his purpose. God can make beauty out of ashes. I'd had time to see the errors of the prodigal brother-in-law, so I privately asked Dad Crouse for his forgiveness. He replied, "I'm the one who was wrong. What is it that you want, Jack?"

To which I replied, "We just want your approval, Dad".

He stared blankly, "Our approval?" Maybe Mom and Dad needed our approval, too. It was a great Christmas we'd never forget. Everyone needs to HEAR that they are approved, loved and respected. The epilogue to this "Parable of The Prodigal Son's Brother-In-Law" is that a couple years after I got my heart right, Dad caught me in our garage while he was smoking a cigar and said out-of-the-blue, "I'm ready, Jack."

"You're ready for what, Dad?"

"To accept Jesus Christ", he replied with a smile. As we pulled up a couple of boxes to talk, he added, "My only regret is that . . . I have to admit my mother-in-law, Ethel, was right all these years!"

You see, Dad was *"Called according to God's purpose"*, too.

28

Operation Speed

"Jack, take $35,000 and set as many records as possible with our new C30 engines", challenged our program manager. Wow, that was like giving a teenager a new convertible, a bottomless credit card and instructions to drive his friends around the country, FAST. Then, to my amazement, he continued, "You set most of the records. We know you are gracious enough to share them with our friends in the industry. Have fun. I wish I was going with you!"

We did just that, starting with our friends at Petroleum Helicopter, Inc. in Lafayette, Louisiana. At that time, next to the U.S. and Russian military, PHI had the third largest fleet of helicopters in the world; most powered by our engines. By leasing one of their Sikorsky S76 helicopters, utilizing two of our upgraded C30's, we proceeded to set or beat over a dozen speed, distance, altitude, time-to-climb and coast to coast records. We incorporated some flights into practical applications, like one weight-class speed record flown from the historic first off-shore oil rig in the Gulf of Mexico to a hospital in Houston . . . simulating an emergency medical evacuation rescue highlighted by local media, all good advertisement for PHI and Allison.

While operating out of Lafayette, we utilized many of their pilots and ours, spreading excitement to their staff and encouragement to ours. I held my attempts until departing Lafayette to Indianapolis, setting the heavyweight class distance record non-stop to Detroit. We installed three large rectangular fuel tanks, giving us wall-to-wall fuel storage across the aft cabin with jump seat space for a couple of riders. We were on our way enroute New York City to attempt the first coast-to-coast helicopter record, ROUNDTRIP!

In NYC, I picked up two of our company pilots, Harry and Fritz. Departing at daybreak the next day, we proceeded westbound stopping only three times for fuel in Indianapolis, Wichita, and Albuquerque. During fuel stops we would refuel, check the ship and be airborne within ten minutes . . . pit stops inspired by our Indianapolis auto racing. Nighttime found us over the Grand Canyon with the 3rd man sleeping in shifts atop the rear tanks. We cleared the San Juncito Mountains at 12,000' to take advantage of the westerly flowing Santa Anna winds, passed over the Seal Beach Radio Beacon in Los Angeles completing the first East to West helicopter flight in less than one day, only 19 hours. Turning back eastward at the coast, we made a high rate descent into Riverside Airport for fuel. Passing through 7,000-feet in the descent we heard two muffled "boom, booms" from the rear compartment. Checkout while refueling indicated everything was okay. We only fueled to half the auxiliary tank levels, since we would have better winds after we crossed the desert heading east.

Our second and final refueling eastbound was at Saint Louis. We bypassed Lambert International due to weather lowering below 500-feet and less than a mile visibility. Heavy weather was laying over the whole Eastern part of the continent; the Appalachians would certainly have heavy rain and low visibilities and ceilings. These conditions were already reported in NYC, not encouraging for night operations even in an all weather helicopter. While fueling we grabbed a hamburger at the restaurant overlooking the ramp.

Anxiety set in as we moved toward that final take-off for NYC. We'd have to make our final decision enroute before passing over the Appalachians. Running to the ship while tucking the last remnants of hamburger in our flight suits, we were stunned to find the big Sikorsky sitting in the center of a 200-foot diameter lake of jet fuel glistening in the ramp lights!

Apparently, those two muffled "boom, booms" in California were two of our large fuel tanks rupturing during the high rate descent after clearing the mountains. The fuel vents were large enough to vent fuel burned but were not large enough to return heavier air to empty tanks during descent ... too much outer pressure ruptured the upper seams in two tanks. Since we only filled the tanks half-way in California, they didn't show leakage until they split when full here on the ramp. God can be seen in the whole operation, had the tanks split at night enroute in weather, ground observers may have seen the explosion only as a bolt of lighting in the clouds. He made the decision to terminate the flight when weather conditions could have become disastrous to the foolhardy. The next day weather was

Jack, Fritz Harvey, and Harry Sutton are welcomed from the record setting flights by Allison's CEO, Dr. Blake Wallace. Over a dozen pilots were utilized in setting 15 U.S. and World Records with the company's new Model 250-30, 650 HP Engine.

reported below minimums up and down the entire East Coast. Yes, this was a minor disappointment, but well worth it to see . . . the glory of God.

Go Design an Aircraft!

"Jack, what is the best general aviation airplane to re-engine with our 450hp turbo-prop?" asked our Small Engine Program Manager.

"The Beechcraft A36 Bonanza would make a winner," I replied without hesitation. "It's a stout airframe and already recognized as the Cadillac of single engine reciprocating aircraft. It's the doctor/lawyer/businessman's choice . . . the top of the line, without having to retrain to upgrade to a twin."

"Go design it and bring us back a sketch layout and your ideas of how it should be built," my manager concluded.

I grabbed my flight test mechanic and friend, George Cummins, "Bring your tape measure. I've got some paper; let's find an A-36 and layout a new aircraft!" The resultant offering was a sleek, almost 2 foot stretch of the already aerodynamically clean Bonanza.

We offset the engine weight loss in the nose by adding additional luggage space. Auxiliary fuel tanks with vertical winglets would be added to give it a star class appearance and extended range. Meeting with our Vice-President the next day, the program was approved from the pencil caricature.

This configuration was first offered to Beech Aircraft who had just terminated their own single-engine turboprop project with a larger engine and pressurized airframe . . . priced almost as much as their successful twin-engine King Air. Even though our approach seemed feasible by some of their engineers, it wasn't accepted. Their Starship Program was draining corporate coffers. The first prototype was built by Soloy, an aircraft conversion company in Washington State. It was ready for flight in a mere 60 days from go-ahead. Following first flights, Allison determined they would handle direct sales of this product line rather than have the conversion company merchandise it. Whoever would have thought real estate, helicopter charter and amusement ride sales would qualify me to become Chief Pilot, Supervisor of Flight Test AND Turboprop Sales Manager? Another job that came in the slipstream was to oversee building of the conversion kits and future Model 250 conversion programs.

Within a few months a handful of distributors were signed for the Prop-Jet Bonanza. I always appreciated the confidence and trust of Joe Boyd of Tradewind Turbine in Amarillo, Texas. When Soloy raised their conversion price by several thousand dollars the night before signing . . . he said when all others were ready to head home, "Jack, I believe in this ship, count me in!" First production aircraft were delivered to the dealers at the Annual Bonanza Society meeting in Boston, Mass. Roses and daughter-in-law Mindy's chocolates were setup in each of the attendee's rooms, along with a personal copy of the National Aeronautics Association's World Record Book. Featured on its cover was "The Allison Prop-Jet Bonanza" with "Smiling Jack" and his crews tucked on the inside covers.

In the midst of this triumphful joy, Sharon received a call that her father died. Another hard trip home, but she was comforted by the fact we knew where he was. "I'm ready", Dad had said in the garage, "to accept Jesus Christ!" Dad was now with Him.

217

Jack Schweibold, Chief Test Pilot for Allison Gas Turbine
Division of GM, points to new World Speed Records being
added to a map at Allison Flight Operations, Indianapolis.
Already holding the greatest number of World Helicopter
Records, Jack is setting out with his company teammates
toward a new goal — with their Allison Turbine Aircraft featured on these covers they are planning to make Indianapolis
not only the Automotive, but soon also an Aeromotive Speed
Capital of the World.

Cover Aircraft: Allison 250-B17 Turbine powered A36 Bonanza,
holder of nine speed records including Tulsa to Indianapolis
at 266.43 mph and Reno C-1c 15/25 km closed course at
234.89 mph.

The Allison World Record Team has claimed over 50 World Speed, Climb, Distance & Altitude Marks in the past few months—all accomplished within normal engine operating limits. Several of the members stand above with the 250-C20S powered Soloy Cessna 206G, from left to right— Paul Nielsen, Nathan Watkins, Brian Halsey, Harry Sutton, Daniel Black, Jerry Marlette, George Cummins, Larry Chambers, Mark Schweibold, Jay Penner, John Beetham and Jack Schweibold.

Indiana Senator Richard Lugar presents, in his Washington, D.C. capital office some of the over fifty U.S. and World Records set or captured by Allison's crews. From let-to-right, Larry Chambers, Jay Penner, Senator Richard Lugar, George Cummins and Jack Schweibold hold the diplomas for:

- Speed
- Altitude
- Distance

In:

- Land Planes
- Seaplanes
- Amphibians
- Helicopters

29

Ask the King

The Nehemiah Story

Have you ever had a burning desire in your heart, one that you think is righteous and needed in every respect; however, one that is just physically and financially out reach . . . and fought at almost every level? If the answer is yes, read along these accounts of how it was accomplished in my career . . . by following a formidable example in scripture.

After we assembled the Prop-Jet Bonanza Dealership network in the US, I saw a need to expand it overseas, first into Europe. I had already alienated my General Manager. He told me three times in one sitting that he would not let me, personally fly ships across the North Atlantic. I should have taken the compliment, "You are too valuable for the corporation to lose". The rejection and admonishment for daring to ask three times left me shaken.

At that time in our church, Pastor Don Tyler was challenging us from the Book of Nehemiah toward another building program. I always appreciated Don's fiscal teachings to get consensus, have most of the money in the bank and then build like mad in faith. Studying along in the Bible with his sermons each Sunday, I could see from already scrawled notes that he'd preached this before. It was still very applicable and effective. The graphic 25-foot "giving thermometer" sitting next to the podium grew rapidly until it burst at the top, indicating a construction go-a-head! God set in my heart to implement my own Nehemiah approach, which meant I needed to get my attitude right first.

Nehemiah, who had been captive in Persia, was burdened to return to Jerusalem and rebuild the walls of the destroyed city walls. In Nehemiah Chapter 1, he stated,

"For some days I mourned and fasted and prayed before the God of heaven. 5 Then I said: "O LORD, God of heaven, the great and awesome God, who keeps his covenant of love with those who love him and obey his commands, 6 let your ear be attentive and your eyes open to hear the prayer your servant is praying before you day and night ..... I confess the sins we Israelites, including myself and my father's house, have committed against you."

Yes, I fasted, prayed and confessed my arrogance of effectively telling my managers to let me fly where and do what I wanted. After a significant period I set another meeting with management but first I prayed the end of Chapter 1, *"1 O Lord, let your ear be attentive to the prayer of this your servant and to the prayer of your servants who delight in revering your name. Give your servant success today by granting him favor in the presence of this man."*

Nehemiah and I obtained those audiences and I learned that he continued to pray through that and all future meetings and activities. I did likewise! We both laid out well defined and coordinated plans. Nehemiah would conscript workers in Jerusalem and we would contract ferry pilots to get our ships to Europe. The King granted Nehemiah's requests and my manager (my king) granted mine, with an expanded task to examine the paramilitary market for a T-34 War Bird Group who had installed one of our Bonanza Turbo-prop kits. We were on our way to the Continent!

The French Connection

I have to admit, he may not have been king, but my boss was right. Why fight the lousy weather over the North Atlantic? The contract pilots flew our Bonanza and Prop-Jet T-34 to France while Sharon and I relaxed in the backend of TWA. Both of the ships were waiting for us on the tarmac when Jay Penner and I arrived to set up our displays at the Paris Air Show . . . or "Pavilion", as the French title it. It has been a bi-annual event since the turn of the 19th century, starting with hot air balloons. This was my third trip to the extravaganza. One thing I'd learned . . . everything from floor space to food is extravagantly expensive.

These frogs (Frenchmen) really know how to rip a buck while moving at half speed. Sharon and I stopped in a small bookshop near our hotel on Avenue des Champs Elysees to purchase a tour guide of the city written in English. One person welcomed us, a second led us to the appropriate shelf, a third accepted it at the counter, a fourth cashiered and a fifth made us wait as she wrapped it . . . while we strained to escape the store. "Why, all this inefficiency?" I asked.

"Well, our unemployment is lower than yours!" responded the one person willing to admit speaking English. Normally, they want to force you to deal with their dying French language.

"If it weren't for all of the American tourists returning to see where their relatives died defending your country, you'd have no economy!" I muttered as Sharon pulled me from the store. We did have to admit Paris probably has more interesting sights in one city than anywhere else in the world. From the Eiffel Tower to the Louvre, they're hard to beat. The "Champs" never shut down, the beggars, entertainers and musicians are at the same location day after day and night after night. Sharon, having toured Europe with me before and Jay's wife, Paula, learned to negotiate the subways and visit sites on their own. One day on their way to Sacre-Couer (Sacred Heart) Cathedral, they were eyed-down by the local girls. The neighborhood women wanted Sharon and Paula off their street, as they strolled down Rue "Pigalle", pronounced "Pig Alley" . . . verbally descriptive for the districts business.

Meanwhile, back at LeBourge Aeroporto (same field where Lindbergh landed), we had displays set to attract civil buyers and military arms merchants, the latter being key attendees at the show. There was an obvious element of military police stationed around the entire show. On the USA Building were squads of armed U. S. Marines and Army Guards, well before the infamous 9-11. While the USA self restricts who it will

225

sell advanced technology, the French seem pleased to sell or be an intermediary for armament to **anyone** . . . making this the melting pot of aviation and munitions sales agents.

"Welcome to LeBourge main pavilion building at the bi-annual Paris Airshow"

Our job, secure a sale for our Prop-Jet Bonanza and appointments to demonstrate the re-engined T-34 military trainer. This thirty year old trainer's airframe was similar to the Bonanza's and it utilized one of our 450 hp turboprops in place of the old 225 hp recip, giving double the power.

During the week, the show is open only to paid attendees and vendor guests. On the weekend, it's open to the public of France . . . free for every school kid in town, a zoo! We set to secure our business early. By the end of the second day we were able to announce in Aviation Daily's Convention newspaper that we had preliminarily signed Eichenberger Aviation as our European Prop-Jet Bonanza Agent.

Eichenberger's Paris Display is shown here, highlighting O & N Aircraft's conversion of the Cessna Pressurized P210 to a 450 HP Allison Turbine

In the first few days we also set appointments with the Turkish, Dominican Republic and Columbian governments. The only immediate catch was that Jay and I would have to help Werner Eichenberger ferry five other small Cessna Aircraft he purchased at the show to Switzerland, then he would test fly our ship in Zurich. Well, anything to close a deal!

Before we left the show that year, we solved an amazing puzzle. At previous pavilions in Europe, we had noticed a number of "FAA looking" gents, all toting field glasses, quietly walking around writing down the tail numbers of various aircraft. Occasionally, they would ask a few casual questions about the installation. Here-to-fore we had only been with our engine displays indoors and never had the opportunity to question these inspectors; this time we grabbed one by the arm and questioned HIM! "Just what are you guys doing with all these notations?" I asked.

"Well mate", he responded, "we are all members of Aero Pubs. They are kind of like your pilot Aero Clubs. We can't afford flying and normally don't have licenses but we love aviation. These logbooks aren't filled with flight hours but with aircraft SPOTTINGS. One bloke at the end of the bar will shout out an aircraft tail number he saw somewhere and another person in the pub would reply with where that plane was to confirm a sighting. It really gets exciting and this is a great place to sight hundreds of sporty ships."

I couldn't resist replying, "Blimey, mate, sounds awesome … just like our Bird Watching Society!" Despite regulations, Americans still have freedom and means to fly.

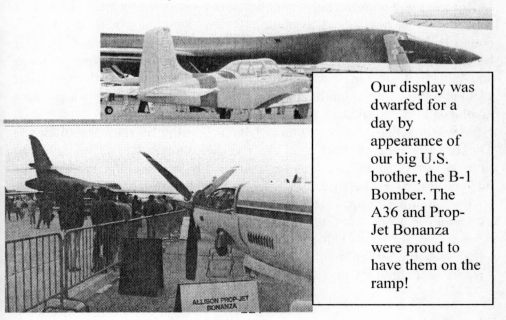

Our display was dwarfed for a day by appearance of our big U.S. brother, the B-1 Bomber. The A36 and Prop-Jet Bonanza were proud to have them on the ramp!

The Swiss Legend

Never will I forget the first day meeting Herr Werner Eichenberger. He was to meet my commercial flight landing at Zurich International Airport. After clearing customs, I entered the spacious, nearly vacant lobby. Nobody in sight appeared to be scouting for an American stranger. I stopped in the center of the modern marshaling room, dropped my bags and waited. As the cases hit the concrete floor, a tall, animated, 60's looking gentleman came whirling onto the upper escalator dressed in a green hospital gown and street trousers. An I-V needle taped to his wrist was trailing tubes flapping in the breeze. Half way down the escalator he bellowed out, "Hair Schvybolt, Velcom to Swizerlandt!" It was my friend-to-be, Werner. That morning he was rushed to the hospital with a gall bladder attack. Apparently, upon reaching my arrival hour, he ripped himself out of the emergency room to meet this fellow aviator from America.

While negotiating introductions and meeting his fraulein secretary, he threw my three big bags on what looked like a shopping cart. He ran full speed toward the upward climbing stainless stairs yelling, "Watch these carts go on the escalator. Swiss ingenuity makes them super OK!" Sure enough, rubber "ZZZ's" bolted to the bottom of the cart wedged into the steel stair until the tread retreated at the top.

This encounter eventually generated our recent Paris meeting where he had accepted an invitation to evaluate the Prop-Jet Bonanza. Now I was ferrying one of his Cessna 150's to Switzerland, alone. After take-off from LeBorgue there were no further radio calls until reaching the border. Just sightseeing; I was in a powered glider, hanging over the French countryside at a mere 300-500-feet and 80-miles per hour. I was able to sit back and enjoy the continent sweeping under my feet. Castles, chateaus and cathedral steeples seemed to brush my heels. I glided over what seemed like endless landscape paintings of the impressionist painters displayed in the Louvre.

After crossing western France, I landed in the Swiss town of Basel. Tucked in a little projection in the river, it appeared to be as much in France and Germany as in Switzerland. My mind envisioned eras of intrigue played out here during the last wars. The tower directed taxi to the customs holding ramp, I deplaned and stood alone, awaiting a barrage of inspectors. No one responded, and then I saw Werner waving me to the other side of the ramp, behind the customs gate.

He was motioning me through, I hesitated . . . I didn't want to be shot. "Where do I show my passport?" I quickly asked.

"Don't start a bad procedure," he snapped back, "Put it away! Pilots can go almost anywhere in Europe on their flying license. Just flash your FAA License to anyone that asks. No one did. However, one agent asked who I was and Werner replied in German, "He's one of my American Pilots." Man, I was privileged to be inducted into Swiss ranks, learning that my associate was a legend in his country . . . as a "Father of Aviation". He packed Jay and me onto a Swiss Air flight. I expected to meet his daughter, a Swiss Air captain but she wasn't piloting our ship that day. We flew back to LeBorge to pickup the Bonanza, T34 and our wives. I could hardly wait to fly them all into Werner's Buttwil (Boot-ville) Airport, his private airfield in the Swiss Alps.

Alpine Shangri-La

Shangri-La has been a mythical place throughout history . . . but not for aviators. It exists in its fullest richness at Werner's Buttwil (Boot-ville) air haven on the edge of the Swiss Alps. Jay and the girls had not been here before, so I had to call Jay's attention back to tighten our formation flying before making a low level pass over the grass strip. "Jay, I'll take the Bonanza in first. This is the ship we're selling here," I instructed over our company radio frequency, which probably belonged to someone else in Europe. "Buttvil UNICOM (Universal Inter Communication for small airports) this is Allison Prop-Jet Bonanza, flight of two aircraft for a low level fly-by," I transmitted, hoping someone would understand the English.

"Jack! … Ve've ben vaiting fer you," Werner responded in broken excitement.

"Roger, we'll come over downwind," I advised, assuming they would clear traffic. A downwind pass added 20-40 knots visual speed due to the relative wind over the airfield. Jay was tucked snugly above my left wing. Sitting in the cockpit on the left, I could peripherally just

229

see his propeller. Jay's position in his clear tandem glass cabin gave him full view of us at all times. My job would be to clear the area and miss obstacles like trees, his job was to follow. As we crested a 6,000-foot mountain top, Buttwil came into sight, an emerald field of green riveted at 4,000-feet on the side of the descending hills . . . overlooking a valley cascading hundreds of feet below.

"Awesome!" I could read Jay's lips as I saw him flip thumbs up. Paula sat to his rear, smiling. We didn't have to discuss this routine. We'd duplicated it many times, from the Oshkosh Air Shows to the Reno Air Races. Jay watched my cue, just a nod as we passed high overhead the group forming below. Sharon, well experienced by now, secured loose items within her reach. Then we pealed into a right rolling wing-over and a screaming dive to the far end of the runway . . . actually dropping below to stay out of their sight as the mountain fell into the valley. Using the trees and cliff as a screen to hide from the onlookers, we only had to pop a little aft stick to clear the trees at redline speed and then drop just off the grass on the flyby. Clearing the far end of the short strip in seconds, we pulled up into a near 4G vertical climb and zoom maneuver. Entering opposing ¾ rolls on top, we circled and rejoined at the far end of the field for a formation landing. Utilizing full reverse thrust at touchdown for minimum landing rolls, we made our turns backing up (this feature had already permitted us to command the record books for STOL aircraft). Without hesitation, we took off in opposite directions for a couple more passes of minimal aerobatics. I could see Paula's face turning green in the sun, Sharon emptied her purse in the side door pocket and said, "One more wingover or roll . . . and my spaghetti ala bolognaise from lunch goes in the purse!" If we were going to make a sale, we'd already clenched it; we taxied in to an eager crowd.

Our treat was yet in store, lunch in their aero club restaurant run by Werner's wife, Margaret. It and the small operations building sat in a Swiss style structure overlooking the field. Our girls opted to sit out lunch. Outside could be heard the gentle toll of cowbells above on the mountain. An occasional airplane would take-off on a training flight or tow mission while gliders swept silently through the treetops back to earth on parallel grass strips. On a previous visit Werner had slipped me into his Enstrom Helicopter, asked me if I could fly it and turned me loose with an autorotation … told me to recover to a hover. I asked to take it to the ground. A perfect engine out landing, "Remarkable!" he said, in mutual respect, even on his turf. He had almost every conceivable type of aircraft operating from his kingdom.

Werner's exposition on the ecological requirements to maintain the natural look of the area revealed his tenacity to agonize through endless local and state government paperwork and regulations. This trait obviously qualified him to work with FAA. In building the strip, he had to buy land elsewhere to plant at least one tree for every tree he cut down. The entire field had to be tile drained and reinforced UNDER the sod. While he needed new hangar and office space, nothing could be built . . . any add-on was still pending, years away, if ever. All aircraft were held to a maximum decibel level of noise which required mufflers that reduced engine horsepower, already critical at these altitudes in summertime. Runways could not be extended; all of these elements made the quiet, high performance, load-carrying Prop-Jet Bonanza a great alpine candidate for Buttwil! We would be demonstrating the next few days to some of the local aero club members, 1000 strong. Hopefully, they would be utilizing it in transporting sightseers to view the Matterhorn and other peaks that rose majestically across the valley.

It had been a long day culminating an equally lengthy week of sales and entertainment. Nightly continental suppers don't begin until 8-10 pm, way past our 5 pm Indiana mealtime. With today's extra flights, battling unintelligible French controllers and the girls being concerned for our safety while awaiting our return . . . we were all exhausted. Our small but clean second story Zimmer accommodations were welcomed; we slept well under the down comforters.

Yes, Werner's group bought the Prop-Jet Bonanza the following week. As God enabled Nehemiah to rebuild the city walls of Jerusalem, I'm convinced God is likewise involved in landing aircraft . . . or landing sales contracts!

30

Expedition to Ephesus

Clandestine Weapons Cash

Following other demonstrations elsewhere in Switzerland, Jay and I put our wives back aboard TWA in Zurich. Once they were heading home, Jay readied the T-34 for departure to Turkey. I met with a couple of munitions dealers. Funny, we had to go to the "peace loving" Swiss to find a source of armament compatible with our Beechcraft T-34 Mentor. Hundreds of these ships are still used as primary trainers around the globe in third-world countries. Our goal was to market upgrade-engine packages, extending the ship for use as a paramilitary vehicle another thirty-five years . . . but we needed access to some significant weaponry to hang from easily installed hard points beneath the wings.

Walking into a small two room office, my thought was, "How can they be selling armament here?" After introductions and a cup of espresso, one of the men pushed a desk button and full wall doors automatically spread back. They exposed a wall of technical manuals on almost every aircraft and weapon built, from many nations. What wasn't available in hard copy was quickly accessible in the second room's files of microfiche (film).

Their answer to our interest in weapons was not just a mere "Yes" or "No" but . . . "What do you want, how many, when and where delivered and how much cash do have?" This was the end of the rainbow. We had hit the pot-of-gold for which we were searching! Before we left, they assembled a portfolio of surveillance cameras, guns, rockets and bombs suitable to start or end a war in most any country; just the information needed to complement our military demonstrations. Hey, how did I suddenly get so far from Air/Sea Rescue?

Once back at Buttwil, I received a frantic call from Jay; he was arrested and fined $1,500 U.S. "We used to keep $5.00 in our socks to get bailed out of the pokey in Mexico, Jay!" I replied, "But I don't have $1,500 in BOTH socks. What happened?"

"Well, I was performing a preflight inspection on the ship at Zurich's ramp. I drained the fuel sumps into the water inspection cup and threw a quarter cup of fuel on the ground, as we always do. Then, sirens sounded and fire trucks and squad cars surrounded me! They hosed down the whole ramp and wrote me a $1,500 citation for contaminating Switzerland with hazardous chemicals. Help!" Fortunately, our "Swiss Legend", Werner Eichenberger stepped forward and pleaded ignorance for the "American Waste Makers" and cleared Jay . . . saving us both the job of becoming "overly creative" with company expense reports.

Expedition to Ephesus

I departed Switzerland for Ankara, Turkey on Swiss Air with an associate from our Washington State conversion shop, Tim Koestor. We left Jay with one of Werner's Flight Instructors who was familiar with flying through Italy and the Mediterranean countries. They would jointly fly the T34 into Turkey's Air Training Command Headquarters located near the ruins of Ephesus. Tim and I would rendezvous with some of his local Turkish contacts for demonstrations to their Air Force. It seems that every country from Japan to Jakarta needs to grease the palm of a local rep through commissions . . . to help us with contacts, customs and language. We found our Ankara contacts in the central marketplace working out of a small 15' wide strip office. It appeared to have existed as a street bazaar well before the crusades. Once inside, there was room for two chairs, a couple of desks and a curtain hiding whatever might be lurking in the rear. A handful of men seemed to be passing in and out, handling important business matters. Two of them stepped forward and introduced themselves in clear English. These were our emissaries to drive us 300 miles to Turkey's Air Force Base on the Eastern Adriatic coast.

We spent the next few hours traveling adjacent rug and souvenir shops negotiating the "best" black market exchange on U.S. dollars. Everyone wanted them; it was a bidding exercise for our associates to prove their negotiation skills. The only problem was we must conform to the custom of a shot of tea out of the same "genie" looking pot in EVERY kiosk. After we had secured a sufficient wad of lira (2,000 to a U.S. dollar), a similar excursion was taken in search of the best airline tickets for our return flight to Istanbul. It seems any one-room hockshop was also a travel agent and could barter transportation anywhere in the world . . . "But only the 'best price' could be obtained in the old quarter of Ankara!" we were told. I was beginning to appreciate our intermediaries, but with all the tea, I needed to GO! Figuring there had to be a toilet or at least a pot behind

234

those woven curtains, I asked to GO. The old quarter was a walled city built on a hill, similar to many medieval towns. I was escorted through the 5-foot rear of the stall, then a plank door. I was standing outside the wall, on a cliff. Gravity took care of sewage. I quit drinking tea.

By noon the next day we were enroute to Ephesus in the youngest Turk's twelve-year-old Buick Rivera. His young German wife of just two weeks sat next to him in front, with his boss next to her. Tim and I had the comfort of the full back seat. Boss was a middle-aged, stout man that always referred to his "special" contacts as being, "From my same school." We never knew if that was a university, military, high school or kindergarten. Even the General we were to meet was from his "old school". Young Turk was just happy to be with his wife as they cuddled close during the beginning of the trip. I believe this was to be their honeymoon. About an hour out of the capital, on what was the major road across Turkey, the same one on which the Greeks, Romans and Mongols had traveled, we could see traffic halted at the top of a far hill.

We discussed our schedule with the air force in two days, our accommodations on the coast and time we might have to tour the ruins at Ephesus. Soon we came to stopped traffic. We could see the cars backed up in our lane a mile or so in front where there were some obstacles atop the hill. Cars began filling in behind us as far as we could see. Unexpectedly, a dust trail formed behind us and a whole lane of traffic passed us on the brim to the right, eventually stopping in a solid line. Now we had two solid lanes heading west. Two hours passed and two more lanes of traffic formed westbound on our LEFT! Men and women started milling around and tempers were getting HOT! According to the grapevine, there were center line painters ahead and the military had traffic stopped in both directions.

You already have the picture. Four rows of cars, trucks westbound, and four rows of cars and trucks facing us eastbound . . . on a TWO-lane road! After two and a half hours, we could see the flags dropped. The whole four lanes, bumper to bumper lurched forward about one hundred feet and STOPPED! Nothing moved . . . until we could see a highly packed produce truck start waving side-to-side. It was finally toppled over, off the side of the road and rolled down the drainage embankment! Things were getting serious. Tim and I quietly rolled up the back windows.

Occasionally we would inch forward as cars were removed and jockeyed for space. In another hour and a half we met our first eastbound car, scarred by abuse; fistfights were breaking out. Young Turk decides he will inch into a left center lane that was forming . . . then we hear a

235

HOOONK blasted by the tri-axle stone truck to our left rear. Young Turk ignores the warning and moves a few more inches forward and to the left. A continuous HOON-N-N-KKK was sounded from the truck's air horn as it moved forward in slow motion style ripping the right rear fender, next to my left hip, from the old Buick. Tim turned to me, and under his breath said, "Jack, you and I have had some dangerous moments in aviation but . . . we may be very close to death!" I nodded in mute agreement.

Young Turk exploded in anger. He leaned to the floor and picked up a tire wrench, turned backward out of the window and was pulling himself to the roof . . . when his wife tackled him around the waist and pulled him back to the seat, knowing armed conflict could terminate her new husband. The planned six-hour trip eventually ended after eighteen hours, leaving with us a better understanding of why and how the Middle East flares into violence, as Paul wrote to the nearby church at Colossi.

Col: *3.8 "But now you must rid yourselves of all such things as these: anger, rage, malice, slander, and filthy language from your lips."*

The City That Disappeared

Pulling into the Ephesus area, we saw nothing but flat farm plain with a few trees in the distance. Little Turk drove what was left of his battered Buick into an old gravel parking lot. The only thing that gave us a hint we were near anything, was an empty tour bus and a car older than ours sitting without two of its wheels. We walked through a sagging wire fence and paid an old man and woman a small entry fee. They were also hawking sexual fetish replicas from the Temple of Dianna to the departing bus passengers. I think the old man and woman lived in the abandoned car. Still we saw no hint of a city.

Once we crested the hill, we stood in awe atop the Amphitheater. It sat as it was almost two millennia ago, when the Apostle Paul was run out of town. He probably hadn't preached from this stage but from a small synagogue about two blocks away. At the base of the hill, a long boulevard, once lined with statues and stalls, ran downhill from the amphitheater to the harbor. Paul had been a tentmaker here for a few years until his evangelism put a dent in the local silversmiths and artisans business selling trinkets and fetishes from adjacent stalls. The temples to their sexual goddess dwarfed the little Jewish synagogue many times over. It was easy to see how Paul and Timothy were outnumbered. It should give a lot of us Christians today increased faith to see what God can do through a few who are sold out to Him.

 The empty foundations and ruins were still being reclaimed, a picture of what Nehemiah saw as he returned to rebuild the walls with unskilled labor. Like the cities of Tyre and Nineveh, Ephesus disappeared from attack of enemies, not from invading armies but from a river silting its harbor bringing mosquitoes, malaria and obviously it had its share of social disease. The city lay discarded for hundreds of years until . . . we tourists arrived!

The next morning we met Jay who had flown the T-34 in the previous day. We drank the prescribed amount of tea with Turkish Air Force generals before Jay took to the air with the evaluation pilots. Since older men blackout during aerobatics way before young bucks, I was happy to let "young" Jay demonstrate to his hearts content. I sat with the Egyptian Air Force staff, occasionally flew the older pilots and enjoyed tea . . . after I checked that headquarters had a latrine!

They'd never seen an Allison flight crew before; even though they had been flying Allison powered Lockheed C130's. They didn't even have a current set of engine maintenance manuals for their big birds. I don't know which was the bigger hit, the promise of getting them new manuals or holding an evening dinner for their pilots. Everyone we'd flown showed up for the food and FILLED up. Like most other pilots we'd fly around the world, they couldn't understand how Jay and I . . . "Could be such good aerobatic pilots and not drink alcohol." I'd long ago learned drinking contests only cheapen your product and yourself. It was a good visit. The Turks are still flying Allison engines and I still enjoy reading Paul's letters to their local churches . . . with new understanding.

NE 4:6 So we rebuilt the wall till all of it reached half its height, for the people worked with all their heart.

Our team had performed with all their heart and completed our goal; we'd secured our European Distributor. Once back home we quickly outfitted the T-34 and a second Prop-Jet Bonanza to extend our circuit into South America. As in Nehemiah's building of the wall, it was time to step back and regroup the troops. We had enjoyed the backing of a good central ally in Werner Eichenberger and our other European manufacturers for any required maintenance. This time we would be flying independent of any known repair facilities or friendly associates. Therefore, like Nehemiah's hostile atmosphere we mustered extra help.

We wouldn't need long range tanks to cross the Caribbean, so we had room for another person in each aircraft. The maintenance gap would be filled by George Cummins, our Chief Flight Mechanic riding shot-gun with Jay in the aft seat of the T-34. Soloy's associate, non-pilot sales representative for Central and South America, Vic Symonds, flew with me aboard the Bonanza. He arranged a cadre of stops . . . and he was relatively fluent in Spanish. We loaded each ship way beyond normal weights, but being licensed "Experimental", we had latitude to throw extra advertising material, tools and equipment aboard. Our four-seat rear cabin was piled floor to the ceiling and when George finally ran to the T-34, he carried a sizeable unplanned cylinder to their two-seat tandem ship. Once he had his helmet on, I called, "What are you sneaking aboard, George?"

"It's my own oxygen system. We are going to be in the Northern Andes and you pilots don't turn our masks on until reaching 12,000 to 14,000 feet. I like mine at 8,000, like every other airline passenger!" he snapped back.

"Where is mine?" pipes in Vic, sitting next to me, "I'm a chain smoker!"

"To bad, Victor", I jested, as we applied throttle for take-off, "Like George used to, you'll get more sleep." The take-off from Indy for Miami took more than normal runway length.

31

Island Hopping

Flying low level out of Miami, we hopped across numerous spits of sandy white islands; some were countries of their own. Our first touchdown was in the Caocus Islands, the last fuel stop before the Dominican Republic.

Jay, hung at a relaxed distance below the right wing, as the clouds drifted lazily over the Caribbean islands.

To say Caocus was laid back would be a gross understatement. It took us time before we could find someone, anyone. Finally, we climbed the tower stairs, which reminded one of climbing a forest ranger tower. We had talked to a person on landing. We found him kicked-back; he let us know we were probably interrupting a snooze. Yogi Bear would have been more attentive. "Is there anyone around below?" we asked.

"Nope, dare won be n'other plane in fo an h'or or so, no sense rush'n . . . you mine tri da snack bar down da ramp." One thing, you could see most of the island from up there, at least what part hadn't blown away in the last hurricane. Nothing moved. Over at the snack bar, we did find a lone person to make us a sandwich with week old bread and to call someone to fuel the planes. Eventually they were fueled. When paying the gasman, we asked, "Where do we file International Flight Plans?"

"Right here with me," he responded. As I passed him the yellow copy, he turned and slipped it through a mail slot into an adjacent room.

"Where does it go from there", I questioned, assuming there was a clerk on the other side to transmit it to Flight Service and our next destination.

"Oh, it stays right there", as he proudly opened the door to a small 10 x 12 foot room with its floor completely covered with similar yellow slips, yielding a three-foot mound near the slot. "Somebody will find it if you come up missing!" Our hearts sunk, NO body will ever know if we WERE missing; at this moment, we suspected what might have happened to Amelia Earhart! All was quiet on the next leg toward the Dominican Republic. We knew that like Nehemiah, we had severed communication with any outside support.

Our landing at Dominica found an active border war in process with Haiti. It would be a day or so before the appropriate pilots and officers would return from maneuvers to evaluate the ships. We were transported to a "Western Hotel"; passing through streets of muddy squalor marked by lines of children queued to fill old plastic jugs with water. Lean-to shelters looked like card houses of miscellaneous material remaining from the last tropical storm . . . stacked, awaiting the next wind to change tenants. It would be easy to find our way back; we had traveled the only concrete byway.

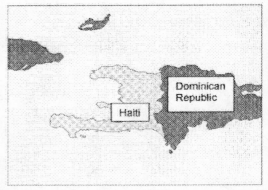

This Nehemiah experience was becoming too surreal. Our three or four days on the island permitted us to demonstrate that our ships could easily patrol the entire Haitian boarder with appropriate armament to deal with the rebels. Before leaving, George checked the ships for damage from small arms fire, which we'd apparently dodged. At that time neighboring Haiti was advertised as the poorest economy on earth. It must have been so, because they were indeed hurting if they were trying to tear down Dominican walls to get in. Vic would need to outperform Nehemiah if he could find money to sell our product here. Even taking all of their tired T-34 recips in trade, it would require another $400,000 per ship to turbinize. There wasn't that much in the whole country. It was time to move to oil rich Venezuela.

Drug Riddled Caribbean

Crossing the southern Caribbean on one tank of fuel, we landed at Vic's dealer prospect, Alberto & Son. They were officed on the beach airport at Maiquetia, a southern suburb of Caracas. Weather reported a 300-foot ceiling, dictating an instrument approach. This is one place we didn't want to miss the turn onto the localizer, centerline. Sheer cliffs rose vertically 4,000' just a quarter mile from the beach . . . and they were bringing us in at 1,500 feet. Not able to fully understand the controllers say TURN, I diligently conformed to the approach chart. Breaking out at 400', the mountains JUMPED at the wingtip. A miss would have been a SMASH!

It was a busy field, a surprise since it was located on the coast. Pulling our two ships up at the customs office, we were forcibly quarantined by armed guards . . . and they appeared miffed. We hadn't been expected. No one had called in our flight plan. We envisioned the yellow copy still perched atop the pile on the floor. The custom agents intentionally made us wait. They searched the ships for contraband. We didn't even have a Band-Aid, so were finally cleared west on the ramp to Alberto & Son's small office.

Walking in the door we felt right at home, pictures of the Indianapolis 500 featuring Alberto posed with his race cars covered the walls. A smiling and jovial Alberto leapt into our life and made us want to do business with the exuberant Venezuelan. "Alberto, your face is badly burned, I didn't think you were racing anymore. What happened?" queried Vic. His story stood the hair on our necks.

"A month ago two men came in this door for helicopter flight lessons. My son, he is a Helicopter Flight Instructor. So, we said okay. We had two ships, a Hughes 500 with your Allison 250 engine and an old Sikorsky S55".

"Yes, I've flown them both", I knowingly interjected.

"Son is out flying the 500 right now and will be in soon," he continued. "Well, the whole thing looked a little stinky, so I went along down below in the Sikorsky. After we were airborne, both of these *drug*

241

dealers pulled guns and we were highjacked. They forced us to land at a shack of theirs in the desert, to teach them to fly there. I was handcuffed to the ships ladder below, while Son taught them to fly."

"What about fuel?" someone asked.

"They had barrels of gasoline stashed at the shack. We flew all day, every day," he answered. "After ten days we knew they were close to killing us and taking the ship. They had already discussed how they were going to use it. In desperation, on what we thought was our last approach into the desert, Son flew us into a palm tree. We flipped and crashed to the ground, immediately catching on fire. The men fled and my son grabbed the fire axe under his seat and chopped me out . . . to freedom. We both got burned!"

Wow, just like Nehemiah's wall builders, they stood guard with their swords. . . .

NE 4:13 "Therefore I stationed some of the people behind the lowest points of the wall at the exposed places, posting them by families, with their swords, spears and bows. 14 After I looked things over, I stood up and said to the nobles, the officials and the rest of the people, "Don't be afraid of them. Remember the Lord, who is great and awesome, and fight for your brothers, your sons and your daughters, your wives and your homes."

I don't believe Nehemiah had combat such as this. I was anxious to meet his son . . . of whom, "Dad was very proud"!

Climb Out of That Hole

In Air Force Flight School I always felt sorry for Cadet Sullivan who was constantly challenged by upperclassmen with, "All right, Mister, climb out of that hole you are standing in!" He was the shortest man in our class, at the very bottom of the height profile to qualify for the cockpit. It was a similar problem we would face in Venezuela. In Caracas, 10 miles over the hills from Alberto's office, the city lay in a basin surrounded by 10,000-foot mountains. Their regulations stated that only twin-engine aircraft, with climb gradients capable of jumping over the peaks, could land at their largest city. We had just the answer, a single engine Prop-Jet Bonanza that could scale those mountains at any weight. What a market!

Unfortunately, just as with Nehemiah, the local politicians got in the act and wouldn't change the rules in our short time. They wouldn't permit high performance *single engine airplanes* . . . even though we strapped them in and climbed, at full weight, straight over their peaks.

Before we left, we got to meet Alberto's 21-year-old son, a fine young man who let me explore the hillsides in his Hughes 500. He let me do the flying. He was a little apprehensive at first, casually rewrapping his burned hands to hide his tenseness. Then I challenged him to an engine out spot-landing contest. We both had fun!

At least temporarily thwarted by the feds, we fueled up and headed onward toward Columbia, abandoning Alberto and Son to deal with their locals. We had only seen a small glimpse of Latin American politics but could see they were similar to Nehemiah's. We recognized we didn't have enough money in our pockets to change things overnight. Alberto & Son would continue their charter activities, negotiate to change regulations, and fly tourists to the chain of islands just north. Paradise spots like Antigua and Rocca sounded more romantic to a 21-year old young man than battling mainland druggies.

Bogotá couldn't be made non-stop; consequently we topped the fuel tanks for the trip's longest over-water leg, direct to San Salvador, a small island in the sun belonging to Columbia. As we filed our International Flight Plans we wondered if anything was ever done with them or were they, too, lying around to gather dust in an empty room?

Point of No Return
Two hours off Venezuela on the flight to San Salvador Island, we passed "the-point-of-no-return". With not enough fuel to turn back and no other airport options . . . we had to reach San Salvador Island. Fortunately, the low frequency radio beacon on the island was high power; we'd even picked it up as we climbed from Alberto's. However, we were also

starting to pick up cloud tops on the far horizon . . . ominous thunderheads. With several hundred miles yet to go, it was doubtful they would be on the other side of our destination ... like Nehemiah, it was again time for serious prayer. The clouds kept looming higher but not looking any closer. This indicated they were still distant and TALL.

We were only a few degrees from the equator; the atmosphere is thicker and taller in this region than it is over Indiana. While big thunderstorms occur at home, they build higher in the southern, moist Caribbean. A whole line was forming from left to right across our course; there was no choice to go around them. They weren't forecast. This must be a quick squall line, the very worst; typically narrow but can be violent. At 200 miles from the front, our storm scope was picking up a solid line of continuous lightening strikes, from South America to the Mexican peninsula. We climbed to 22,000-feet. George was hugging his personal oxygen bottle in the rear of the T34, he was smiling. Once within fifty miles of these giants, towering another 30,000 to 40,000-feet further overhead, San Salvador was still beyond another 5 to 10 miles. The storm was advancing toward us.

Neh 4.9 *"But we prayed to our God"* . . . from each aircraft, we prayed on the radio. First me, then Jay, George, yes and even Vic! "That God would get us through it and hold us together", Jay's aerobatic ship was

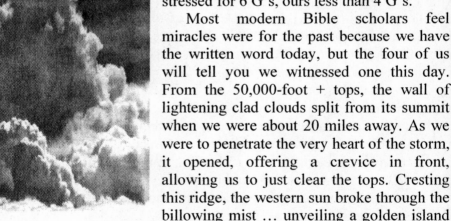

stressed for 6 G's, ours less than 4 G's.

Most modern Bible scholars feel miracles were for the past because we have the written word today, but the four of us will tell you we witnessed one this day. From the 50,000-foot + tops, the wall of lightening clad clouds split from its summit when we were about 20 miles away. As we were to penetrate the very heart of the storm, it opened, offering a crevice in front, allowing us to just clear the tops. Cresting this ridge, the western sun broke through the billowing mist ... unveiling a golden island and runways 25 miles beyond. An even greater miracle, Victor praised God, too. Nehemiah built his wall; God tore ours down.

Invisible Aircraft

As we picked up San Salvador approach control for landing, we encountered a pleasant surprise that surpassed clearing the thunderstorms.

Where control and tower language is supposedly available world wide in English, it had deteriorated at times into indistinguishable Spanish. Now, out of the blue we are talking with a guy who sounded as if he were from back home in Indiana. We learned that he might have been. In the 80's we'd heard rumors of covert U.S. involvement in Central America. Now we were beginning to experience its fringe elements. On landing, we noticed, as we  would when departing Columbia in Cartahania, the presence of U.S. controllers, a variety of aircraft including AWACS, some painted black . . . and U.S. troops.

These facts were not widely publicized at home except in "Schwartznegger" type movies. It was a deterrent that we would soon learn was necessary to control drug traffic from Columbia, an anti-U.S. takeover in the Panama Canal, and "unfriendlies" controlling a hostile regime and warfare in Nicaragua. With Cuba off-limits for decades, the entire Caribbean seemed to be struggling with various cancers; hopefully they were curable. We would learn to ignore this presence. The men and equipment were to be invisible . . . apparently, they didn't exist.

The instrument approach into Bogotá later in the day went without incident. Jay and I had memorized the letdown charts, knowing we'd be communicating with a series of radio handoffs to a series of Pedros and Gonzalezs. We were right. On landing at nearly 13,000-foot density altitude we saw why turbine aircraft shine here. Airplanes need lots of power at these altitudes.

The local aircraft dealer, his wife and son met us as we deplaned. Obviously a Columbian aristocrat, this fine gentleman had seen his business decimated. It fell from top foreign sales dealership for his American manufacturer . . . to no sales of new aircraft during the past two years. His property on the airfield boasted a pool, tennis court and empty assembly hangar for South American deliveries. He had arranged a week's presentation of our aircraft to the Columbian Air Force; he certainly was the key contact to have in this volatile area.

The very first courtesy at hand was for Vic to complete a dual, a challenge previously agreed upon if the dealer secured the visit to his Air

245

Force. We and his family all lined up behind the flight office building. I hadn't known why Vic brought his weapon in a traveling case. It had bounced around in the cabin for the past two weeks. Both men stood opposite each other. Neither Jay, George nor I had offered our services as seconds. Victor would only have one shot at this. The referee shouted, "Serve!" Vic fired the first shot . . . the tennis match was on. His opponent at seventy-five would normally be an easy kill for the forty-ish Vic, but the Dealer was on his home ground . . . with lungs trained at 13,000' density altitude all of his life. The match ended after the first set as Vic lay with a mortally wounded pride, gasping for air and coughing up coal tar from his life-long chain smoking. Vic may not have won but, like Nehemiah's wall warriors, he was our champion!

32

Running the Gauntlet

City of Beauty

Jay was excited. In a couple of days, we would travel to Cali to visit the Columbian Air Force Academy. Yes, he was excited to fly but he added, "Cali is the home of beautiful women. Miss Columbia lives there and was crowned Miss World a few months ago." Well, I don't know if Jay was right about all the women in town but it was a beautiful, modern city. While judges, politicians and businessmen were being kneecapped (machine-gunned), all planes were being searched on EVERY landing and take-off. Drug lords and guerrillas controlled the cocaine-rich mountains and most of the business economy lay in shambles. This area, resting

between the mountains and the Pacific on a 3,500 foot high plain, boasted relative peace, solitude and safety. The entire city and nightlife exuded a Riviera style gaiety, except for the slightly conspicuous riot police.

The dealer had set an excellent military presentation, one full week. The first day would involve our providing separate staff and student briefing with an engine ground school. The second through fourth days would permit one-on-one flight demonstrations for each instructor and senior students while the fifth day would be debriefing by their staff. It was just like stepping back thirty years in time to my military flight training. Similar barracks, hangars, support buildings and even T34's. I probably flew one of these very aircraft. It looked like our government cut a base out of Texas and transplanted it, fully outfitted, to Columbia. I can still picture a handful of Columbian students who went through training with me. Two years away from home made them homesick. It took awhile to overlook their morning ritual of raw eggs cracked into a glass of juice, with a lower body hair quickly added and gulped in one swallow . . . to cure homesickness!

Jay's excitement carried onto the flight line; in fact, all were concerned that we wouldn't see a repeat of one of the last U.S. sales delegations to this base. While we had with us a re-engined old T-34 recip, a major aircraft manufacturer had built a new military version on a larger airframe with twice the horsepower. When demonstrating here two years before, they ran up against the South American "Macho Syndrome". In Europe where pilots tend toward gods, Latin American pilot stripes convey POWER! The pilots apparently had an "ups-manship" contest. Finally, one crew, while coming out of an aerobatic maneuver, pulled the

As each of the Columbian pilots flew our ships they were awarded an "Allison Flight Shirt", complete with shoulder epilates. By the time we left we had re-uniformed the entire force, they proudly wore them the next few days.

wings off and crashed in the middle of these buildings . . . killing both pilots. Hopefully, this scenario was still fresh enough in their minds that they, too, didn't want a repeat disaster.

The dealer had several dinners set for us to entertain their Air Force principles. One evening was spent with several prominent businesspersons. One, a statesman who published high quality, full-page fold-out books for children made clear his compatriots' position concerning us constricting their drug trade. "Mr. Schweibold," he started officially, "Consider if . . . our positions were reversed".

Yes, I'm praying we don't take out another hangar.

"What do you mean?" I countered.

"Well, your country gets concerned when our nation's product, the coco bean is converted to cocaine. You come down here with your politicians and military and try to wipe out the industry. In reverse, America has factories that build steel and guns that you sell to us. We don't come to America and try to close down your steel and munitions plants. Here in Columbia we convict our people who USE guns or drugs. Why doesn't America convict your people who use drugs? Without your dollars, our drug lords would be out of business and our economy and my plant could go back to normal." He sounded a lot like Nehemiah, effectively paraphrased, "Go away and let us rebuild our walls here in Columbia!"

Pilots love to discuss the finesse of aerobatics

I didn't have a counter comment. We shouldn't judge another man until we've walked in his shoes or tried to get a job in his country. The balance of the evening was enjoyable. I learned how Columbian natives glue those intricate books, by hand . . . the same books that Sharon was home reading to our grandchildren.

"Lockdown" In the Embassy

On our flight back to Bogotá, the dealer pointed out where a mudslide below had wiped out a whole town of tens of thousands earlier in the year. "A volcanic earthquake triggered the slide", he concluded. Looking under, I could see a scar several miles wide down the mountainside ending in an even wider and longer debris trail along the valley river. I had landed on the rim of Mt. St. Helen's a few weeks after it erupted. Life can end quickly anywhere in the world.

"OK, men", announced Vic, once we landed and he'd called his California office. "Alberto (a new Alberto) just received final approval for demonstrations to the Guatemalan Air Force. We need to find the U.S. embassy and obtain our visas". This was a bonus and a welcome change as we could fly back home inland, rather than hopscotch across the Gulf of Mexico. Walking up to our U.S. embassy was refreshing. It had already been "hardened" following the recent car and truck bombing of our embassies in the middle-east. It was a newer building, surrounded by concrete buttresses positioned away from the major structure. Double entry doors shielded the interior from any outside blast waves. The extra doors also slowed down personnel for inspection by armed guards. It is getting easy to recognize storm clouds on this trip, these indicating the tempest headed for the United States as our own borders become more porous.

As we secured our visas, a siren sounded announcing the embassy was under "Lockdown". We hardly had time to gather up our paperwork as guards secured the doors. In a few minutes, the horn resounded . . . coupled with the announcement, "All-clear". No comments were offered when departing. We didn't learn until returning to the hotel that . . . five other embassies in the world were simultaneously hit, some penetrated by terrorists, three in South America. Nehemiah's wall only circled Jerusalem. America's extends around the world.

Before leaving Bogotá, we toured the dealer's empty assembly hangars and found to our surprise that he had underwritten his son, an aeronautical engineer, to design and build a small six-place passenger/cargo aircraft for the South American market. It would be built out of readily available components suitable for the continent's "bush" environment, similar to Canada's approach with their DeHaveland Beaver and Otter aircraft. We could see the ship was already of such size that it would need the power of our Model 250 Turbo-prop. This was a true find, an emerald in the rough, found laying on a Columbian ramp on our safari into South America. This could become our biggest prize!

Guatemalan Gauntlet

It was an effortless formation climb out of Bogotá, since we started at 11,000 feet. George had worked hard keeping the aircraft maintained and looking good and Jay and I had managed to hold aerobatics within bounds; at least both ships still had wings. Vic recovered from the tennis dual and we noticed his chain smoking diminished, conservation of lung power at our altitudes brought discipline to daily routines. The Air Force gave a very favorable critique on our installation and upgrading of their T-34's to Allison turbines. Funding availability would require a longer term answer and would be Vic's task once home. I'd anchored a return trip to sign the Columbian dealer's son's new aircraft to use our engine. It had been a productive visit. I could see George strapping on his oxygen mask as we continued our climb toward the Panama Canal. Upon filing our flight plan we found we were not welcome in Panama so we made a shorter final stop in Cartahana, Columbia, staying overnight in a hovel only one notch above facilities in the Dominican Republic.

Our next day was non-stop to Guatemala where we were greeted by 18,000-foot, quad (4) volcanoes looming 10,000-feet **above** the Guat City Airport. Here, Vic had an effervescent friend, Captain Alberto. I can't remember if Alberto had been in the Air Force or if "Captain" was a macho moniker adopted for his Latin American flying. In any case, everyone we met in his country knew Alberto. He was blessed with a lovely wife, Maria, and two beautiful girls. These ladies formed a team to run the office while he handled charter flight operations and hangar maintenance.

We had a two-day window with air force headquarters in "Guat City". It seemed they were preoccupied with more important matters, but Alberto assured us we'd get a fair demo the next day at their East Coast flight center.

He was right; demonstrations were accomplished and cordially received at that base. Following lunch the morning of the third day, we headed back to Guat City. As we were taxiing out in both aircraft, their commander came running after us, "Senior Jack," he called. "You'd better top your fuel tanks. Our military has just declared a coup, taking over the major cities and airports."

It seemed strange to be in the middle of an official coup. We knew once we left the military base we could be considered foe rather than friend. It seems we have been on many sides of many governments this trip. For the moment, we were in a country not even yet recognized by the U.S., and Alberto could be considered a man without a country.

251

Flying back to Guat City equated to Dorothy and her crew following the Yellow Brick Road enroute to the capitol city of OZ. We didn't know what we'd find. Once the Volcanoes were in sight, Alberto called the tower in English, "Guat City tower, this is Turbine Bonanza Two-Five-Zero-Alpha-Tango, flight of two, 25 miles East for landing".

The controller responded, "Bonanza Alpha Tango, this Quat City Tower, we have small problem since you left, Alberto. Our military has staged a coup and taken over the government and our AIRPORT!" Sure enough, reaching the field we saw the whole 12,000-foot length of the sole runway and parallel taxiway covered with tanks and trucks . . . scattered to command the field. "Bonanza flight of two, enter a 2 minute holding pattern at the marker beacon. We'll let you know when the field reopens." That was 3pm.

"How much fuel do we have, Jack?" Alberto asked, still flying the plane.

Checking the quantity and our fuel flow, I responded, "A little over two hours at this altitude. Maybe longer if we go higher."

"We'll stay here. The airliners will stack up overhead and we can be first to land," Alberto rationalized. I could tell he was a sharp pilot the way he finessed the holding pattern. Two hours and twenty patterns later, Alberto called the tower, "Palo, this is Alberto, when is this coup going to be over?"

"Alberto," the tower operator replied, "You know, we have not had a good coup for over two years, and it may be several days!"

Alberto turned to me and asked, "Can you guys land in 300-400feet, between army tanks . . . on that cross taxiway?"

"You bet!" I said, with a gulp, "But how about the tanks?"

Ignoring my question, Alberto snapped to the tower, "Palo, it's 5 pm. You know my wife, Maria. She'll have my rear-end if I'm not home for supper! Tower, Bonanza Zero-Alpha-Tango is declaring a fuel emergency and landing immediately!" Then he switched radio channels and called his hangar, "Maria, get the hangar door open, NOW!"

I called Jay to form up behind me and we landed in formation, right on the taxiway heading for the hangar . . . taxiing in with engines running. As Maria closed the door, we shut the engines down. Stepping out of the planes and dropping to the floor, I expected to see men running in with guns drawn. No men, no guns, we took the ladies and went out for dinner. As with Nehemiah, God was in command!

The Volcanoes Erupt

Checking in with the company, I found God's reason for being trapped in Guat City the extra day. "Jack, you seem to be in just the right place at the right time" explained my boss. "The Engineering Department reports they have a handful of 250-C30 engines in MD-500 helicopters flying down there . . . and they are flunking the daily power checks. Instead of just cooling your heels in the tropics, how about going over to the seismographic guys and investigate the problem?" he concluded. Whenever you are traveling for a company, they always picture you lying on a beach, basking in the sun while occasionally taking a break from the bar to telephone or write your reports. These past six weeks had been one long series of prepping, fueling, sales work and training while fighting the elements . . . ranging from weather to armies. It was no use remonstrating.

"OK", I said as jovial as possible, "I'll change hats and hit the pavement . . . as far as the armed guards permit". Fortunately, the company's flight office was on the field. They were flying brand new 500D's, similar to Howard Hughes' ship in which we set our first records, only upgraded with double the horsepower and an extra main rotor blade. "Should make them an excellent high altitude machine," I thought to myself. We'd flown a 500D in Indy for a period while working out inlet configurations. I had a good idea what might be the trouble.

In talking with their manager, I was able to examine their test records. Periodically, the pilot would take seismographic teams to the surrounding 18,000-foot volcano peaks. Before take-off, the pilot would make a run-up and check engine gages against performance charts. This would determine if the engine was meeting specification power. If it didn't, there would be no flight until it was examined. Mysteriously, on most occasions, nothing was found wrong, just power shifting around.

The next stop was the airport weather desk to get a copy of weather readings for the days in question. You guessed it, good weather, good power; stormy weather, heavy clouds or high winds . . . low power. The problem was that we suddenly had an outstanding engine that could **forecast** violence at the mouth of the volcanoes! The reason it was so intelligent . . . was it had a well-trained pilot coupled to the flight controls. One that rationally didn't want to die! It was the same old South and Central America pilot machismo, "Captain Gonzalez" is too brave to turn

253

down a dangerous flight to the volcano tops exploding with wind shear, violence and weather . . . making the mission unsafe or even impossible on instruments or with 80 mph+ knot winds. Those peaks might even be 23,000' high density altitudes, depending on temperature! So instead, Captain Gonzales "sucks wind", tilts his eyes as he reads the gages and . . . the engine FLUNKS its health check for the day. Overlay of the power check charts and bad weather days confirmed the analysis. It was recommended the pilots become professionals, recognizing and admitting that GOOD aircraft and GOOD pilots have limitations; also, that management must accept the fact that under certain conditions, there would be no flying and, revenue would be lost . . . not men and aircraft.

Our problems, poor engine power and the coup, evaporated; we headed for Costa Rica ... rejoicing!

NE 12:31 "I had the leaders of Judah go up on top of the wall. I also assigned two large choirs to give thanks."

No Place like Home

Our three-day courtesy stop in Costa Rica was to visit their Police Department, which had already purchased five of our 250 powered Cessna 206 fixed-wings. This peace loving, laid-back little country, squeezed between the

militants of Nicaragua and Panama, is an enigma in the Central American political arena. Costa Rica depends totally upon the benevolence of good ol' Uncle USA for its defense; otherwise, they secure domestic tranquility with the police department equipped with their Allison powered Cessna's. Not an all bad deal, both ways.

On the airport within the police compound, it's easy to spot the country's Aero Club . . . yes, we were warmly welcomed!

After demonstrating our newest products, we were free to roam the small country at will, the safest I'd felt on the whole trip. We could always find someone eager to speak broken English and send us on the next turn in the road. In several of the villages we were able to find hand carved craft objects in native woods; items we'd never seen in the world's "el'touresti" shops, where everything looks the same. Victor was working on a spit of Pacific Coastal land to purchase, but I think the potential of the Nicaraguan gorillas looking over his patio from the northern border just a mile away dissuaded him. In fact, as we were again flying Northbound abeam Managua, immediately offshore Nicaragua's territorial waters, Managua Radio called and said, "American aircraft just west of Managua, immediately head out to sea or we will perceive your flight as a hostile act!" With Jay's ship looking like a U.S. military paramilitary we made a formation turn 30-degrees further into the Pacific.

During a stop in Mexico, George determined Jay's flying with a "wing low" lately, was not due to Jay being tired … but that the T-34's wing was loosening. All of our high "G" maneuvers had taken its toll. We pulled George and all equipment out of the T34 to lighten its weight, put Vic on an airline to California, slowed our speeds and limped back to Indianapolis for repairs and rest.

It had taken Nehemiah's group 52 days to rebuild Jerusalem's walls, it would be years before the city was restored . . . his final words were,

NE 13:30b *"Remember me with favor, O my God."*

Likewise, it had taken our team the same period to build a foundation for our engines to grow, to plant our dealership in Europe, to fully evaluate re-engining T34 military aircraft, to secure a new aircraft installation in Columbia, to sign a sale in Mexico, to salvage a helicopter fleet in Guatemala and most of all … to successfully and safely complete our mission. You see, we didn't have just four or five scraggily men on our team. Like Nehemiah who had hundreds of his countrymen, we also had hundreds of warriors. We had a manager and total support of our company underwriting the trip and others performing the most important task of all. They were praying for us. "Like whom?" you may ask …

- Wives and families
- Fishing friends, like the Richard Miller family
- Flying friends, like the David Whites
- Family Flight Surgeon friends, the Blacks
- Believers at work
- A whole church family, nearing 2,000, etc., etc …

Allison built over 25,000 of this engine series to power nearly 75 **different** aircraft; I had the privilege to fly all but two or three. Jay went on to fly with Pan Am, George to serve as a Missionary Aviation

255

Mechanic in Africa and Vic to re-engine part of the Columbian Air Force ships.

God blessed us all. If we ever think we do things in our own strength, we are wrong. Our final words upon landing at home were the same as Nehemiah's:

"Thank you for remembering us with favor, O our God!"

The next time you face a desire of your heart that seems overwhelming and too big . . . read and <u>wear</u> *"The Book of Nehemiah"* . . . it is a blessing!

33

God Provides

One of God's names is Jehovah Jireh, "God will provide". These have been some of His unusual provisioning:

Emergency Landing Sites lead the list: During test flying, I have been forced to the ground inadvertently more than 295 times in single engine aircraft, more failures, if you count multi-engined airplanes. That means, I'm just flying along when the engine suddenly, without warning, quits or a tail rotor falls off . . . next, I'm heading for the ground in a plane, sea plane or helicopter for an impending impact . . . each one could be another vignette in this book. God always provided a suitable landing site; an aircraft was never damaged upon touchdown. Skeptics might reply, "That was just luck or chance, there is no God".

Well, I'm here to say that the odds in flying and suffering immediate full to the ground forced landings ... with a 295-0 record, is like making 295 straight passes on a craps table! First, I'm not that good. Yes, we try to fly with emergency landing areas reasonably available but much of the time we are at the mercy of traffic vectoring or cross-country over woods, mountains and water. Next, once we get close to a touchdown point that may have looked good from hundreds or thousands of feet, it can turn to manure when you're ready to touchdown, i.e. boulders, ruts, stumps, fences, trees, cars, etc. A shopping center parking lot, a miniature island, small openings in woods, driveways, remote airfields, an opening between sorrel cactus, a pond, the only flat rock on a whole mountain range to skip off, to a multiplicity of farm fields, etc. etc., He had them there.

I always knew the price of crops to settle the $/acre reimbursement for what we tore up . . . but we never injured a ship or person. God <u>always</u> provided a special landing spot!

1 Peter 4:11 If anyone serves, he should do it with the strength God provides, so that in all things God may be praised through Jesus Christ. To him be the glory and the power for ever and ever. Amen.

257

P.S. In all of emergency landings, I don't believe any were for running out of fuel. That's not saying the engine wasn't breathing fumes a couple times. We have even stopped at a remote Stuckey's that had been closed for the season in the Northern Rockies. We were the first new visitors in over a month. Happy for a big sale, the owners, who lived in a rear apartment, were happy to throw in two free lunches – just for the company.

Comfort: Our oldest son, Scott was killed in an automobile accident when he was twenty-nine. There is probably nothing harder in life than losing a child. We expect our parents and even our mates to be taken before us . . . but, certainly not a child. I failed to have adequate empathy and understanding for those who had lost an unborn child or even a distant relative, never allowing them sufficient opportunity for grieving the loss. I gained a new perspective on their grief the night we stopped at Sharon's folks in Toledo returning from Boston. Mom asked us to call our son, Mark, back in Indianapolis . . . he was given the responsibility of telling us about Scott's wreck when returning home after work in the foothills outside of Athens, Georgia. We were informed that the driver behind Scott saw him swerve to miss a motorcycle that lost control on a bridge. Scott likewise lost control, plunging over the bridge to his death.

But God had already comforted. Two years earlier we had been on our knees in prayer for that son. He had been lost to drugs and alcohol. While on the floor next to each other, Sharon and I cried out to the Lord in prayer and lifted Scott up to Him until we could hold our arms no more . . . we gave Scott to Christ at that time. Scott had been free of those chains for more than a year. In fact, he had just been home for a couple of weeks in sound mind and body, even testifying to his brother, Brad, that faith in Christ was his sole source of getting through rehab. The autopsy reported him to still be free of stimulants. He had given his life for another as the driver testified.

Our Lord, family and friends wrapped their loving arms around us. As was our custom, our family led the graveside funeral. Brad led the service from scripture, Mark gave the Eulogy. Mindy, Nancy and Leesa marshaled the children. Our pastor closed in prayer with John 14:1-6 and his staff stood, probably one of the first times they didn't have to officiate. A friend, Jim Black asked to take pictures, a kindness normally shunned. One of Sharon's friends sang. My brother Robert came from Toledo. Dozens of friends and family flanked us in support . . . as I looked back through the attendees recently; those people are still cherished today.

God had a year before prepared a recovery period for us. Within a couple of days Sharon and I left for Sidney, Australia to attend the Federation Aeronautique Internationale's Annual Meeting to receive The Tissandier Diplome as Airman of the Year. Coupled with a ten day vacation in the northern jungle and the Great Barrier Reef, we had an opportunity to reflect on God's goodness in giving us Scotty for almost thirty years. Only in years to come, when Scott's two daughters graduated from Pensacola Christian College as teacher and nurse, married two fine Christian men and started bringing us great grandchildren . . . would we truly understand the comfort He would continue to bring us through Scott. We still claim

Proverbs 22:6 *"Train a child in the way he should go, and when he is old he will not turn from it."*

We just never know how *old "old"* is.

Joy in Family! He gave us an abundance of grandchildren. During one of my travels, Sharon decided to let our older grandchildren parachute into the night. It was an exciting event. She took one of my old parachutes and strung its twenty-eight foot canopy over a huge limb of our backyard sugar maple. She had previously helped them make Indian costumes for the tribe and gave instructions on how to form a tepee. From this new structure, they played war games throughout the day and at night they slept in it . . . including grandma. Here, Holly, Harmony, David, Kelsey, Steven, Daniel and Karin launched what would become an annual "Cousin's Night".

These events would be a challenge to plan and keep secret through the year. They included trips to amusement and theme parks, B & B's, motels, theater productions, etc. Occasionally we'd just stay home around the pool, or have an activity like a Treasure Hunt or an "Un-birthday Party", celebrating everyone's birthday for the coming year. Without a doubt, the most remembered Cousin's Night was the last year we had them all together . . . the summer before our oldest granddaughter; Holly exited the clan by marriage. It began in early spring when I sent out a letter to each one on grocery bags with the edges "burned".

It set an imaginary stage for "The Last Train out of Paris", an escape of the Schweibold family from Germany in the early 40's as Hitler invaded Europe. The letter stated that since we were a Christian family, we couldn't tolerate the persecution and ideals of the Nazi regimen and were going to escape through Italy to France and then to Switzerland.

259

Each person would have to plan and pack a costume to wear so that we could cross the border of each country without being recognized.

As they arrived at our home, the whole family was dressed in "USA" shirts for family passport photos needed for entry into America.

After a photo session in the back yard, we left their parents and headed in a couple cars for downtown Rome (Indianapolis) to begin the adventure. Dinner was set in the Old Spaghetti Factory. After supper, we stepped out of the restaurant into two waiting horse drawn carriages. The children were surprised and immediately entered

into the spirit of intrigue and escape across the Italian border to France. Once we got to Indy's Monument Circle, they could visualize arriving in Paris. Eventually, we pulled up at the old train station for our attempt to get on "The Last Train out of Paris".

We all ran through the station and arrived at our train . . . it was a real Pullman sleeper. The Holiday Inn, built around the station, has rooms in a number of cars parked on the original train platform. Luggage was already in place and we changed into our disguises. The boys were in one car and the girls in another. We met in the boys car and all took parts in performing the murder mystery game, "The Last Train out of Paris". Our youngest, Kimberly, remained in "Germany" with her parents, she was too young to survive the escape. The cast of characters follow:

Princess	Holly
Performer	Harmony
Banker	David
Journalist	Kelsey
Pilot	Steven
Arms Dealer	Daniel
Designer	Karen
Duke Major	Derek
Detective	Kristin

Sharon and I were dressed as conductors and moderated the murder.

Everyone got into their character for the occasion and no one guessed Holly was the bloody assailant; bludgeoning the victim to death, changing disguises, cramming the body in a trunk then hefting it onto the baggage car. The full cast stumbled to the pool exhausted. The next morning around breakfast and family devotions we relived the magic of the event as we all returned to reality . . . from Schweibold's Cousin's Night.

Answers: Mid-way in my career I accepted an assignment by the Helicopter Association International to develop the first FAA Flight Instructor Refresher Course, "all helicopter" syllabus.

The Helicopter Association International's Annual Meeting of 25 years ago in Tucson has grown many-fold in size.

After writing the full three-day course, I split the subjects up between some of the very best instructors in the country, Don Harvey, Nick Lappos, Vern Albert, Alacia Lane, Gary Young and many others. We presented it to the nation's instructors in one hour segments running for 2-3 days. I took Turbine Engine Operations and Fundamentals of Instruction. While Turbine Engine Operations was a snap, I agonized over Fundamentals of Instruction.

Prayer remained my only option to find an example for the "Levels of Learning", i.e. rote, understanding, application and correlation. My hardest maneuver to learn was brought to mind, recovery from inverted flight . . . when I split "S'd" out of the sky to qualify for my pink-slip in aerobatics. I thought I'd learned it all, but I hadn't yet. Once I passed the check ride, I knew I'd learned the ROTE by memorization, UNDERSTANDING by doing the maneuver and APPLICATION by applying it to rolling a helicopter upright when getting upside-down in jet wash. I thought *CORRELATION* came when analyzing the maneuver, WRONG.

Right then, it hit me. "EUREKA!" That's it, when my flight instructor threw me his back cushion to use the day he pink-slipped me . . . he knew I wasn't holding the control stick fully forward. As I rolled the ship with the stick, my arm became shorter for-and-aft, pulling the stick back and sucking the nose down (being inverted) and diving in a split "S". His cushion gave me the extra two-inches I needed. I finally had the answer, Step 4, the final step in the FAA Learning Process: CORRELATION and a winning lesson for the course's 22 year run. It took almost a lifetime to learn, repeat, apply and *correlate* this one lifesaving maneuver in the learning process. As Bill Gothard used to say, "PBPWMGNFWMY, Please be patient with me, God's not finished with me yet."

Career Enjoyment: I've had the privilege of attending all but a handful of the Helicopter Association International's 50 plus annual conventions across the nation. The one depicted above was in Tucson 25 years ago; it has grown ten-fold. Besides Paris came regular events at Oshkosh and Lakeland Experimental Aircraft Associations, Dayton Air Shows and the Reno Air Races. These activities developed camaraderie in a yet small fraternity of people who lived aviation.

O & N Aircraft's Pressurized Turbine P210 sits in the shadow of the Rivera Hotel. It was taxied down Las Vegas streets at 2 AM from the airport . . . with 50 other aircraft. The only danger might have been to the 1,000's gawking from their hotel balconies.

It was at the Reno Air Race where Sharon received her first taste of that emersion. Previously, she had been nonplus in exhibiting any extended interest in the sport, figuring the other male addicts in the family were enough. But something happened at Reno. We had four others on our team for that display and record setting activity. The first day we arrived with a one-day pass. Then I bought five all-week passes for the team. After handing them out on departure at the end of the day, Sharon asked in bewilderment, "Where is MINE, don't I get one?"

"Well, no," I replied. "You said you were going to stay in the hotel and read for the week."

At this point she ripped the last ticket out of my hand saying, "Get your own pass, I loved it!" From this point, she was in the stands ALL day and was always engaged in future flying activities as able. In fact, on return to Indy her Jabez prayer kicked in . . . in full force . . . she sought out a flight instructor and started flying lessons. Sure fooled me, I guess we should never assume we are immune from anything!

Sharon was back at the Reno Air Race all next week where she took this snapshot of the event's record setters: Chuck Yeager, Larry Chambers, Marie McMillian and her teammate, Jack

People: When I returned to Columbia to help coordinate installation of our engine in the new aircraft we found on the previous trip, I had time to spend in the duty free shop at Bogotá's Airport enroute home. The jewelry case displayed an exquisite collection of Columbian Emeralds: necklace, earrings and bracelet combinations. At $2,400 a set, divided by 200 for the Columbian exchange rate, they were bargains at roughly $120/set. Remembering what Sharon said about the Japanese pearl bargain I decided to get her a set, even though she didn't particularly like emeralds. While the saleslady was wrapping it, I decided that I better get a set for Nancy, Mindy, Leesa, Holly, Harmony, Kelsey, Karen, and Mom Crouse. I picked out ten sets, roughly 24,000 pesos, I mentally figured. A lot of money, but Christmas shopping for the ladies was finished.

As the clerk tallied the purchase, I gave her my credit card. She called the card for approval and I signed the receipt. As I took the receipt, I looked at the 24,500 figure and asked her if she'd take U.S. dollars instead. "Of course", she replied. I knew she'd probably sell the $1,250 US on the black market and pick up 5-10% or save at least the credit card charge.

"The credit card would be best, I guess", I finally decided. I can get rebate points.

At that point a distinguished Columbian traveler who had been watching said, "That's a sizable amount of cash to be carrying!"

To which I replied, "I always carry an extra $1,000 overseas, for emergencies".

The clerk entered into the conversation at that point, "Señor that will be $24,000 U.S., please".

"Aren't those prices in Columbian Pesos?" I gasped, "Divided by 200 for US Dollars?"

"No, señor, they are in US dollars", the clerk corrected.

I grabbed my charge receipts and passport, apologized, thanked the distinguished gentleman and ran for the darkest airport corner. Boarding the aircraft I passed my friend sitting in first class, he asked me to join him in his empty seat. "No thanks", I said, "This big spender is sitting in economy!"

Had I left it on the credit card, I wouldn't have known until Sharon received the bill for $24,500. The only thing we had worth that much was our grandchildren and their parents wouldn't have let us hock them! On the flight home I thanked God for providing that man to save me.

Passports: Our final one is stamped with the blood of Jesus Christ, our citizenship is in heaven. Thank you, God, for providing something we couldn't earn.

Phil 3:20 "But our citizenship is in heaven. And we eagerly await a Savior from there, the Lord Jesus Christ...."

34

Stretch Yourself Daily

I recently heard a secular physiologist say, "You should do something dangerous every day". While I don't agree with the total premise of this statement . . . utter foolishness can lead to serious injury, death, loss of reputation or financial disaster . . . I believe it has some merit. Going out on a limb for God and trusting in the Lord daily can strengthen us and enliven our life by seeing God at work. Our Pastor, Kim Kauffman, refers to this as "I spy God". Such practice has produced many of this book's positive chapters.

As we get older, the tendency is to withdraw into a protective shell. This will quickly bring boredom and decay into our life! On retiring from GM, I took a three-year contract as sales manager for O&N Aircraft Company in Pennsylvania, selling out their production each year. Then, Sharon and I stepped out in faith and have pursued work in our church since. I took on establishing a lawn and prayer path after new construction on the church's thirty-five acre site, eventually ending up on staff as Senior's Director and Elder. Sharon gravitated toward teaching women and now has eight-hundred women under her ministry in a variety of weekly Bible courses. While various physical trials occasionally interrupt our service, our goal is to keep serving as our energies permit.

One place I needed stretching was in my attitude and trust. I'd always considered "short term mission trips" to be a boondoggle. After all, "Why not just send the missionaries you visit the cost of your trip and not mess up their lives by descending on them for a week or so?" Until, as an Elder, I was challenged by our Missions Director, Dale Shaw to develop an aviation ministry trip. I grit my teeth, set aside my negative belief and fears and stepped out to go on such a trip. I called a missionary our College Park Church supported, Dan Moulton, a maintenance engineer for planes of the Northern Canadian Evangelical Mission. He was unable to accommodate our trip because of his wife's current battle with cancer, "See, I told you we were just imposing on God's troops", I confirmed to Sharon.

Then I remembered an old friend, Dan Kelly, Director of the Missionary Aviation Institute, a segment of Piedmont Bible College in Winston Salem, NC. Maybe they could use help painting a hangar or washing aircraft for a week. I called. He blew my excuses right out of the water! "Jack, we do need help!" Dan exclaimed. "Last week Moody Bible College announced it is shutting down their aviation training after 50 years and we are going to pick up half of their students, doubling our enrollment. We don't have facilities to handle them. Can you help us extend our eating area?" BAM, where I couldn't see any need for a short-term-mission-trip before, I was suddenly presented with a legitimate need. There was no backing out now.

Gideon's Law shortly became a force. When we had eight confirmed travelers, we were winnowed down to four. A new opportunity to back out and close the whole trip presented itself, but since our grandson, Daniel was still eager to go . . . I was stuck with the mission.

Up to the last day, I could still make excuses: back pain, sore feet, age, etc. Our assignment came by letter, "Build a whole lunch room, 24' x 24' on an existing slab in four days; to include: full frame construction, siding, insulation, electrical, doors, windows, drywall and exterior/interior paint". Soon I found out the other men felt the same, in shock. We drove 600 miles east in fear, trepidation and PRAYER.

God mightily answered our prayers. Nard, 74, met us with materials and sketches of the layout. Our teammates, Kelly (an aircraft mechanic) and Daniel (15, who'd just helped build our son, Brad's home) were capable of all construction tasks. Ethan (16) and I were effectively their helpers. Ethan took on much of the "mighty men's" moving and was nicknamed "Sledge". In small ways we became a blessing to many on the airfield as we lightened their load by meeting the crunch schedule for this space. We completed the entire task, except for final interior paint, in just three and one half days. They repaid in kindness by giving our men orientation training flights in a Piper J-3 Cub, Cessna 172 and Cessna 182. Our drive home was a wonderful trip . . . relating our many "I spy God" encounters.

The next year, three of us joined three new teammates, Harry, Larry and Ruth making the original trip to Canada to minister with the Moultons. Funny, little anxiety was noted in the previous attendees to North Carolina but fear and trepidation was again seen in our new members. The game of "I spy God" was just as exciting! We again saw answers to prayer in accommodations, work, food and transportation. Our eyes were opened to the great work being accomplished by the Moulton's ministry, helping take the gospel to eleven million Canadian Indians living on 2,000 reservations . . . by airplane, airwaves, satellite TV and publications. Our church's changing the title from "mission" to "vision" trips was valid; we started to get a better glimpse of God's vision. Oh, about our fears of over-burdening the missionaries . . . their tears of joy exceeded ours on these trips. Let's not be afraid to stretch ourselves daily!

"The cure for age - is interest, enthusiasm, and work, Life's evening will take its character from the day which has preceded it. You will always find joy in the evening, if you have spent the day well!" George Matheson

Dan, Harry, Ethan, Jack, Dan M. and Larry fly from the Saskatchewan River

Symphonic Flight

I heard William Buckley being interviewed on the radio regarding his recent retirement. He was asked why he also gave up his racing yacht. "Effectively", he said, "expenditure of resources no longer balanced pleasure." He was speaking, at his age, of physical not financial assets. He also alluded to losing the ability to, ". . . finger the keyboard on the piano as I would like", to be a similar loss. It sounded like he and I shared similar interests, racing in the wind and music. Oh, no, I can't play an instrument but for those of us who are musically illiterate, watching or listening to a symphonic orchestra can still be exhilarating. I have always admired our children and grandchildren; they each learned to play an instrument. That may be the reason I've never been enamored with supersonic flight, very little relative motion, "feel" or sound. The one thing I have been able to satisfyingly engage in through music is letting favorite scores play through my mind while flying in different settings. I agree with Buckley, who is also writing his autobiography, when he says, "You can't take memories from us. They just become more vibrant as we reflect on our past".

Most vivid is the Grand Canyon Suite filtering in my mental ears while skirting closely the outer walls of giant thunderheads; watching internal flashes of lightning, glowing from darker inner regions and viewing new layers of vapor self-generate and climb majestically in rainbows of sun glint. Only a wingtip away from the inferno . . . it can be as smooth as glass, like standing riveted in awe on the Grand Canyon rim, observing its potential violence just a step away. Just as breathtaking as  walking a mile on the very edge of the canyon cap rock. Silence abounds but the "Thunder Storm" portion of the Grand Canyon Suite rumbles in my ears.

Likewise, flying aerobatics in a fighter or turboprop trainer to crescendos from Superman, chasing herds of wild horses in a helicopter and attempting to separate the pack from the lead stallion to "Flight of the Bumble Bee", or just making a perfect landing to the "Nutcracker Ballet" . . . allows this pilot, with flight controls in hand, to conduct the entire concert. God gives us a varied way to play music; we can all be His musicians.

Valentine Month

One of the most significant errors made during my life was not to tell Sharon more often just how beautiful she is and how wonderful she has made our marriage. I knew how lovely she was . . . but didn't want her vanity flamed. When I told her about this one day and asked for her forgiveness, she broke down and cried. She said, "I didn't think you felt I was attractive. Talk about cruelty to your mate, this topped them all!

So-o, a few years ago I picked up on a challenge by a speaker at our men's retreat, "Make Valentine's Day special for your wife!" I decided she was more worthy of . . . a Valentine MONTH! To gear up for the event I scoured the stores for a number of assorted cards. She liked an occasional religious one. Also, knowing she liked surprise gifts, I picked up a couple dozen simple dollar store items (I liked the cheapies) and to top off the ensemble I threw in 3-4 nighties for times SHE selected to be moments of "special" intimacy. All of the items were wrapped neatly (I normally slapped packages together with duct tape) in Valentine colors and sparkly bags. I laid them out in an impressive presentation with a bouquet of roses.

Each day she could select a card, gift or piece of wearing apparel . . . and before the flower petals wilted, new flowers were in place.

WOW, how wildly she responded to this long-deserved attention! Overwhelmed you may think? She wasn't, I was . . . by her exuberant response! It was a GREAT month. We both agree the neatest thing we received out of the month were the comments overheard from our grandchildren, like, "My grandma and grandpa REALLY love each other!" One of greatest gifts we can give our children is to let them see our love in action.

What have I done for an encore? You're right, repeat it each year . . . only now I have a whole year to think about her and plan for letting her know how much I love her. The third year's February grew to a daily typed page of notes augmented by copies of favorite photos. I know she has saved them.

Eph 5:25-27 Husbands, love your wives, just as Christ loved the church and gave himself up for her to make her holy, cleansing her by the washing with water through the word, and to present her to himself as a radiant church, without stain or wrinkle or any other blemish, but holy and blameless.

Old Pilots Never Die . . . They Just Fade Into the Sunset

The Bible tells us in Ecclesiastics 3:4, there is a time . . . a time to weep and a time to laugh. Personally, I *choose* to laugh at most things, even those I should weep over. I think it is better medicine than pills. Modern medicine has proved that joyful people of faith tend to live a longer than average life.

Attending a church retreat last year, Sharon and I were challenged to come up with a piece for evening entertainment. This was our offering from a mind cluttered with a lifetime of aviation quips . . .

I started with . . . "Tonight you will hear SOME truth; the rest . . . will be mostly JET WASH!

Sharon steps in:

Sharon: "I don't know what happened, we had a great career in aviation, and now with 25,000 comics out of work . . . you want to be a standup comedian!"

Jack: "Well, we need to tell them about one of the greatest things that did happen was when the company approved you as my copilot in experimental aircraft . . . why don't you climb aboard this *imaginary plane* and we'll tell them about some of our adventures . . . and explain some

272

common aircraft terminology. Do you remember what the preflight check is?"

Sharon: "Yes, that's that big check you always wrote before you went pleasure flying . . . and forgot to enter!"

Jack: "How about the *pre-flight run up*?"

Sharon: "Oh, that's where we'd all run up for quick boarding"

Jack: "Yeah, after I'd already spent 15 minutes getting ready in the rain!

How about the *Take off roll*?

Sharon: "That's that long period of time you would be looking at the airspeed indicator and yelling about the extra passengers, baggage and scuba tanks!"

Jack: "What was one of your jobs on take off?"

Sharon: "To watch for fuel being siphoned out of the wing tanks . . . you occasionally forgot to fasten the fuel caps.

Jack: "Why was that so important? We never had a fire . . ."

Sharon: "It was to prevent an engine failure . . . an engine failure is the point when the fuel tanks become FULL . . . FULL of AIR!!!"

Jack: "Let's tell the group what the controls do, what do the ailerons do?"

Sharon: "That's easy, they BANK (Sharon holds out arms and rolls into a bank) . . . actually that's where he's got this plane financed!"

Jack "Now, show them a STEP BANK . . ."

Sharon: (Roll steeper) that's a bank that was charging him HIGH interest!

Jack: "What are some of the things I taught you about flying: For instance:

Jack:

• "Pilots?" ... Sharon: "Never fly with someone BRAVER then I am!"

• "Speed, slow like a Piper Cub?" . . . Sharon: "Oh, it's the slowest and safest airplane; it can just barely kill you!"

• "FAST, like our propjets?" . . . Sharon: "Since I was in charge of maps . . . you've NEVER been lost, until you are lost at 400mph!"

• "And Weather?" ... Sharon: "Weather reports are horoscopes with numbers"

• "What did you like best about flying in weather?" . . . Sharon: "Nothing!"

• "How about Over Water Flights?" . . . Sharon: "There are more planes left on the bottom of the ocean . . . then submarines left in the sky!"

Jack: "What was your favorite airplane we flew?" Sharon: "Helicopters!"

Jack: "Why helicopters?"

Sharon: "Because . . . you'd always land at romantic places"

Jack: "Like at the downtown heliport or the Sedona Cap Rock restaurants for dinner?

Sharon: "No, I mean alone in the desert or on a remote beach!"

Jack: "Oh, you mean on that Florida Key? When two nosy planes and a speed boat came to see if we'd crashed!"

Sharon: "Or on a mountaintop!"
Jack: ". . YEAH!"

Jack: "What was your most important job in the cockpit?"

Sharon: "PRAYER!!!"

Jack: "Yes, besides that!"

Sharon: "Reading your maps and approach charts, you can't see up close . . . especially on night landings."

Jack "Why night?"

Sharon: "Because I learned those things you called flashlights . . . were only metal tubes to carry dead batteries!"

Jack: "Speaking of landings, look at this beautiful setting sun. This is going to be a night landing, you know that a good night landing is mostly luck and two good night landings are ..."

Sharon: "ALL LUCK!!!!!"

Jack: "Well, in that case, since you and I have already had a lot of GREAT landings together . . ."

Sharon: "You mean . . . NEVER land!!! -. . .

Jack: YES! God's old pilots never die . . ."

Jack/Sharon in unison (arms about each other with other arms outstretched as wings, departing): "They just fly off into the sunset **TOGETHER!!!**"

35
Life is an Adventure

If you haven't figured it out by now, life has been a wonderful adventure! Oh, you say, "God doesn't promise us a *wonderful adventure*", I think he does. Consider impending death . . . and right at that moment He steps in, reaches down and hands you another brand spank'n new life! That would be an exciting event, wouldn't it? This happens every morning when we wake; an opportunity to accept a new day in Christ and <u>choose</u> to walk in His righteousness.

King Solomon, the Bible's pillar of wisdom summarized life better than I can:

Ecc 9:7-9 Go eat your food with gladness ... for it is now that God favors what you do... Enjoy life with your wife ...Ecc 12:13 here is the conclusion of the matter: Fear God and keep his commandments, for this is the whole duty of man.

If you haven't yet lived this magnificent adventure with Christ, call on Him for salvation today:

"For God so loved the world that he gave his one and only Son, that whoever believes in him shall not perish but have eternal life". [JN 3:16]

May you enjoy YOUR own fantastic journey as I have enjoyed mine
. . . ***In the safety of His wings***

Epilogue

Since this book was dedicated to my family, one of their first thoughts will be, "Where are *my chapters*?" Well, they own those precious episodes . . . just as you own yours, and their chapters can only be told as seen through their eyes. I am confident that their adventures filtering through precious minds will be even more exciting and meaningful than mine. I close by challenging them and you, as my reader and friend, to . . .

DT 4:9 "Be careful, and watch yourselves closely so that you do not forget the things your eyes have seen or let them slip from your heart as long as you live. Teach them to your children and to their children after them."

277

All of these aircraft flown by one model turbine engine(s) and tested or evaluated by one pilot.

The author, his flight crews and family were featured on covers and in articles of dozens of magazines, record books and newspapers around the world.

Printed in the United States
46996LVS00004B/205-228